MAXIMUM GOVERNMENT, MAXIMUM GOVERNANCE

Maximum Government, Maximum Governance

Reframing India's Macroeconomic Discourse

SASHI SIVRAMKRISHNA

MANOHAR
2019

First published 2019

ISBN 978-93-88540-05-6

Published by
Ajay Kumar Jain *for*
Manohar Publishers & Distributors
4753/23 Ansari Road, Daryaganj
New Delhi 110 002

Typeset by
Kohli Print
Delhi 110 051

Printed at
Replika Press Pvt. Ltd.

For him [Keynes] the only real economic constraints that limit our policy options are scarcities of real resources—of labour, skills, machines, factories, land, raw materials, exhaustible resources. If we cannot make use of them this must be due to institutions, superstition or to our own stupidity. We should be wary therefore of the argument 'There is no money for it' and always ask whether there is any real scarcity involved or not. This naturally leads to a critical attitude towards institutions, especially financial ones. Institutions, this definitely is Keynes' view, have to be such as to make the full use of available resources . . . Keynes therefore had no respect for financial orthodoxy—the gold standard, balanced budgets, sound finance—in so far as they merely hindered a rational use of available material resources.

JOSEF STEINDL

Contents

List of Figures 9

Preface 10

Acknowledgements 11

Introduction 17

PART I: MAINSTREAM MACROECONOMIC DISCOURSE

1. Economics and Macroeconomics 29
2. The Classical and Keynesian Macroeconomic Paradigms 35
3. The Neo-Keynesian Paradigm 51
4. Monetarism and the Decline of Neo Keynesianism 56
5. The 'New' Macroeconomics 62
6. From Stabilization to Growth and Development 73
7. A Summary of Neoliberal Macroeconomics 81

PART II: POPULAR MACROECONOMICS DISCOURSE IN INDIA

8. Putting India's Current Macroeconomic Policies in Perspective 87
9. India's Neoliberal Policy Framework 95

PART III: MODERN MONEY THEORY (MMT)

10. Modern Money and Economic Sovereignty 127
11. Fiscal Deficits in a Modern Money Economy 139

12. The Hierarchy of Money 149
13. Banking and Endogenous Money Theory 158
14. Monetary Policy in the MMT Framework 174
15. The Sectoral Financial Balances (SFB) Model 184
16. A Summary of Insights from MMT 207

PART IV: REFRAMING INDIA'S MACROECONOMIC DISCOURSE

17. Maximum Government, Maximum Governance 213

Bibliography 235
Index 237

List of Figures and Tables

FIGURES

2.1	Key Macroeconomic Variables for the US during the Great Depression	37
3.1	Key Macroeconomic Variables for the US during the Golden Age of Capitalism	52
6.1	Key Macroeconomic Variables for the US during the Great Moderation	74
6.2	Economic Policy Priorities of the European Union	77
7.1	Divergence in Real Wage and Productivity Growth in the US, 1948-2015	84
9.1	India's Declining Private Sector Investment (Gross Fixed Capital Formation)	96
9.2	Credit Growth and Interest Rates, India, 2009-16	99
12.1	The Hierarchy of Money	151
13.1	Credit Expansion in a Growing Economy, India, 1951-2016	163
13.2	Horizontal and Vertical Aspects of Money	165
14.1	India's Liquidity Adjustment Facility (LAF) Framework	178
14.2	Actual Movement of Call Money Market Rates in India within the LAF Band, June-September 2017	179
15.1	India's Sectoral Financial Balances	191
15.2	US Sectoral Financial Balances	192
15.3	The SFB Template	194
15.4	Shifts in India's Sectoral Financial Balances, 2012-17	196
15.5	Divergence in Real Wages and Productivity Growth in India, 1983-2013	202
17.1	The Aggregate Demand Curve (AD) and Shifts in the AD Curve	221

17.2 The Aggregate Supply (AS) Curve and Shifts in the AS Curve 222
17.3 The Pure Keynesian Situation 223
17.4 Shifts in AS without Shift in AD—Inadequacy of Pure Supply-side Measures 224
17.5 The MMT Argument 226
17.6 Increased Expenditure without Adequate Increases in AS 227

TABLES

13.1 Balance Sheet of the Reserve Bank of India, 1949 and 2015-16, Select Entries 164
15.1 India's Sectoral Financial Balances 192

Preface

Macroeconomics, as I was taught during my Master's programme at the University of Mumbai (then Bombay) back in the early 1980s, began with the classical model and the Keynesian critique, followed by the neoclassical synthesis, ending with Friedman's monetarism. As far as I recall, we were not introduced to rational expectations theory then. My introduction to the 'new' macroeconomics began at Cornell in 1985 with a reading of papers by John Muth (1961)[1] and Thomas Sargent (1973),[2] which essentially claimed the inefficacy of fiscal policy, not just in the long-run but even in the short-run. In fact, I don't recall hearing the name of John Maynard Keynes too often (if at all) in my macroeconomics courses at Cornell. Looking back, this is not really surprising because the mid-1980s were a period of economic and political transformation that brought with it the resurgence of free market principles across the world and globalization of economies. Macroeconomics was reduced to a dynamic optimization problem of firms and individuals, an extension of static optimization that was covered in microeconomics. From that point onwards my interest in macroeconomics plummeted and to a large extent my interest in mainstream economics too. Not only was the mathematics getting me but the whole exercise seemed completely out of sync with reality.

I recently came across a paper which reminded me of the macroeconomics that would be, and I am sure still discussed in academic seminars:

> One can further show that if the initial distribution is a Dirac point mass, the limiting distribution is a travelling wave with ã = ó v 2á. If the distribution F is a travelling wave . . . productivity $z = e^x$ is on average growing at the constant rate ã and hence one can say that the economy is on a 'balanced growth path' with growth rate ã.[3]

The economy might be on a balanced growth path but reading

this surely threw me off balance. What has Paul Dirac[4] got to do with macroeconomics? When I checked Google for the definition of 'Dirac point mass', it only got worse: 'Intuitively it is a mass infinity in one point, so that the integral with respect to this mass is 1. Formally, it is a linear functional on the space of continuous functions with uniform convergence on all compact sets defined by Dirac_x_0(f)=f(x_0) for all such continuous functions f.'[5]

Not surprisingly then, after completion of my Ph.D, I took a long sabbatical from economics and when I returned to research more than a decade later, my focus was on application of basic microeconomic principles to specific issues that I encountered as part of my field engagement in India including solid waste management, self-help groups, water distribution and contract farming. My interest in documentary filmmaking led me to make a foray into environmental and economic history. All this was exciting but I remained unhappy with my relative unease engaging with macroeconomic issues which after all caught the headlines everyday. At the same time, the 'new' macroeconomic theories had somehow never convinced me of their relevance except perhaps for their hegemonic influence. India was an even more complex and challenging context to simply 'apply' macroeconomic principles to understand debates; to me a political economy angle seemed indispensable in making sense of what was happening.

It is here that my detour into history helped; I developed an understanding of money and also the history of the rupee on which I wrote a book, *In Search of Stability: Economics of Money, History of the Rupee.* It gave me a (re)entry into macroeconomics. The scope of the book was, however, temporally restricted to the beginning of the end of the Bretton Woods era (1971). To extend my research on the rupee from 1971 to the present I needed a framework for analysis that not only captured the context of the floating exchange rate regime that arose in the post-Bretton Woods era but also stressed the importance of money in macroeconomic analysis.

Quite by chance, I came across Modern Money Theory (MMT), which offered fresh insights into the world of modern money and how the macroeconomy really functions. MMT was not just a strong critique of, but more importantly provided a constructive alternative to mainstream macroeconomics. At last I was able to construct arguments on the macroeconomy with conviction. Unfortunately, MMT has not been widely accepted by the mainstream, neither in the West nor in countries like India. Though I have written a few pieces for *The Wire* on MMT, I thought a more complete narrative would be topical especially in times of political churning and economic distress, particularly related to the issues of unemployment and rising inequality in incomes and wealth.

NOTES

1. John F. Muth, 'Rational Expectations and the Theory of Price Movements', *Econometrica*, 29(3): 315-35.
2. Thomas Sargent, 'Monetary and Fiscal Policy in a Two-Sector Aggregative Model', *American Economic Review*, 63(3); 345-65.
3. Y. Achdou et al., 'Partial Differential Equation Models in Macroeconomics', Philosophical Transactions of the Royal Society, October 2014, http://www.princeton.edu/~moll/PDE_macro.pdf
4. Paul Dirac was a great quantum physicist.
5. http://at.yorku.ca/cgi-bin/bbqa?forum=ask_an_analyst_2007 &task=show_msg&msg=3855.0001

Acknowledgements

First and foremost, I must thank the MMT community for sharing their insights so openly on the Internet through papers, videos, interviews and blogs. Without access to these resources, I would never have gotten to know of MMT. Of course, any errors in the book are solely mine.

I have always been able to share my thoughts on MMT with many friends and colleagues. Amongst them, I must make mention of Amalendu Jyotishi and Rajesh Madhavan who have on several occasions given me a patient hearing and helped bring clarity to my thoughts.

The Foundation to Aid Industrial Recovery (FAIR) supported me, especially during the early years of my research on MMT. Unlike the US, Indian academia and even the popular media is far more open to new ideas in economics. We do not seem overly dogmatic when it comes to economic theory. I enjoy this freedom to work on areas of my choice without the rigidities of adhering to particular schools of thought. Given my temperament this has been a great boon to me.

Last but in no way the least, I must thank my wife Preeta and son, Kartikeya for once again supporting me in my endeavours. Spending long hours working at my desk at home is a luxury I have enjoyed in spite of the several stresses and strains of mid-life years.

SASHI SIVRAMKRISHNA

Introduction

At the very outset, it is important to delineate the meaning of neoliberal or orthodox macroeconomics to avoid any confusion over the use of these terms in our discussions.

> Neoliberalism is a policy model of social studies and economics that transfers control of economic factors to the private sector from the public sector. It takes from the basic principles of neoclassical economics, suggesting that governments must limit subsidies, make reforms to tax laws in order to expand the tax base, reduce deficit spending, limit protectionism, and open markets up to trade. It also seeks to abolish fixed exchange rates, back deregulation, permit private property, and privatize businesses run by the state. . . . Neoliberal policies aim for a *laissez-faire* approach to economic development.[1]

Neoliberal macroeconomics, built on the pillars of free market principles and minimum state intervention, has dominated economics discourse and defined the narrative for more than four decades beginning in the 1970s. The pursuit of neoliberal economic policies brought with it economic growth and development for countries across the world but not without serious repercussions that gained visibility in the aftermath of the global financial crisis (GFC) of 2008. Perhaps the greatest failure of this paradigm has now been recognized as growing disparities in income and wealth between individuals, households and regions, exasperated by stagnant real incomes, high rates of unemployment as well as chronic private-sector indebtedness. Moreover, over this period the tables have turned on the support for globalization; the advanced (Western) countries that pushed for it in the 1980s are increasingly threatened by low-cost imports from, low wages in and immigrants from emerging economies while the latter view globalization as an opportunity for rapid growth and development. Once again, we must be cautious with such generalizations as there are many who support economic globalization in the West just as there are significant numbers of people in the developing world who feel constrained or threatened by the neoliberal economics edifice.

The world now stands at the crossroads between two competing economic paradigms; one that argues for the status quo wherein neoliberal economics remains the pillar of economic policy—globalization of trade, capital and even labour flows, central bank independence, government austerity, low and stable inflation, de-unionized labour markets and supply-side structural reforms to enhance private sector investment—while the other, quite like what was once the domain of the left, seems to want a return to a more statist or, at least a more interventionist world—protectionism from foreign trade, de-globalization, localism, restrictions on global labour and even capital flows, greater role for the government through expansionary fiscal policy and limits to central bank independence.

Once again it would obviously be naïve to generalize and compartmentalize policies of governments across the globe into such simple categories, for the real world is far more complex where shades of both paradigms coarsely blend into each other. Nonetheless, within a relatively short span of just a few years, a rather clear trend is emerging, especially in the West on the political support to these economic predilections; politically liberal parties to the centre and right-of-centre are clinging on to the neoliberal paradigm (for example, Merkel in Germany, Macron in France, Trudeau in Canada) whereas the new wave of politically 'illiberal'[2] populist-nationalist leaders (for example, Trump in the USA, May in UK, Le Pen in France) are opposing at least some of the fundamental propositions of neoliberal macroeconomics—dilution of central bank autonomy, larger fiscal deficits especially with tax cuts to the rich—although without an economic paradigm that supports their beliefs or from which they can draw upon.

In emerging economies, particularly India, the situation is even more complex given that the privatization/liberalization phase remains incomplete and globalization is still considered an opportunity for rapid growth. While the present National Democratic Alliance (NDA) government led by Prime Minister Narendra Modi of the Bharatiya Janata Party (BJP), since 2014, could be labelled as populist-nationalist, the economic policies seem, broadly speaking, neoliberal given its support for global trade, capital and labour flows, privitization, fiscal consolidation and broad adherence to market principles. This economic tilt to neoliberalism was succinctly captured in the BJP's 2014 election slogan, 'minimum government, maximum governance'. However, since 2016, economic and political commentators have noticed a perceptible change in India too with greater economic interventions by the state[3] (for instance, in medical product pricing—stents and knee joints, protection for Indian steel manufacturers, the call for buying Indian products, agricultural loan waivers, higher taxes on luxury goods, the hesitance towards labour reforms[4] and to an extent even authoritarian as for instance, demonetizing the rupee and suppressing the Reserve Bank of India's autonomy.

The reason for growing state activism across the world is plain; a market economy is simply too impersonal, detached and mechanistic to accommodate and respond to widespread, complex and intense social, cultural and economic tensions and conflicts that have built up over the last several decades. And it is unlikely that even those who believe in the basic tenets of neoliberal macroeconomics will dismiss the necessity for greater state activism in tackling some of the most jarring economic problems that could potentially destabilize countries: unemployment, inequalities of income and wealth, jobless growth, poor infrastructure, inadequate and unaffordable social sector services like health, education and sanitation as well as the socio-cultural frictions emanating from greater international labour mobility.[5] No government today in a functioning democracy can leave these entirely to the market and private sector to resolve. The assertion of the state over market forces therefore cannot be undermined and is instead turning even more compelling.

While it seems that nationalist-populist leaders are challenging economic neoliberalism by veering towards greater economic intervention by the state coupled with varying degrees of right-wing state authoritarianism[6], the 'politically liberal'[7] leaders are clinging on to economic neoliberalism. Yanis Varoufakis, former Finance Minister of Greece and a professor of economics, succinctly brings out[8] the dissatisfaction over the latter—politically liberal, economically neoliberal—combination that came to power in France in 2017. There is hope that a space will emerge across nations that combines a more politically liberal worldview while at the same time questions some of the basic tenets of economic neoliberalism that stifle the economic role of the state.

Soon after the French elections in 2017, the politician and writer Pavan Varma pointed out that India too cries out for a *new political paradigm* with a liberal, centrist leader (à la Macron) who promises and delivers 'good governance, economic growth, equity, ethics, tolerance and social stability'.[9] While political leadership is indispensable, Varma fails to consider the need for an accompanying economic paradigm—a paradigm, which unlike neoliberalism, does not constrain the state from playing a larger role in tackling the most critical issues of unemployment and inequality.

Soon after the results of the 2017 Gujarat elections were announced, Manish Tewari, former Union Minister in the United Progressive Alliance (UPA) government raised a most pertinent question on the future of strategy of the Congress:

> The shift in India's trajectory has left the Congress vacillating between doctrinal socialism and a gold rush towards a new neoliberal economic order for more than 26 years now . . . how does it square up with building an economy for 99 per cent of Indians who have not benefitted from neoliberalism?[10]

There seems to be a crying need for liberal politics combined with non-neoliberal economics; but what is this economic paradigm that can pose a *realistic* challenge to neoliberalism? To me the answer is Modern Money Theory (MMT). The insights revealed by MMT point out to the necessity for, and an opportunity to proactively use fiscal policy by governments in a *modern economy*—an economically sovereign country which issues its own fiat currency. MMT is based on an understanding of modern money and a description of how the monetary system actually works rather than a theory built on obscure assumptions. Academically, MMT is not 'new'; it is ensconced in the post-Keynesian paradigm and its basic tenets have been elaborated by economists such as Abba P. Lerner, Wynne Godley and Hyman Minsky decades ago. However, it saw a revival in the 1990s with the works of relatively few economists like Warren Mosler, Randall Wray, Stephanie Kelton, Scott Fullwiler, Eric Tymoigne and Bill Mitchell. Since then it has gathered a small following in the West but has been largely ignored by Indian economists in spite of its utmost relevance.

My modest aim in writing this book is to introduce Indian readers to MMT and at the same time attempt to reframe macroeconomic discourse that is presently obsessed with the neoliberal macroeconomic premise of reigning in public debt and fiscal deficit to arbitrary (low) levels. It is also pertinent to add that the book *does not claim theoretical originality* or in making advances to MMT;[11] instead I use it as a framework to trigger debate on macroeconomic policy. Moreover, MMT's greatest challenge today is not the basis or veracity of its claims (that I hope the reader will be convinced of) but on how to *change the narrative*, which still remains under the hegemonic grip of neoliberal, orthodox, mainstream macroeconomics.

Part I of the book is an introduction to mainstream macroeconomic discourse beginning with a chapter that locates macroeconomics within the broader definition of economics. This introduction, however, is not an academic survey of the literature; instead, it is to provide readers with the essential tenets of mainstream economics as it has evolved over decades. The emphasis throughout Part I is on money, fiscal and monetary policy as well as inflation and unemployment. In particular, I highlight a critical mainstream economics proposition that the macroeconomy is financially constrained—both the government and the commercial banking system—which brings into focus an overriding concern over the fiscal deficit target and savings rate, respectively.

The book is thereafter divided into three further parts. In Part II, I discuss the popular discourse on macroeconomic issues and policy in India that has broadly aligned itself with mainstream economic theories. Once again, I must emphasize that I do not attempt a survey of Indian economics and policy literature. Instead, I focus on how mainstream views have filtered into and been absorbed by popular macroeconomic discourse. Although there seems to be wide consensus on economic policy there are some opposing arguments too but these only serve to keep the debate brewing and do not fundamentally alter the orthodox perspective on the working of a modern economy. The danger I see in the current discourse is that many of the ideas emanating from questionable theories and models are being reduced to the level of common sense—once this happens it becomes almost impossible to propose new alternatives. Post-truth economics after all preceded post-truth politics.

In Part III of the book, I embark on my primary objective—introduce and explain the basic tenets of MMT. While these tenets directly question some of the mainstream macroeconomic tenets, I do not reduce this to a one-to-one debate. Moreover, the reader will feel a disjoint between parts I and III of the book; this is not something that can be bridged. MMT is not an extension of mainstream theory—it is a different, an alternative—macroeconomic paradigm. Most importantly, MMT fundamentally alters our understanding of an economy with a modern monetary system that allows us to reframe macroeconomic discourse and rescript the narrative. In a nutshell, MMT rejects the mainstream view that an economy, at a macroeconomic level, is financially constrained. The overriding concern or even obsession with fiscal deficit and public debt target numbers needs to be given up and instead the focus of policy must be turned on real resource and governance constraints.

Given my own acceptance of and adherence to MMT, money finds a central place in the book. In fact, a major problem with mainstream macroeconomics is the assumed neutrality of money. As I argue in the book, this is the most unfortunate assumption in mainstream discourse which influences policy choices. Moreover, the assumption that banks are mere intermediaries between savers and borrowers has also undermined the role of commercial banking (and bank money) in a modern economy as well as its contribution to financial crisis.

Finally, in Part IV of the book I attempt a reframing of macroeconomic discourse by drawing upon insights from MMT but at the same time addressing some of the unequivocal concerns that policy-makers face in a country like India. I must reiterate at the outset that the book does not provide solutions to all present issues; rather, by reframing the discourse it hopes to open up new lines of discussion which until now may have been dismissed as 'unaffordable'.

There is also another question that needs to be addressed; to whom do we take the MMT message? MMT has to make a breakthrough in the *popular* macroeconomic discourse if it must stand a chance of being heard by the political class. In an age when the media not only influences but also shapes the public's political choices, MMT must be taken to a wider audience in order to engage with the political class. The book is therefore aimed at the general interested reader, economic commentators, policy makers, think-tanks and students of economics and other social sciences who may have been compelled to imbibe mainstream macroeconomics without even realizing the existence of alternative theories and descriptions of how the economy works and fails. Only wider public awareness of the true constraints to economic growth and development can exert pressure for institutional and political change. With the feedback loop between the popular domain and political establishment becoming stronger, MMT stands a chance of breaking through the current impasse.

The resistance to change is not so much the politician as much as mainstream economists and the institutions under their control. Not only does mainstream academia dominate, influence and sway macroeconomic discourse, but it is less receptive—even hostile—to heterodox ideas. Discussions amongst orthodox macroeconomists are usually 'apolitical', mathematical or statistically dense but otherwise, trite. And except for certain nuances, everyone agrees with everyone—that's why they even called it the 'New Consensus Macroeconomics'—until the GFC of 2008 ruptured this make-believe world.

Unfortunately, the crisis itself was not able to dethrone mainstream economics, which continues to rule the roost in most academic and economic institutions across the world. Nonetheless, there is an undercurrent of frustration with the neoliberal world view, which, as mentioned earlier, has manifested itself in the rise of illiberal nationalist-populist leaders in many countries around the world.[12] While MMT could well be appropriated by these forces,[13] it also provides an opportunity for progressive forces—those socially, politically and economically aligned to the centre and left-of-centre—to build a new political narrative with a new economics that brings employment back into focus.

The overriding objective of this book and more generally of MMT is to dislodge the notion which neoliberalism has drilled into our heads—that the government is financially constrained—and instead realize that it is not finance but governance that needs to be put on the pedestal so as to effectively and efficiently navigate through economic (or real) resource constraints that an economy confronts in order to achieve full employment and high economic growth.

NOTES

1. http://www.investopedia.com/terms/n/neoliberalism.asp
2. Fareed Zakaria, 'America's Democracy has become Illiberal', *The Washington Post*, 29 December 2016, https://www.washingtonpost.com/opinions/america-is-becoming-a-land-of-less-liberty/2016/12/29/2a91744c-ce09-11e6-a747-d03044780a02_story.html
3. See, for instance, Rajeev Deshpande and Sidhartha, 'Three years of Modi Government: State Plays Bigger Role in Economic, Social Change', *Times of India*, 26 May 2014, http://timesofindia.indiatimes.com/modi-government/news/three-years-of-modi-government-state-plays-bigger-role-in-economic-social-change/articleshow/58847819.cms
4. These were perhaps the reasons for the early resignation of Arvind Panagariya from the NITI Aayog in August 2017. See, Mihir Sharma, 'The Inside Story of why the BJP's Biggest Policy Champion May Have Jumped the Modi's Ship', 10 August 2017, http://economictimes.indiatimes.com/news/economy/policy/how-india-lost-another-champion-in-the-form-of-arvind-panagariya/articleshow/59996454.cms
5. See, for instance, the TED talk by the billionaire capitalist, Nick Hanauer, 'Beware, Fellow Plutocrats, the Pitchforks are Coming', https://www.youtube.com/watch?v=q2gO4DKVpa8
6. Subodh Ghildiyal, 'NDA@3: Hindutva + Pro-poor Message Corners Opposition', *Times of India*, 26 May 2017, http://timesofindia. indiatimes.com/modi-government/news/three-years-of-modi-government-hindutva-and-pro-poor-message-corners-opposition/articleshow/58848189.cms

7. An interesting quote provides a clear notion of 'political liberalism'; 'by liberalism . . . I mean the generosity of spirit, an attempt to comprehend otherness, a commitment to the rule of law, a high ideal of the worth and dignity of man, a repugnance for authoritarianism and a love of freedom' (Alan Paton at Yale University), http://www.thefreedictionary.com/Politically+liberal
8. Yanis Varoufakis, Well Done, Macron: Now We Oppose You, Livemint', 22 May 2017, http://www.livemint.com/Opinion/9wrfH33mgcAVREYVbd50BK/Well-done-Macronnow-we-oppose-you.html
9. Pavan K. Varma, 'Can India do a Macron?', *Times of India*, 27 May 2017, http://blogs.timesofindia.indiatimes.com/toi-edit-page/can-india-do-a-macron-the-country-cries-out-for-a-liberal-centrist-leader-who-can-take-on-both-left-and-right/
10. Manish Tewari, 'Gujarat Election Results: No Better Time for Congress to Reanalyze Policies, Politics', *Hindustan Times*, 19 December 2017, http://www.hindustantimes.com/analysis/gujarat-election-results-no-better-time-for-congress-to-reanalyse-policies-politics-manish-tewari/story-iqaXbxB0OsG2g0Fhn9DG8J.html
11. MMT has been extensively discussed in blogs, You Tube and working papers. There is relatively lesser number of papers published in formal journals than mainstream economics. I have drawn extensively from these sources. Moreover, theoretical advances to MMT have slowed down; most of what had to be said has been said. As many MMTers suggest, attention must now be turned to framing and marketing, getting people and policymakers to listen and dispel some of their rigid beliefs.
12. See, for instance, League of Nationalists, *The Economist*, 19 November 2016, https://www.economist.com/news/international/21710276-all-around-world-nationalists-are-gaining-ground-why-league-nationalists
13. In fact, Donald Trump said something that MMTers have been trying to convince people for a long time; 'This is the United States government. First of all, you never have to default because you print the money. I hate to tell you. So there's never a default.' Dylan Mathews, Donald Trump on the debt: 'You Never have to Default because you Print the Money', *Vox*, 9 May 2016, https://www.vox.com/2016/5/9/11639292/donald-trump-default-print-money.

PART I

MAINSTREAM MACRO-ECONOMIC DISCOURSE

CHAPTER 1

Economics and Macroeconomics

DELINEATING THE SCOPE OF ECONOMICS

To make this book self-contained, I begin with my take on what economics is and what makes macroeconomics distinct from the other, microeconomics. A compulsive start to any question today begins with Google. When I keyed in 'economics' two meanings appeared:

- The branch of knowledge concerned with the production, consumption, and transfer of wealth.
- The condition of a region or group as regards material prosperity.

These definitions are rather vague. Everything and anything seems to be a part of economics. Let me therefore articulate a more precise definition of economics.

People (and many animals too) live in groups and with this, division of labour amongst members of the group becomes inevitable, bringing with it specialization and higher standards of living. Imagine a life where you had to do everything yourself from growing tea to building your own house, let alone putting together an air-conditioner. Note that I have not said assembling because you would also have to make the tubes and wires, the blades and fasteners! What about mining and smelting? And who will design the air-conditioner and provide electricity? It is obvious that without division of labour we would never have progressed beyond hunter-gatherers.

Perhaps it was the need to facilitate the division of labour that people chose to live in groups. Whatever may have been the case, the division of labour generated the need for organization of production of goods and services as well as distribution of produced goods and services among members of the group. The economy, or the organization of production and distribution of goods, then becomes essential so that all tasks that have to be done get done and all members of a group get an appropriate share of the produced output. But who organizes this production and distribution of goods and services?

Consider, for instance, a tribal society where tasks and responsibilities are allocated according to traditional social and cultural norms. Distribution or who gets what share of the produced goods is also decided on a similar basis. The chief of the tribe is entrusted with ensuring that norms and customs are adhered to so that rules are not broken arbitrarily. Enforcement has to be strict because breaking rules could mean that some jobs never get done, which may even impact the tribe's survival. Or consider a feudal society as it prevailed in India where the caste system 'assigned' occupations by birth and also decided who got what and how much of the output. While these allocations may not be socially just, it did ensure that all tasks that had to get done got done. Finally, central planning as it existed in erstwhile Soviet Union (USSR) was also considered a viable and rational way to solve the economic problem of organizing production and distribution. Economics, at least the mainstream version, however, does not delve into a study of such economic systems where traditional norms and customs, politics and compulsion or a central plan directed the allocation of resources and distribution of the produced goods amongst members of a society.

DEFINING ECONOMICS

So what is economics in the modern sense of the word then? To me, economics is the study of the economy, i.e. how the economy is organized or, in other words, how society decides on who produces what and how much and who gets what and how much of the produced output of goods and services. But here comes the crucial point; economics studies how a *market system* goes about doing this, not other economic systems. We are really not interested in how production and distribution is organized in a tribal community, a feudal society or a centrally planned economy. I, therefore, propose the following definition of economics:

Economics is the study of production and distribution of goods and services *in a market system*:

(i) how the market system works,
(ii) how 'well'[1] it works,
(iii) when/why does it fail to work well, and
(iv) what can be done to set the failures right and by whom.

The market system comprises markets or institutions that bridge demand and supply across place and time through exchanges that take place by *bringing together* buyers and sellers under a 'single roof' and generating price signals from the *cumulative* desires and abilities of all consumers and producers. Individual consumers and producers then react to these signals which either work as an incentive/disincentive to buy and sell more or less. A market system is a network of these interconnected markets that encompasses the entire economy or the entire sphere of production and distribution of goods and services. It goes beyond individual markets like those for automobiles and toothpastes. Thousands if not millions of markets develop for every conceivable good and service including labour, which are then interconnected with all other markets through price signals that impact consumer decisions, sales, inventories and profits and thereby regulate the allocation of resources to each market, the quantum of output that is produced as well as who gets what share of that output.

Adam Smith, some 250 years ago, used the expression 'Invisible Hand' . . . a hand (that could be interpreted as the hand of God) that guides us in our actions but something which is not seen. This Invisible Hand is the market system, a system in which economic activities of society are organized through mutually beneficial voluntary exchanges between buyers and sellers on the basis of information transmitted in the form of price signals or prices. It is price that tells us, individually and collectively, what society wants us to do and how the total output is to be divided amongst us.

The market system guides exchange, making the division of labour possible and smooth, allowing specialization, increasing productivity and consequently enhancing our standards of living.

While economists have devoted a lot of time to understanding how and how well the market system works, the study of market failure is equally if not of greater importance. Do price signals always encapsulate all information on scarcity or surpluses? If they do not, we end up with an inefficient or sub-optimal allocation of resources or market failure. 'Microeconomics' studies market failure in individual markets and finding solutions for such failures. In general, the reasons for market failure (and their solution given in brackets) include market structure reasons like monopoly or oligopoly (regulation) and non-market structure reasons like asymmetric information (screening and signaling), risk and uncertainty (insurance or hedging) and externalities (taxes or creating markets by assigning property rights). For instance, the cause of climate change is considered to be the inability of, say, the market for coal-based thermal energy to price greenhouse gas emissions resulting in too much pollution or what is called a negative externality. Assigning property rights over pollution and enforcing caps on the quantum of pollution permissible can create a market for carbon and generate a price at which exchanges or carbon trading can take place.

MACROECONOMICS

Sometimes market-system failure takes place not just in specific markets but across most markets of the economy, all at the same time; this is *market failure on a grand scale* which leads to a contraction of aggregate output of the economy (Gross Domestic Product or GDP) and rising unemployment, or what are called recessions or depressions. The approach to understand such instances of market failure is the subject matter of macroeconomics. In other words, macroeconomics restricts itself to the study situations where there is simultaneous failure in broad categories of the market for goods and services, the labour market as well as in financial or credit markets. At an even deeper level macroeconomics questions whether the causes of market system failure on a grand scale are mere 'imperfections' of a microeconomic kind or whether there is a fundamental problem with market capitalism; one that does not guarantee full employment as the natural outcome of free market interactions even when microeconomic imperfections do not exist.

It is important to reiterate that economics (or what is sometimes called microeconomics) as well as macroeconomics are both concerned with the same questions pertaining to the market system. Microeconomics is not restricted to delving into problems of individuals or individual firms as the term might suggest. The 'micro' actually refers to its foundations; it begins from an understanding of an optimizing consumer and a firm's behaviour. Furthermore, microeconomics does deal with issues that have 'macro'-level significance. For instance, market failure in financial markets because of asymmetric information could have nation-wide or even global repercussions. Similarly the impact of climate change arising from externalities in the energy market may have important implications for human civilization itself. Unlike their early predecessors, present-day mainstream macroeconomists argue that market failure on a grand scale ultimately arises from micro-level failures in specific markets. For instance, unemployment may be on account of inefficiencies in the labour market; minimum wage laws, asymmetric information, and so on. It is argued that the need for a 'different approach' developed by early macroeconomists (Keynes and the neo-Keynesians) may actually be a weak one. But Keynesians, especially post-Keynesians and MMTers, believe in the inevitability of crisis in and the intrinsic limitation of self-acting market capitalism in ensuring full employment.

The scope of macroeconomics goes beyond the study of market failure on a grand scale to the devising of instruments and the institutional apparatus to set it right—*stabilization policy.* Here the emphasis is on taming the business cycle, containing unemployment and inflation, rather than engaging with issues pertaining to improvements in standards of living. The latter facet of macroeconomics falls in the domain of economic growth and development. While growth is easily measured as the rate of change of GDP, development is more social in nature than either stability or growth. It includes issues like regional inequalities and inequalities in distribution of incomes and wealth, gender discrimination, the environment, health and education. Economists have proposed measures of development like the Human Development Index (HDI) to track the performance of countries in relative terms over a period of time.

There is another question that macroeconomic discourses in developing countries like India must address; can we use the theories developed in the West relevant to their own economic conditions be 'applied' to issues facing us? Or do we need an alternative paradigm with fundamental differences in macroeconomic theory? The answer is that although the economic environment that developing countries operate in may be different from their Western counterparts, the macroeconomic principles as well as certain institutions (like the Ministry of Finance/Treasury, central banks, modern banking sector, etc.) are not really unique to warrant a distinct theory. To cope with structural differences (like trade and exchange rate policies, role of public sector, informal sector, financial markets and volatility issues, etc.) models do need modifications, but this can be done with the existing tools of economic analysis.

NOTE

1. 'Well' in economics is referred to as 'social welfare' and is defined as the sum of consumer and producer surplus.

CHAPTER 2

The Classical and Keynesian Macroeconomic Paradigms

MACROECONOMIC SCHOOLS OF THOUGHT

Broadly speaking, there are three schools of thought in economics from the left to the right; Marxist, Keynesian and classical. The difference between these schools of thought essentially boils down to one major issue—the role of the state in a capitalist market system. While Marxism saw the ultimate demise of capitalism and the market system for their exploitative nature, the Keynesians and classical schools believe in the overall ability of the capitalist market system to organize the production and distribution of goods and services. Although Marxist analysis does provide deep insights into capitalism, I do not think a discussion that rejects the capitalist market system *in toto* is particularly relevant at present. I therefore exclude Marxist thinking from the present discourse.[1] The reader may or may not agree with this proposition.

It is important to elucidate that Keynes' ideas are not really in sync with those of the radical left. He was a believer in the overall efficacy of the free markets system except that state intervention was necessary when aggregate demand was inadequate to sustain full employment. Unlike Marx, Keynes was not in favour of central planning as a substitute for a competitive market system. Many believed that through his theory, Keynes was able to resurrect the market system from its collapse on a grand scale during the Great Depression of the 1930s, which may have, left to its own, been the basis for a communist revolution in the 1930s. It is a coincidence and an interesting bit of trivia that Keynes was born just days after Marx died, in 1883.

In the context of market capitalism, the two dominant and relevant schools of thought driving mainstream macroeconomic discourse today are therefore the Keynesian and the classical. Within the Keynesian paradigm there are sub-schools of thought that are considered mainstream (neo-Keynesian and new Keynesian) whereas some are kept out of the mainstream (post-Keynesian). While this book focuses on MMT that draws upon post-Keynesianism, we present in this chapter some mainstream Keynesian ideas that influence popular macroeconomics discourse. To the right of the Keynesians are the classical economists who believe that the role of the state should primarily be confined to the provision of public goods like street lighting, policing and defence services, education and health where market failure is inevitable. The government, however, must not manage the business cycle since the market system can correct itself even in case of market failure on a grand scale. The classical school too has evolved over time into many different paradigms, each with its own set of idiosyncratic assumptions and policy proposals. In many ways we are driven to favouring the propositions of these schools of thought by our own life experiences and world view. At the same time, the popular discourse (drawing directly or indirectly from academia) does influence our world view and in a democratic country, the policy responses of the political establishment too.

CLASSICAL MACROECONOMICS

Macroeconomics as a distinct field of enquiry began with the Great Depression of the 1930s when several markets were drawn into a crisis, simultaneously; the markets for goods with large unsold inventories, the labour market with high rates of unemployment and even financial markets with multiple bank failures. As sales fell, companies cut back production that led to a vicious circle of falling output and rising unemployment. This was a definitive case of market system failure; how could one ever justify 25 per cent of the labour force being out of work when they were willing to work? And this indeed was the situation in the US as illustrated in Figure 2.1 with data for key macroeconomic variables during this period.

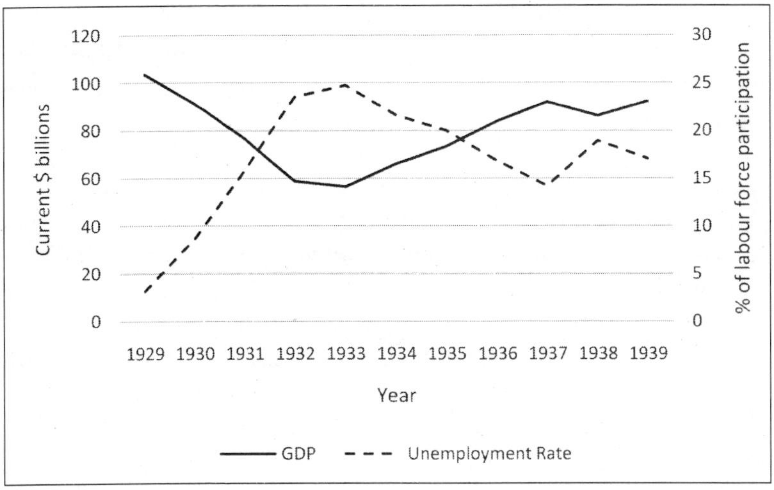

Source: https://www.bea.gov/scb/pdf/2012/08%20August/0812%20gdp-other%20nipa_series.pdf

Figure 2.1: Key Macroeconomic Variables for the US during the Great Depression

What were the causes of the depression and possible solutions to alleviate the situation? The prevalent belief then was that the market system would correct itself out of the crisis. The reasoning was based on the works of the classical economists of the eighteenth and nineteenth centuries, which included Adam Smith, David Ricardo, John Stuart Mill and Jean Baptiste Say. While their work never really dealt with recessions or depressions in the way we understand them today, there was some oblique reference to it in the work of Say who argued that a general glut or an excess supply cannot exist in all markets simultaneously. This is because 'supply creates its own demand' or what is referred to as 'Say's Law'. This idea—which at first seems rather counter-intuitive—implicitly supports our widespread belief in the market system and is still relevant in today's economic debates.

Why would anyone want to supply a good or service to others? The answer is because s/he desires to buy something else in exchange for these good or services. Consider, for instance, a barter economy with two individuals, Crusoe and Friday. Suppose Crusoe specializes in catching fish while Friday gathers coconuts. Why would Crusoe catch fish? It can either be for his own consumption or because he wants to exchange fish for coconuts with Friday. Why else would he want to catch fish? The planned supply of fish for exchange therefore means a demand for coconuts.

In a world of barter, to buy something a person must sell and *to sell implies the desire to buy something*. At a macroeconomic level, any increase in supply must automatically mean a creation of new demand in the economy for that is indeed the purpose of increasing supply in the first place. Starting from a position where demand is equal to supply, this need not mean that what is newly being produced and supplied is automatically demanded. This could therefore result in an excess supply of these goods. However, there must be an increased demand for some other goods leading to an excess demand for them in that market.

Say's Law argues that there can never be a general glut; an excess supply in all markets concurrently. An excess supply (surplus) of one or more goods could exist but only when balanced by an excess demand (shortage) in some other market. Put in the context of aggregate markets, the law may be interpreted as follows: while there may be an oversupply of produced goods (say, automobiles), this must be balanced by an excess demand for labour. As wages rise the excess demand for labour gradually diminishes. Meanwhile, a rise in wages increases the demand for automobiles but at the same time decreases their supply by increasing the costs of production so that the excess supply in the product (automobile) market declines. These changes would, however, have further implications on the demand for and supply of automobiles as well as labour. Through a series of iterations, market forces would, via price adjustment, work quickly (it is assumed) to abolish excesses and shortages across markets. Even though this description of the economy was challenged by Keynes, it continues to hold sway in macroeconomic policy through its emphasis on the need to *unshackle supply rather than focusing on policies that create demand.*

The classical view on recessions and depressions can also be articulated from a micro-level view of the labour market where labour is exchanged between people and firms, voluntarily. Consider a situation of unemployment, i.e. where more people are willing to work than firms wish to hire; an oversupply of labour would lead to a decrease in wages (assuming no barriers to this decrease exist) and some people leaving the market voluntarily while at the same time increasing the willingness of firms to hire more people (as it becomes cheaper relative to capital so that firms would substitute capital with labour). This will continue until the wage rate equalizes demand for and supply of labour. Involuntary unemployment therefore cannot exist in a free market—all those willing to work at the going wage rate will find work. In other words, equilibrium in the labour market implies full employment and full employment implies equilibrium. Free markets—and labour reforms are essentially to ensure a free market for labour—have the ability to solve the economy's problems of recessions and involuntary unemployment, automatically.

KEYNESIAN MACROECONOMICS

To Keynes, Say's Law was inadequate in providing a convincing explanation of the Great Depression of the 1930s (or the recession of 2008) when coexistence of an excess supply of labour or high rates of unemployment (long queues at employment exchanges) and excess supply of goods (unsold inventories of several goods) became a stark reality. Classical economists, however, attributed such situations to government interventions or other market imperfections like monopolies and/or trade unions preventing price/wage adjustments as well as minimum wage laws that did not allow adjustments towards full employment. To them the solution to the crisis lay in elimination of these distortions—that are rather akin to irritants—so that a competitive free market system could deliver an optimal outcome.

There are several Keynesian[2] arguments against Say's Law: first, labour unions are institutions of the modern world with deep roots and cannot simply be wished away. Second, 'sticky prices' including that of labour (wages) as well as of goods and services (due to the existence of monopolies, oligopolies and strategic behaviour,[3] monopolistic competition and brands, etc.) are a reality of capitalist economies. The incapacity of prices to bring about a balance in supply and demand often implies that changes in quantities (output) do the job, giving rise to people being laid-off or unemployment. In other words, if price cannot fall to clear excess supply then a firm may simply cut back production to match demand. But sticky prices per se are not the essence of Keynesian theory—as the New Keynesians[4] seem to think—after all there really is nothing substantial in this over what the classical economists were saying. In fact, sticky prices and wage inflexibility reduce Keynesianism to just a special case of classical theory.

Third, Keynes' core concern was the fluctuation in aggregate expenditures. More specifically, uncertainty and speculation are rife in any capitalist economy and decisions of firms to invest can be volatile. What happens if firms, reacting to some bad news (say a stock market crash or a geopolitical event), decide to cut back investment spending? This decline in aggregate expenditure could result in a vicious circle of slackening demand, fall in sales, rising inventories, layoffs and falling wages. All in all, a recession sets in.

To the classical economists, this poses no serious problem since rising unemployment would result in a fall in wages, which in turn increases quantity demanded of labour by firms and a reduction in quantity supplied of labour by individuals. The labour market will return to equilibrium, i.e. where no involuntary unemployment exists. But Keynesians pose a counter-question; what if firms *during a recession*, seeing wages fall sharply, fear that workers will have less to spend and therefore cut back production, anticipating weak demand. This may lead to a decrease in demand for labour at any going wage rate, resulting in a vicious cycle of falling wages and greater levels of unemployment. As wages begin to decline and before equilibrium can be restored at a new wage rate, firms once again cut back production and consequently decrease their demand for labour so that unemployment persists.

Finally, Keynes pointed out yet another problem with classical theory, in particular, with Say's Law; the latter was generally *valid only for a barter economy.* Say and the classicists were convinced that barter was merely a simplifying assumption so that the introduction of money would not change anything in the analysis. Money after all was just a means of exchange and a store of value (utilized for future consumption) and the classical economists had unearthed the workings of the *real* economy, the exchanges of actual goods and services below the veil of money. Keynes, however, argued that the introduction of money could invalidate the premise of Say's Law that a general glut cannot exist.

Returning to our earlier example, what if Crusoe catches fish not only to exchange these for coconuts with Friday but also demands money as a distinct good? Crusoe now catches fish either for self-consumption, to trade for coconuts, or to (now) trade for and accumulate money. In other words, people demand money for its own sake—as a financial asset—and not merely as a means of exchange. Supply would therefore not create its own demand (for other goods). A desire to accumulate money could then lead to a general glut in product markets—long queues at the unemployment exchange and unsold inventories of goods could indeed coexist. And most importantly, *this could happen irrespective of whether or not we have labour unions and other market imperfections.*

The excess demand for money is essentially *hoarding*; the desire to hold money for its *own sake*, causing a shortage in the demand for goods and services, an undesired increase in inventories, a fall in the general price level (deflation) and ultimately a fall in production. This general glut would in turn cause a fall in the demand for labour and consequently higher levels of unemployment. During a recession or depression the desire for hoarding is even more. People, in fear of losing their jobs, may hoard more and firms cut back on production. Failing banks and financial institutions (like in the 1930s and even during the 2008 crisis) may further drive people to even hoard their savings 'under mattresses'. At the same time, banks may not be willing to lend to firms and even other banks in lieu of firms and banks going bust. Hoarded money therefore does not find its way back into circulation, throwing the economy into a vicious cycle of falling consumption and production and consequently, a depression. The logic of Say's Law could therefore be flawed in a monetary economy; supply may not create its own demand making government intervention necessary to revive a faltering economy.

THE CLASSICAL COUNTERAR-GUMENTS TO KEYNES

Although Say's Law proved inadequate to deal with recessions in a monetized economy, classical economists[5] found a way out of the dilemma. What if this recessionary process can be halted by ensuring that hoarding (savings, primarily by households[6]) is always matched by an equal quantum of dishoarding (investment, primarily by firms[7])? The classical economists believed that this balance is automatically achieved in a capitalist market economy by way of a *market for loanable funds*, which operates like other markets where price signals, namely interest rates, equilibrate demand and supply. Widely disseminated by popular textbooks, the classical loanable funds model provides a basis for many neoliberal arguments in popular macroeconomics discourse.

In the classical loanable funds model, the quantity demanded for loanable funds (or investment) is considered inversely related to interest rates; lower interest rates induce firms to demand more loanable funds for investment. The quantity supplied of loanable funds (or savings) is positively related to interest rates; higher interest rates incentivize households to save more. The equilibrium rate of interest, much like the equilibrium wage rate,[8] ensures that savings (S) is equal to investment (I). Now suppose a sudden shock (say a massive stock market collapse) leads to a sharp decline in desired investment so that an excess supply of loanable funds arises ($S > I$). Interest rates will consequently fall, ensuring that savings is brought back to equilibrium with the new level of investment. Hoardings are equal to dishoardings so that there is no possibility of a general glut in other markets. Say's Law holds good. The loanable funds market overcomes the Keynesian argument against Say's Law that hoarding can contract output and generate a general glut. An efficient loanable funds market will ensure that savings (hoarding) will always be equal to investment (dishoarding) through the working of the price (interest rate) mechanism.

KEYNESIAN RETALIATION

Keynes, however, did not accept the classical view on interest rates. He argued that interest rate changes may not be adequate to bring savings and investment into equilibrium so that changes in aggregate output and income may be warranted. In other words, interest rates could turn 'sticky' at low levels and thereby unable to balance savings and investment fully. In such a situation, aggregate income would have to contract to *force* quantum of savings (which depends on incomes) down so as to be on par with investment.

Unlike the classical world view, Keynes thought that the demand (I) and supply (S) of loanable funds would be rather inelastic (insensitive/unresponsive) to interest rates. The savings function is inelastic because when interest rates increase (decrease) some people may desire to save more (less) while others may actually decide to save less (more) because they are able (need) to get the same return from a lower (higher) quantum of savings. For example, if my target return from savings is Rs. 10,000 and interest rate is 20 per cent, then I must save Rs. 50,000. However, if the interest rate falls to 10 per cent then I would now have to save Rs. 100,000 to earn the same absolute return of Rs. 10,000. A fall in interest rate increases my level of desired savings. Of course, there are some individuals who may wish to save less at 10 per cent given the decline in incentive to save. These contradictory responses may then lead to a rather inelastic aggregate savings function which is not as responsive to interest rate changes as assumed by the classical economists. Keynes, therefore, considered savings to be a function of income rather than interest rates.

To Keynes, the investment function too would be rather unresponsive to interest rate changes, especially during a depression. Do you think a large automobile company would set up a new plant during a major economic downturn simply because borrowing rates fall by a few basis points, say, from 1 to 0.75 per cent? Decreases in interest rate, given the state of dismal expectations and the relative share of interest payments in their total costs, may not be sufficient to incentivize firms to invest more. There is yet another possibility; a decline in interest rates may leave households with lower disposable incomes which contracts spending. This may have an adverse impact on sales and consequently a decline in investment demand of firms.

Hoarding (saving) decisions are made by different people and for different reasons than decisions to dishoard (invest); hoarding and dishoarding are unlikely to be equal at all times. In the context of inelastic savings and investment functions to interest rate changes, a shock that results in a severe decline in investment may not be brought into equilibrium with savings (*S* remains in excess of *I*), even if the rate of interest falls to zero. Keynes, moreover, ruled out zero or negative nominal interest rates as an impossibility due to the 'liquidity trap' argument (discussed below) wherein interest rates hit a floor at some positive interest rate so that the only way for equilibrium to be restored in the loanable funds market is by forcing the quantum of savings to contract, not in response to interest rates but rather in response to a sharp decline in aggregate output and income. To put it simply, when price cannot bring demand and supply for goods and services into equilibrium, changes in production, output and income are inevitable. This was Keynes' explanation of the Great Depression; its root cause being an exogenous collapse in investment demand that shrunk aggregate output and incomes that forced a consequent decrease in savings by households.

One of Keynes' major contributions was, however, to supplant the classical loanable funds market with the money market where interest rates are determined. Let me sketchily explain Keynes' theory of money or liquidity preference where interest rates are not a reward for saving but compensation for parting with liquidity or hoardings. The equilibrium interest rate is determined in the money market or the market for liquidity given demand for and supply of money or liquidity. People demand liquidity (cash being the most liquid asset) not only for transactions (as a means of exchange) but also for speculative purposes (as an asset). The idea was that at low interest rates (i.e. return on alternative assets[9]) people would desire to hold more money whereas when returns or yields on alternative assets are high, the demand for money is low. Moreover, at low interest rates, small increases in interest rates could lead to heavy capital losses,[10] making cash a more attractive option to hold. The demand for money (liquidity or cash) is therefore inversely related to interest rates. If the central bank determines the total supply of money in the economy, then the equilibrium interest rate is where the demand for money is equal to the supply of money. By increasing the supply of money, the central bank could lower interest rates as people buy alternative assets with surplus liquidity, driving up the price of these assets. With the interest rate falling, people will now be willing to part with liquidity at a lower price for new investment. This could trigger increases in investment and consequently, output and income. This also becomes the basis for Keynesian monetary policy.

Keynes further argued that at low interest rates the demand for money curve becomes perfectly elastic or in other words, the demand for liquidity is infinite. Any increase in money supply will simply be held as cash balances rather than purchase of other assets so that there is no chance of interest rates falling further; this is called the liquidity trap. When increases in money supply cannot lower interest rates and thereby induce people to part with liquidity, the only instrument available to the government to achieve full employment is fiscal policy. While the inability of interest rates to bring about savings and investment into equilibrium are compelling for an economy in recession or depression, there is a role for monetary policy in 'normal' times, when there is some slack in the economy although nowhere close to a liquidity trap.

Some economists point out that although nominal interest rates may not be negative (i.e. when you pay the bank to hold your money), real interest rates[11] could be so if the inflation rate is increased. However, achieving inflation in times of recessions or depressions is not easy as it sounds; Japan has been trying to reach positive inflation rates for decades as well as Europe and the US too, post-2008, have been struggling to achieve an inflation target of + 2 per cent. In any case, if negative nominal interest rates were indeed set (especially on savings or deposits although not on lending) then equilibrium in the loanable funds markets can be restored without contraction of aggregate income and a consequent contraction of savings. Given that people could always hoard cash instead of holding a deposit in a bank at a cost, negative interest rates, however, become possible only in a cashless economy like Sweden,[12] providing additional policy space to mitigate an economic recession or depression.

It is important to make one additional comment on the loanable funds model since it continues to influence popular conceptions on the role of savings and interest rate determination; the level of investment in an economy is savings constrained. Any increase in savings would lead to a decrease in interest rates and a consequent increase in the quantity of investment demand. Moreover, in the classical model, the quantity of money plays no role in the determination of interest rates; the real (or natural rate of interest) depends solely on the real savings and real investment. Banks and financial institutions are mere intermediaries in channellizing savings to investment. The classical loanable funds model was extended in the 1930s by Dennis Robertson and Bertrand Ohlin—the loanable funds doctrine—wherein bank credit was added to the supply of loanable funds in addition to savings. Banks, given their ability to create credit, were now in a position to bring down interest rates and enhance the quantity investment demand.

How relevant are these theories of interest rates in a modern money economy? MMTers generally do not subscribe to either, the classical loanable funds or Keynesian liquidity preference model as they do not capture the essence of how interest rates are determined or rather set in today's world. By ignoring the hierarchy of money and the present institutional context of monetary arrangements, they not only complicate our understanding of money and interest rates but are also an incorrect description of a modern economy, resulting in incongruous policy standpoints. We will present the MMT perspective on monetary policy in Part III of the book.

Coming back to our earlier argument; to Keynes, unlike Say's Law, supply may not automatically create its own demand so that a general glut becomes a real possibility. This general glut or recession is caused by inadequate dishoarding (investment) or what Keynesians refer to as a shortfall in aggregate expenditure, which is the sum of net exports (*X–M*), consumption spending (*C*) and private investment spending (*I*).[13] To set this market failure right, Keynes prescribed that the government step in and spend money (*G*) to compensate for the inadequate level of aggregate demand and to employ the unemployed, a measure referred to as 'fiscal policy'. This in turn would raise demand for goods and services and pull the economy out of depression. Increased government spending could, however, lead to fiscal deficits (an excess of government spending over its revenues); however, for Keynes this per se was not a problem.[14] Rather, it is an instrument that the government must use in order to alleviate unemployment. On inflation, Keynes argued that with surplus capacity that would have arisen across industries and agriculture as the economy slipped into a recession, continually rising prices due to increasing demand would not be a matter of concern.

SUMMARY OF HOW CLASSICAL AND KEYNESIAN IDEAS HAVE SHAPED MACROECONOMIC DISCOURSE

Several interesting insights have been drawn from the classical and Keynesian paradigms, which to a large extent shape popular macroeconomic discourse even today.

1. The classical economists saw the market system as working efficiently in clearing markets through the price mechanism. This is true not only in the goods market but also in labour markets as well as the loanable funds market. State interventions or other imperfections (trade unions) cause distortions, which do not allow markets to clear.
2. Economic policy should be directed at unshackling the economy of supply-side constraints. Once this is done, by Say's Law, supply will create its own demand. Temporary excess demand in any market/s will be matched by an excess supply in other market/s. Price changes will take the economy back to general equilibrium, i.e. where all markets clear. This is a continuous process, which is best left to the market system.
3. In the classical model, money acts as a mere medium of exchange—for present or future exchange of real goods—or in more technical language, money is neutral. Economists look beneath the veil of money to ascertain *real* exchanges in the market.
4. According to classical loanable funds model banks and other

financial institutions act as financial intermediaries that channellize loanable funds from savers (primarily households) to investors (primarily firms). These intermediaries bring in economies of scale and overcome information asymmetry, which otherwise make it difficult for savers to find suitable investors. The notion of banks as financial intermediaries has important implications for mainstream macroeconomic modelling—since banks and credit are nothing but a conduit for transfer of funds from savers to borrowers there is no net effect of such transactions on the economy;[15] banking and credit can then be safely left out of the analysis.

5. Household savings are the main source of loanable funds which firms must use to finance their investment plans. An increase in the savings rate (shift in the savings curve) will bring down interest rates and increase the quantity of loanable funds invested. Private-sector investment is therefore considered savings constrained. The only other source of loanable funds is foreign capital inflows. By basic balance of payments (BoP) accounting, such capital inflows automatically imply a current account deficit.
6. The loanable funds doctrine, however, incorporates banks as creators of credit and suppliers of loanable funds. The market interest rates are, therefore, influenced by the volume of credit created by banks.
7. In the Keynesian view, interest rate changes in the loanable funds market may not be adequate to clear an excess supply of savings. This may induce a contraction in output and income, which forces savings down to the level of autonomous investment.
8. For Keynesians, money is more than a medium of exchange and store of value (to be used as a medium of exchange in future). It is also a financial asset and therefore people may demand it for its own sake and not just a means for present or future exchange. This can invalidate Say's Law.
9. Investment in the Keynesian system is exogenous and depends primarily on *expected sales*, making it rather insensitive (inelastic) to interest rate changes during recessions.

10. In the Keynesian paradigm, investment decisions are subject to uncertainty and risk, making the market system inherently unstable. Shocks that cause a fall in private-sector investment can pull an economy into a recession or depression. The shortfall in aggregate demand ($C + I + X - M$) must be made up by increasing government spending (G) or more generally, expansionary fiscal policies. A capitalist market economy may be at equilibrium with involuntary unemployment. Only state intervention through spending will ensure a return to full employment equilibrium. However, Keynes was open to the idea that once full employment is achieved, the economy could thereafter be supply constrained.
11. Keynesians do not reject monetary policy as a tool for stabilization of the economy; changes in money supply through open market operations and/or changes in cash reserve requirements could influence interest rates and consequently, investment demand and GDP. However, when an economy is in a recession and the money demand function is in the liquidity trap zone, monetary policy is rendered ineffective, making fiscal policy the only meaningful option for economic stabilization.

The Great Depression of the 1930s saw the adoption of Keynesian policies by the US government, although some argue that the efforts were half-hearted. However, the massive government expenditure that the Second World War entailed seemed to have ultimately pulled the West out of a depression that had by then lingered on for almost a quarter of a century.

NOTES

1. I have also excluded the minimal state interventionist, free market Austrian school.
2. In the discussion that follows, I mention Keynes and Keynesians; however, I do not use these in a strict academic sense as to whether Keynes actually said or did not say something.
3. Paul Sweezy's kinked demand curve model establishes sticky prices under conditions of strategic decision-making in oligopolistic markets.

4. The New Keynesian School is discussed later in the chapter.
5. It is important to mention that the debate between classical and Keynes(ians) did not happen sequentially as presented here.
6. Firms also save money.
7. The expenditure on new housing by households is also included in investment spending.
8. This rate of interest where the real demand is equal to the real supply of loanable funds is called the 'natural rate of interest' as proposed by the classical economists, Henry Thornton and later, Knut Wicksell.
9. The alternative asset considered by Keynes was a perpetual bond. But the asset could be stocks and other less liquid assets. The interest rate (or yield) on a bond is $i = c/PB$ where c is the fixed coupon on the bond and PB is the market price of the bond. An increase in PB leads to a decrease in i, for a fixed coupon.
10. Suppose i = 0.005, then if $c = 10$, $PB = 2000$. If interest rates increase to 1 per cent from ½ per cent, then $PB = 1000$, i.e. a 50 per cent capital loss.
11. Real rate of interest is the nominal rate less inflation rate.
12. Jon Henley, Sweden leads the race to become cashless society, *The Guardian*, 4 June 2016, https://www.theguardian.com/business/2016/jun/04/sweden-cashless-society-cards-phone-apps-leading-europe
13. This is the simple Keynesian model. In general, aggregate expenditure (*AE*) is the sum of *C, I, G* and *NX* where *G* is the quantum of government spending and *NX* = net exports or exports (*X*) minus imports (*M*).
14. Consider, for instance, what Britain did at the onset of the First World War. It simply revoked its commitment to the gold standard and started 'printing' currency to buy resources for the war. See, Sashi Sivramkrishna, 'Modern Money and the Obsession Over Fiscal Consolidation', *The Wire*, 4 April 2017, https://thewire.in/121017/modern-money-obsession-fiscal-consolidation/
15. This is except for differences in marginal propensities to consume of the two sets of economic agents. This view of banking and credit will be delved into later in our discussion of MMT.

CHAPTER 3

The Neo-Keynesian Paradigm

A SYNTHESIS OF CLASSICAL AND KEYNESIAN MACROECONOMICS

The post-Second World War era saw ideas from both, Keynesian theory and the classical approach synthesized into neo-Keynesian economics or Neoclassical Synthesis[1]; through the use of statistical techniques the objective was to forecast actual GDP and estimate its deviation from the country's potential GDP or level of output where resources are fully employed. This deviation could be set right using either fiscal and/or monetary policies.

The heydays of neo-Keynesianism coalesced with the Schumpeterian idea of 'co-respective competition' and the welfare state—also called 'embedded liberalism'—that resulted in and what is now looked upon as the Golden Age of Capitalism, at least in the West. Some key statistical parameters in Figure 3.1 make it amply clear why this period may have been eulogized in such terms.

Attributed to some of the greatest economists of the twentieth century, including John Hicks, Paul Samuelson, James Tobin, Robert Solow and Franco Modigliani, the neo-Keynesian model ascertained the rate of interest and real output (GDP) which were simultaneously consistent with equilibrium in the product market (where savings were equal to investment, or the *IS* curve) and money market (demand for money equal to supply of money, or the *LM* curve). The *IS-LM* model further incorporated the view that until full employment was attained, interventionist Keynesian monetary and fiscal policies could be used whereas once an economy reaches full employment the classical paradigm became operative. More specifically, during recessions and depressions, when interest rates sunk into the Keynesian liquidity trap zone, fiscal policy was the most

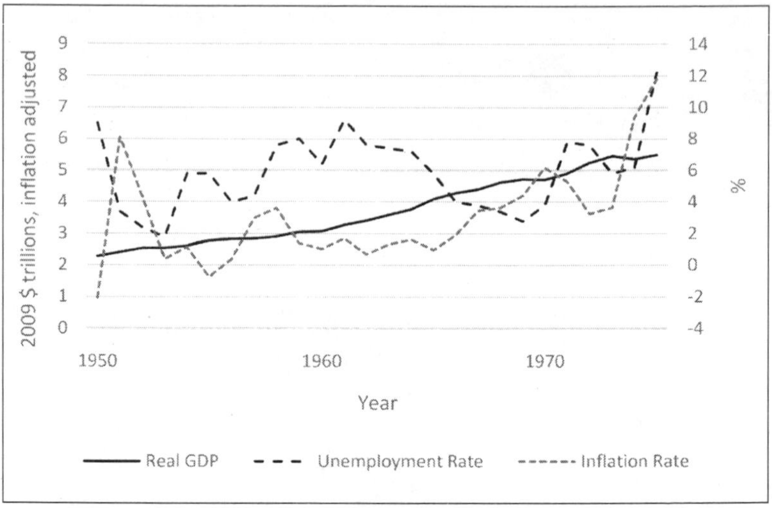

Source: http://www.multpl.com/us-gdp-inflation-adjusted/table

Figure 3.1: Key Macroeconomic Variables for the US during the Golden Age of Capitalism

appropriate policy option while at the other extreme, during booms when the economy is straining past full employment level, interest rates could keep inflation in check. In the 'intermediate' zone between recessions and booms both fiscal and monetary policies could be effectively used to tackle unemployment.

The *IS-LM* curve, however, only indicated the price level (and not inflation rate) consistent with full employment. The Phillips Curve, an empirical relationship between unemployment and inflation rates, not only established a tradeoff between these objectives of macroeconomic policy but also allowed policymakers to predict rates of inflation consistent with any given unemployment rate.

Another contribution of the neo-Keynesian *IS-LM*[2] analysis was to point out that although fiscal policy could be used in reducing unemployment it comes at the cost of affecting the private sector negatively; this is because of the 'crowding out' effect, a term used extensively in contemporary popular discourse. As discussed in the previous chapter, the supply of loanable funds is generated from savings.[3] When the government 'borrows' money for its expenditures, it competes with the private sector for the limited pool of loanable funds. The increased demand for loanable funds raises interest rates and consequently reduces private sector investment. This crowding out effect is now a part of common parlance and is often used as an argument against government spending. The term 'crowding in' is also used widely; however, it is not strictly derived from economic theory but is more an intuitive idea that public spending could raise aggregate expenditure and motivate private-sector firms to invest.

The neo-Keynesian synthesis has been criticized by several economists for its theoretical and empirical inconsistencies and inadequacies—and even by its originator, John Hicks, who later referred to it as nothing more than a 'classroom gadget'. However, there are three specific (theoretical) inadequacies in the model that need mention because they take away from the very essence of Keynes' macroeconomics[4]; first, the role of uncertainty (to which we will return in Part III of the book) which renders the investment function as inherently unstable in a market capitalist economy. Second, the exogeneity of money supply as considered by the *IS-LM* model is problematic. Changes in the monetary base ($M0$ = cash + reserves) induce changes in money supply ($M1$ = cash + bank deposits) through the money multiplier process. The central bank can then reach its target rate of interest assuming that the demand for money function can be estimated and is stable. This view is challenged on several accounts; the exogeneity of money, the money multiplier process as well as institutional mechanism of setting the interest rate by the central bank does not conform to present-day institutional realities. Third, the inability of the *IS-LM* model to establish unemployment equilibrium without the introduction of market distortions and imperfections like wage and price stickiness misses the essence of Keynesian theory, which, as seen above, was the possibility of unemployment equilibrium without market imperfections. These shortcomings effectively rendered Keynes' ideas in the neo-Keynesian view to a special case of the classical model rather than considering it a paradigm shift.

Nonetheless, market capitalism supported by state intervention witnessed rising living standards and abundant social security in the post-War period (1950-70). Complemented by low inflation rates, this was indeed the period when the Western world flourished. Post-independent India too was influenced by neo-Keynesianism along with elements of central planning as practised in the former USSR. Although India did not experience the same growth in living standards as the West, the role of government as a prominent participant in economic affairs became firmly entrenched.

SUMMARY OF HOW NEO-KEYNESIANISM HAS SHAPED MACROECONOMIC DISCOURSE

Let me briefly summarize some insights from neo-Keynesianism that filter seamlessly into today's macroeconomic discourse.

1. The efficacy of Keynesian demand-side fiscal policy as well as monetary policy to manage the business cycle.
2. The ineffectiveness of monetary policy during times of deep recession or depression when the economy has hit the liquidity trap. The need for fiscal policies in times of extreme slowdowns or recessions.
3. The effective use of monetary policy to control inflation in times of boom.
4. The possibility of expansionary fiscal policy crowding out private-sector investment and consumption spending in the 'intermediate zone' between boom and bust.
5. The tradeoff between unemployment and price level or between growth in GDP and inflation based on the Phillips Curve that allows the government to choose from a menu of unemployment-inflation combinations.

The Golden Age led economists to believe that they had finally found the answers to tame the business cycle and establish a set of policy options for long-term growth and stability. The euphoria was short-lived; just two decades after its success, neo-Keynesianism would see its fall and abandonment for a long time to come.

NOTES

1. Although drawing generously from Keynesian ideas, the term neo-classical synthesis was preferred to neo-Keynesian because of anti-left McCarthyism in the US in the 1950s.
2. *IS* stands for product market equilibrium ($I = S$) and *LM* stands for money market equilibrium (money demand or $L = M$ or money demand).
3. This could include the hoardings of households and firms.
4. This is what post-Keynesians highlight, unlike the neo-Keynesians and New Keynesians who focus on market imperfections as the cause of unemployment.

CHAPTER 4

Monetarism and the Decline of Neo-Keynesianism

A PARADIGM SHIFT

Alas, golden ages don't last forever; by the 1970s embedded liberalism, and with it the neo-Keynesian paradigm, came under threat with several important events gathering momentum. First and foremost was the phenomenon of stagflation—growing unemployment with higher rates of inflation. While the neo-Keynesians claimed this to be a result of the oil shocks on account of the war in the Middle East, the pro-market economists argued that this was inevitable due to profligacy of the government. Left-of-centre and some heterodox economists, however, viewed this argument as a ploy to dismantle Keynesianism and with it the growing share of labour in domestic output vis-à-vis the private-sector capitalist class; while labour's share in GDP had grown in the post-war years, the share of the top 1 per cent had fallen from 16 per cent to just 8 per cent of national income during this period.[1] Free trade and flow of capital, embodied in the notion of globalization, were important instruments to tame domestic labour and check rising real wages. Stability in exchange rates was, however, a necessary condition for such global movement in goods, services and capital. With the era of fixed exchange rates abandoned in the early 1970s, volatility under a floating exchange rate regime had to be curbed, which in turn necessitated stable domestic inflation rates. Strong government involvement in the economy and its corollary—the welfare state—could potentially disrupt the process of globalization and prevent the capitalist class from extracting a larger portion of the GDP pie. Pro-market forces, not always conducive to domestic businesses, were unleashed across countries supported by multinational corporations and international institutions, particularly the International Monetary Fund (IMF), the World Bank and the World Trade Organization (WTO).

Although inflation rates barely went beyond 15 per cent in the West, the fear of it cascading into unmanageable levels was enough reason to begin dismantling the neo-Keynesian edifice along with its accompanying institutional apparatus. The alternative? A new wave of economists began scripting a return to free market capitalism—neoliberalism—where state intervention in active management of the economy came to be considered more a hindrance to sustainable growth and development than a necessity. The attack on neo-Keynesianism was theoretically intense and in a race to annihilate it the baton was passed from one 'great' economist to another—John Muth, Robert Lucas, Thomas Sargent, Eugene Fama, Finn Kydland and Edward Prescott; most of them being rewarded with a Nobel Prize for their success in minimizing if not eliminating the role of the state in the efficient functioning of free market capitalism.

But the economist who must be 'credited' for initiating this attack on neo-Keynesianism was Milton Friedman. Although many of his specific policy recommendations have been long been abandoned, he sowed the seeds for a 'new' macroeconomics, one which would dominate the narrative for the next three decades—neoliberal macroeconomics and the return to the classical world view. Much has been written and discussed about Friedman's 'monetarism'; our purpose here is merely to outline some of its basic propositions rather than enter into a technical discussion of the theory itself.

Friedman's most significant achievement was to bring inflation and monetary policy (control of money supply) into the centre stage of macroeconomic discourse while at the same time subduing the role of activist fiscal policy and relegating unemployment to market forces. He began by questioning the efficacy of using fiscal policy—government and tax rates—in taming the business cycle. These instruments of fiscal policy were sluggish and worked with long lags in bringing about full employment and simultaneously keeping inflation rates in check. Friedman also attacked the (neo)-Keynesian idea that monetary policy could be used to influence the real economy and unemployment rate. In fact, monetary easing according to Friedman would only lead to higher inflation in the longer run, without actually lowering unemployment from its 'natural rate'. In other words, policies that tried to lower unemployment from its 'natural rate' would perhaps work only in the short-run at the cost of accelerating inflation in the long run.

The 'natural rate of unemployment' or 'non-accelerating inflation rate of unemployment' (NAIRU) is the rate of unemployment where there is no pressure for wages to increase, which emanates from demand pressures in labour markets. What happens when there is an expansion of money supply due to an expansionary fiscal and/or monetary policy? According to Friedman, this monetary expansion would lead to a fall in interest rates, triggering an increase in investment and consumption spending so that aggregate demand for goods and services as well as labour expands—which in turn results in rising output prices in the short-run. Firms, in response to increasing aggregate demand and falling real wages,[2] increase the quantity demanded of labour. Since workers suffer from 'money illusion' (i.e. they react to nominal wages rather than real wages in the short-run), workers may respond to this increased labour demand of firms at the same nominal wage resulting in a lower level of unemployment from the natural rate. This, however, is the case in the short-run; once workers realize that prices have risen, wage contracts will be redrawn so that nominal wages increase to the full extent of an increase in output prices—the real wages fall back to their original level—the economy is back to square one—employment returns to its natural rate. The only change that has occurred in the process is a higher price level matched by a proportionate increase in nominal wages.

Now if workers build in the history of inflation into labour contracts so as to maintain constant real wages, the only way for policy to be effective is to somehow beat their expectations (as incorporated in their contracts) or, in other words, engage in expansionary fiscal and/or monetary policy that accelerates output inflation beyond the expected rate. However, once again, over time, as explained above, the economy would ultimately return to its natural rate of unemployment—although with an even higher rate of inflation once input prices adjust. Continued expansion in money supply on account of expansionary fiscal and/or monetary policy will not have any long-term impact on the unemployment rate although the economy experiences an accelerating inflation rate. The Phillips Curve which was the mainstay of Keynesian theory was rechristened as the Short Run Phillips Curve while the Long Run Phillips Curve was now vertical implying that in the longer run an economy cannot permanently reduce its natural rate of unemployment using expansionary fiscal and/or monetary policy.

CENTERING INFLATION IN MACROECONOMIC DISCOURSE

Instead of rejecting monetary policy *in toto*, Friedman cleverly recast its role—what it can and should do; the central bank must maintain price stability by ensuring stable growth in money supply as defined by the most relevant monetary aggregates, like for instance, total currency in circulation plus demand deposits ($M1$). For Friedman, rather than targeting unemployment, money supply was the primary determinant of inflation; an increase in money supply would raise inflation and vice versa. Discretion in money supply growth should be avoided; rather growth in money supply should follow a fixed rule and be in sync with GDP growth.

In the working of the market system, price signals are crucial because they contain information on shortages and excesses. By responding to price signals, individuals and businesses eliminate these imbalances and in the process ensure efficient use of resources. Inflation distorts the functioning of the price mechanism in many ways[3] including uncertainty over exchange rates that adversely affects international capital flows, difficulty for firms to distinguish changes in relative prices from changes in the general price level so that use of lower-priced inputs may not take place, rising interest rates as lenders incur losses on capital lent, eroding purchasing power of fixed income earners especially in the informal sector.

Inflation must therefore be maintained at low and stable (predictable) levels. An efficient market system will then propel an economy on to a path of long-term growth in an environment of competition and innovation. The oil shocks of the 1970s and the emerging phenomenon of stagflation (accelerating inflation with higher levels of unemployment) strengthened the validity of Friedman's theory and ensured departure from neo-Keynesianism.

SUMMARY OF HOW MONETARISM HAS SHAPED MACROECONOMIC DISCOURSE

To summarize, Friedman's monetarism shook the neo-Keynesianism and raised doubts over the latter's efficacy.

1. Fiscal and monetary policy could alleviate unemployment in the short-run insofar as they were unanticipated or in some sense were in the nature of 'shocks'.
2. Monetarism denied the efficacy of fiscal and/or monetary policy in the long-term to reduce the natural rate of unemployment—the trade-off as predicted by the Phillips Curve would not hold in the long run. In the long run, the Phillips Curve would actually be vertical meaning that expansionary fiscal and monetary policy would be ineffective in alleviating unemployment although the inflation rate would rise.
3. Money supply was seen as the determinant of inflation and its growth had to be contained. Moreover, it would be appropriate for money supply growth to follow a fixed rule rather than by discretion.
4. Monetarism viewed money supply growth as exogenous and its control was possible through control of high-powered money (HPM or $M0$ = cash + reserves) through changes in the cash reserve ratio (CRR) or through open market operations.
5. The only long-term policy option available to lower the natural rate of unemployment was to alleviate supply-side structural constraints.

A paradigm shift in macroeconomics was once again underway.

NOTES

1. Jason Hickel, *A Short History of Neoliberalism*, http://www. newleft-project.org/index.php/site/article_comments/a_short_history_of_ neo-liberalism_and_how_we_can_fix_it
2. Real wages are the nominal wage deflated by the price level. It can also be thought of as the purchasing power of a nominal wage in terms of real goods and services.
3. The infatuation over inflation by the European Central Bank (ECB) is well known. Their document, Price Stability: Why is it Important for You?, 2009, available at https://www.ecb.europa.eu/pub/pdf/other/ whypricestabilityen. pdf?d216ec331f60449d4afb9fe259eb6cce is a must-read for all those who want to understand the present fixation particularly in the West over 'low and stable inflation rates'. The reasons for concern over inflation in the developing world could be quite different – especially its impact on the purchasing power of the poor.

CHAPTER 5

The 'New' Macroeconomics

FROM THE NEW CLASSICAL MODEL TO NEW CONSENSUS MACROECONOMICS

Friedman's ideas were developed and refined to (mathematical) perfection all through the 1970s, beginning with the rational expectations model. By introducing the notion of rational expectations wherein on average economic agents can predict the future actions of the government, New Classical Macroeconomics propagated a return to *laissez-faire*, effectively relegating Keynes and Keynesianism to history and in doing so altered not only the goal of macroeconomic policy but also the role of the state in managing the economy. First, replacing Friedman's adaptive expectations with rational expectations[1] meant that fiscal policy was 'proven' incapable of affecting output and employment not just in the longer term but even in the short term. Attempts to use fiscal policy to achieve full employment only led to inflation. Second, since policies are likely to have a short-run effect but only with unanticipated monetary policy, there would be an incentive for the government to 'cheat'. To eliminate the use of discretionary powers by the government, the New Classical economists suggested the responsibility for an anti-inflationary policy to be assigned to an 'independent central bank'. It was then the duty of the independent central bank to control inflation using the interest rate (rather than money supply)[2] as their instrument. Of course, the appropriate longer term sustainable policy was to curb the fiscal deficit itself, which would effectively check inflation expectations and thereby minimize the need for curbing private sector's aggregate expenditure components (i.e. consumption and investment spending) through interest rate hikes. Third, the entire Keynesian edifice of forecasting GDP and using policy instruments to counter deviations from the potential level was shaken at its foundation by the 'Lucas critique'; the past is no guide to the future because economic agents change their behaviour according to policy. The structural relationships used in econometric modeling had therefore to be abandoned—and with it, the neo-Keynesian paradigm too. Finally, based on the work of David Ricardo, New Classical economists also 'proved' that fiscal policies financed by bonds were unlikely to have any effect as people would cut back present consumption in order to save for future taxes that will be raised to repay the national debt at some point of time in the future. This is the so-called Ricardian equivalence theorem.

The attack on Keynesianism continued unabated through the 1980s. Another seminal model in the New Classical paradigm that once again negated the economic role of the state was the 'real business cycle' (RBC) approach to observed fluctuations in output and income over the long run. Rather than viewing the business cycle as a response to monetary (or nominal) shocks, RBC theory proposed that the business cycle was an optimal response to random (stochastic) supply-side shocks arising from technological progress. The fluctuations in output and income are the response and dynamic adjustment by economic agents to these random shocks as the economy moves towards a new (general) equilibrium across markets.

The impact of real shocks on the economy are captured by Dynamic Stochastic General Equilibrium (DSGE) models, which are built on the assumption of rational representative agents dynamically maximizing their utilities subject to budget constraints and firms maximizing profits subject to production and technological constraints and then logically solving these equations for general equilibrium. The policy implications from the RBC approach were neoliberal to the core; monetary policy has no effect on real variables (neutrality of money) and fiscal stabilization policy will only reduce welfare given that the business cycle is the optimal (welfare maximizing) response to real shocks and any deviation from that must necessarily reduce welfare. Some insights drawn from RBC-DSGE models are rather astounding. As Paul Krugman tauntingly remarks:

> [According to RBC theory] the business cycle reflects fluctuations in the rate of technological progress, which are amplified by the rational response of workers, who voluntarily work more when the environment is favorable and less when it's unfavorable. Unemployment is a deliberate decision by workers to take time off.
>
> Put baldly like that, this theory sounds foolish—was the Great Depression really the Great Vacation? And to be honest, I think it really is silly.[3]

Meanwhile, the New Classical paradigm was contested by another emerging paradigm in the 1980s: New Keynesian macroeconomics. Drawing upon some of the criticisms of Keynesians against the classical school, they argued that the existing market system could not be considered perfect. Several imperfections exist in markets including nominal wage and product price rigidities, imperfect information, imperfect competition, and coordination failures. Under such conditions continuous market clearing by the market system cannot be assumed; instead, these imperfections may affect real variables like output and employment, particularly in the short-run. The New Keynesians, however, unlike earlier Keynesians, were keen to build a macroeconomic paradigm based on strong microfoundations and therefore began with optimizing consumers and firms. RCB-DSGE provided the appropriate foundation.

Within mainstream macroeconomics a synthesis of both, RBC and New Keynesian approach emerged in the 1990s, referred to as the 'New Neoclassical Synthesis' or 'New Consensus Macroeconomics (NCM)'. The DSGE model incorporating New Keynesian imperfections were used to study the market system response to not just supply-side shocks (technological change) but other random shocks as well. For instance, what kind of adjustments will follow in (say) an emerging economy from a commodity price crash, oil price decline or the Federal Reserve raising interest rates? DSGE models with New Keynesian assumptions and constraints were also built to study the impact of monetary policy shocks on the economy.

It is important to mention that the New Keynesian paradigm encompasses a wide range of assumptions and policy options. At the vintage Keynesian end you have those supporting expansionary fiscal policy especially in recessionary times. In the longer run, however, the fiscal deficit and public debt must come under control and it will, through self-financing when tax revenues rise. On the more neoliberal end we have other New Keynesians who go by several classical assumptions like the loanable funds model, Say's Law, neutrality of money, even oppose fiscal policy and are in favour of austerity. Nonetheless, the general trend in macroeconomics is now to introduce New Keynesian assumptions of market imperfections into DSGE models.

As economic growth surged ahead in between the mid-1980s and 2007, new macroeconomics took credit for having conquered the business cycle—euphorically called the 'Great Moderation'. Celebrating this triumph, Robert Lucas, a pioneer in dismantling neo-Keynesianism commented:

> Macroeconomics in this original sense has succeeded: its central problem of depression prevention has been solved, for all practical purposes, and has in fact been solved for many decades. . . . The potential for welfare gains from better long-run, supply-side policies exceeds by far the potential from further improvements in short-run demand management.[4]

Higher rates of growth and price stability were also accompanied with reduced volatility in some of the key economic real variables including industrial production, output and employment. With central banks independent from government intervention, the short-term interest rate based on the Taylor Rule[5] was used as the key instrument to tame inflation and unemployment when actual levels deviated from their desired or potential levels. It was celebration time for mainstream macroeconomists.

But history repeats itself; even as more complex and intricate NCM-DSGE studies proliferated, none were able to predict the looming financial crisis of 2008. While several economists have criticized DSGE in the aftermath of the GFC, I think Robert Solow's scathing attack is worth mentioning:

> I do not think that the currently popular DSGE models pass the smell test. They take it for granted that the whole economy can be thought about as if it were a single, consistent person or dynasty carrying out a rationally designed, long-term plan, occasionally disturbed by unexpected shocks, but

adapting to them in a rational, consistent way. . . . The protagonists of this idea make a claim to respectability by asserting that it is founded on what we know about microeconomic behavior, but I think that this claim is generally phony. The advocates no doubt believe what they say, but they seem to have stopped sniffing or to have lost their sense of smell altogether.[6]

THE CONTINUING DOMINANCE OF THE NEW CONSENSUS MACROECONOMICS

How did the mainstream macroeconomics respond to such criticisms in the aftermath of 2008? After all, macroeconomists must provide us with an analysis and solutions to market failures and crises, not merely ascribe booms to themselves—which could have been due to exogenous factors like technology, expanding markets and access to cheap resources and labour. Unfortunately, NCM-DSGE models and more generally mainstream macroeconomics has changed little, insisting that their models had got it right in the past and can be modified and extended—incorporating New Keynesian imperfections, along with a government intertemporal budget constraint as well as Taylor rule—to capture the complexities of the real world.

Meanwhile, in India too, the New Keynesian model continues to rule the roost amongst macroeconomists. The Urjit Patel Committee had unambiguously stated on page 12 of its report that it was influenced by the New Keynesian research programme.

. . . [it] had limited itself to the basic three-equation New Keynesian model—or what has interestingly been described as a *monetary model without money*. Such a basic model has little use in actual policy design or analysis . . . [there is a need] to bring together a richer set of New Keynesian analyses of the Indian economy.[7]

It is interesting to note that while Urjit Patel is currently Governor of India's central bank, the author of the article Niranjan Rajadhyaksha is the Executive Editor of one of India's most cogent business dailies. Implicitly, New Keynesianism, one may therefore infer, frames the academic macroeconomic discourse and thereby strongly influences the popular discourse in India as well today. But can a monetary model that has its foundations built on the assumption of a moneyless economy be spruced up to actually shape macroeconomic policy; moreover, macroeconomic policy in which monetary policy (interest rates) is deemed supreme with little room for fiscal policy?

A couple of paragraphs from a working paper[8] by one of India's foremost macroeconomists, D.M. Nachane—the first from the introduction and the other from the conclusion to his paper—captures the present state of the dominant macroeconomic paradigm:

> Additionally . . . the models in spite of being strongly tied to theory, can be 'taken to the data' (to use a phrase which has become standard in this literature) in a meaningful way. A major feature of these models is that their theoretical underpinnings lie in what has now come to be called as the New Consensus Macroeconomics (NCM) which established itself in the 1980s as the *weltanschauung* of the bulk of the macroeconomics profession.
>
> . . . While the DSGE models superficially do give an impression of being 'scientific', a closer look casts strong doubts on the validity of such a claim, rather the theories are scientific but vacuous. . . . The DSGE modelers would possibly plead that they recognize the importance of these problems [real world phenomena] but they are analytically intractable. Economic policy is 'hard' in the sense of being difficult to solve *formally*. . . .

Having read through several NCM-DSGE papers what I find most disconcerting is who decides which is the 'right' DSGE exercise that one should abide by? There are so many, each with its own sets of assumptions, spewing out estimates of how the economy is likely to respond to some random shock. Moreover, on the one hand there is this immense hope that DSGE models are inching slowly but surely to encompass the complexities of the real world but at the end of the exercise we are told that 'further research is needed' or even worse, that DSGE models are plain inadequate and they will forever remain so. But can such an approach really serve as the basis for policy? Imagine that in the field of medical research a scientist comes up with a cure for malaria but without considering the fatal effects of the drug on the liver and kidneys. Will the authorities allow it—or even consider allowing it—to be administered to patients? Or imagine engineers design an aircraft that flies at 2,000 kmph but cannot land. Perhaps from a pure engineering point of view, these are interesting experiments, but would aviation authorities allow such an aircraft to be sold? In macroeconomics, however, such incompleteness is accepted not merely in theory construction but more unfortunately, policies based on such theories may even be adopted.

More specifically, there are three important assumptions in the NCM model—drawn from a paper by Arestis and Sawyer[9]—which need to be highlighted: first, banks and financial institutions are excluded in this model. Anyone familiar with the history of crises in market capitalism will know that most of them have emanated from the banking and financial sector. This is not merely a simplifying assumption but a lack of understanding of modern money, the institutional and operational complexities of a modern monetary economy and plain arrogance in spite of a major crisis that should have undermined their belief system. Second, 'fiscal policy is deemed impotent in this approach by construction . . . this takes the form of the government's intertemporal budget constraint', which states that current debt must be compensated by fiscal surpluses in the future. Once again, does the government actually face a budget constraint like households and firms? Or is this just a blatant flaw in the NCM perception of modern money? Finally, based on the erroneous idea that private sector spends all its income (deficits/surpluses are zero) it follows from basic double-entry book-keeping that in a closed economy public sector must also be left with no surpluses/deficits. The essence of Keynes was to point out the inherent instability of private sector investment demand arising from uncertainties in market capitalism. How can a macroeconomic theory assume that people spend all their income when the root of crises is to the contrary, a lack of effective demand or to put it bluntly, sales? The bottom line of market capitalism is sales (a term that economists find too mundane). Without sales businesses sink and so does the economy. NCM also fails to recognize that when people do not spend their incomes, they desire net financial asset accumulation. And this simply cannot be assumed away. It is no surprise then that Arestis and Sawyer's critique of NCM is sub-titled, 'an unreliable guide for policy'.

While the NCM paradigm proliferates as a science of macroeconomics (with all its fallacious and stultifying assumptions), it leaves behind a policy imbroglio that seems to randomly draw from the world of contradictory macroeconomic paradigms including classical, Keynesian, neo-Keynesian and monetarist theories. This per se may be an acceptable approach to macroeconomics—a separation of science from policy relevance—however, what is missing even in the latter[10] is something that David Colander deems necessary: 'This policy search requires a practical sense of real world institutions, a comprehensive knowledge of past literature, familiarity with history, and a well-tuned sense of nuance.'[11]

With a growing consensus on the absence of these necessary elements of policy-making in the NCM framework, it is only a matter of time before it becomes redundant even in mainstream macroeconomics discourse. Although touted as the framework adopted by economic institutions, the popular macroeconomic discourse still seems to draw primarily from earlier theories—from classical to new classical and Keynesian to neo-Keynesian—that developed until the mid-1980s. The microfoundations approach to macroeconomics is simply too far drawn out from present institutional and political realities to be of policy relevance.

Let me end with a short extract from the lecture notes of an economist at a renowned American university at the height of NCM. His treatment of the government in a modern economy exemplifies the bizarre state of affairs in macroeconomics.

GOVERNMENT

So that we can analyse some simple fiscal policy issues, we introduce a government sector into our simple static model in the following manner. The government makes purchases of consumption goods, and finances these purchases through lump-sum taxes on the representative consumer. Let g be the quantity of government purchases, which is treated as being exogenous, and let T be total taxes. The government budget must balance, i.e.

$$g = T \quad (1.28)$$

We assume here that the government destroys the goods it purchases. This is clearly unrealistic (in most cases), but it simplifies matters, and does not make much difference for the analysis, unless we wish to consider the optimal determination of government purchases.[12]

There seems to be no limit to the nonsense floated in the name of macroeconomic theory-building.

SUMMARY OF HOW 'NEW MACROECONOMICS' HAS SHAPED MACROECONOMIC DISCOURSE

The non-economist takes a lot for granted; after all common citizens believe that most arguments are supported by an edifice of academic economics and economists who know the workings of an economy just like a physicist or engineer knows the working of a nuclear power plant. The popular macroeconomic discourse has therefore imbibed many of the ideas emanating from the 'New Macroeconomics'.

1. Fiscal policy is ineffective not just in long run but also in the short run.
2. Expansionary fiscal policy does not alleviate unemployment; it only causes inflation.
3. To prevent governments from resorting to unanticipated expansionary fiscal policy, it is necessary to have an independent central bank that has the autonomy to set interest rates to reach a low and stable inflation target.
4. Capping the fiscal deficit is prudential macroeconomic policy as it allows the central bank to keep interest rates low and thereby enhance private-sector investment.
5. Business cycles are the optimum response of a market economy to technological shocks. If so, interventionist policies of the state are welfare reducing.
6. Deviations from full employment equilibrium are because of market imperfections. The role of the state would therefore be to undertake structural reforms to remove these market imperfections.

The New Macroeconomics is in many ways a return to the classical world with minimal state intervention in the working of the economy. Market forces can be relied upon to take an economy to full employment. The Keynesian idea of the necessity of an interventionist state to correct the inherent problem of the market system in automatically attaining full employment has therefore been rejected by neoliberal macroeconomists. The epitome of the New Macroeconomics has found expression in austerity policies adopted by several countries in the post-GFC era.

NOTES

1. Friedman's views were based on adaptive expectations. People adapt their behaviour to policies after their announcement. There will be a lag between policy action and change in behaviour of economic agents (say, renegotiating a wage contract) during which time there could be a positive outcome from that policy action. With rational expectations people on average can guess correctly the outcome of the policy. As soon as policy action is announced the economic agents change their behaviour without a lag. The policy action may then have no effect.
2. Friedman's policy instrument was money supply—attempts to control money supply were entirely futile and ultimately abandoned. This is because money supply endogenous and not exogenously determined.
3. Paul Krugman, 'How did economists get it so wrong?', *New York Times* Magazine, 2 September 2009, http://www.nytimes.com/2009/09/06/magazine/06Economic-t.html
4. Lucas, R.E. (2003) 'Macroeconomic Priorities', *American Economic Review* 93(1): 1-14.
5. Taylor's Rule is a guideline for how central banks should alter interest rates to deviations in actual inflation and output (and therefore employment) from their targeted levels. Based on the mandate of the central bank given by the government, weights could be assigned to inflation and output.
6. Prepared statement of Robert Solow, Professor Emeritus, MIT, to the House Committee on Science and Technology, Sub-committee on Investigations and Oversight: Building a Science of Economics for Real World, 20 July 2010, https://web.archive.org/web/20110204034313/http://democrats.science.house.gov/Media/file/Commdocs/hearings/2010/Oversight/20july/Solow_Testimony.pdf
7. Niranjan Rajadhyaksha, 'Adding Heft to Inflation Targeting', *Livemint*, 24 May 2017, http://www.livemint.com/Opinion/awcb2VXiHFhbbQnRnk

O4XL/Adding-heft-to-inflation-targeting.html. Italics my own for emphasis.

8. D.M. Nachane, 'Dynamic Stochastic General Equilibrium Modeling: Theory and Practice', WP-2016-004, Indira Gandhi Institute of Development Research, Mumbai, January 2016, http://www.igidr.ac.in/pdf/publication/WP-2016-004.pdf
9. Philip Arestis and Malcolm Sawyer (2008), 'The New Consensus Macroeconomics: An Unreliable Guide for Policy', Revista Análise *Econômica*, 26(50): 275-95.
10. Abstraction from institutional realities and complexities may be justified in theory building but is not justifiable in design of policy.
11. David Colander, 2010, 'Is the fundamental science of macroeconomics sound?', file:///C:/Users/Sashi/Downloads/IsTheFundamental Science OfMacroecono_preview.pdf
12. Steve Williamson, 'Notes on macroeconomic theory, 1999', http://www.econ.yale.edu/smith/econ510a/notes99.pdf

CHAPTER 6

From Stabilization to Growth and Development

THEORIES OF ECONOMIC GROWTH

Did neoliberal polices deliver a positive outcome since its revival in the 1970s? As mentioned earlier, to many neoliberal macroeconomists the answer lay in the Great Moderation; the period between 1980s and 2007 when the US experienced decreased macroeconomic volatility (Figure 6.1), both in inflation rates and the level of output and employment. Ben Bernanke in his 2004 speech to the Eastern Economic Association argued that it was improved monetary policy, specifically in targeting inflation rather than output and employment which brought about this structural change. While conceding that the Great Moderation could also be attributed to 'good luck' wherein exogenous shocks did not occur or have the same effect as in the Neo Keynesian (Golden Age) period he contemplates the possibility that shocks were actually endogenous and that improved monetary policy had in fact altered the distribution of shocks.

> The Great Moderation, the substantial decline in macroeconomic volatility over the past twenty years, is a striking economic development. Whether the dominant cause of the Great Moderation is structural change, improved monetary policy, or simply good luck is an important question about which no consensus has yet formed. I have argued today that improved monetary policy has likely made an important contribution not only to the reduced volatility of inflation (which is not particularly controversial) but to the reduced volatility of output as well. Moreover, because a change in the monetary policy regime has pervasive effects, I have suggested that some of the effects of improved monetary policies may have been misidentified as exogenous changes

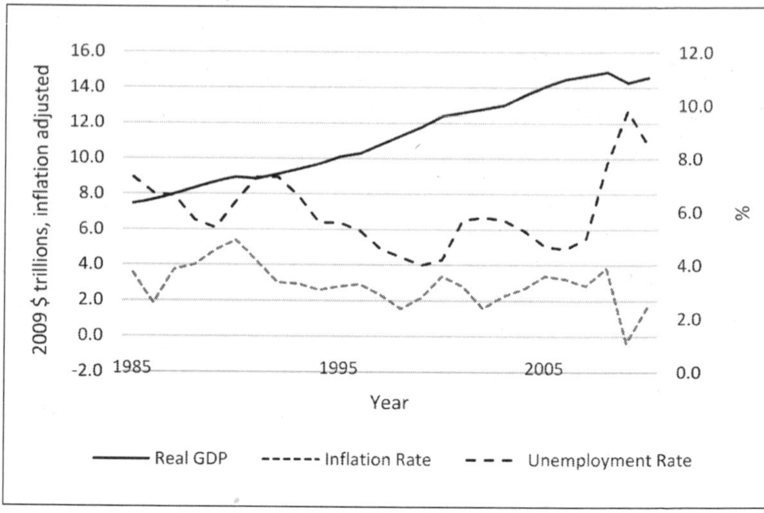

Source: https://fred.stlouisfed.org/series/GDPC1

Figure 6.1: Key Macroeconomic Variables for the US during the Great Moderation

in economic structure or in the distribution of economic shocks. This conclusion on my part makes me optimistic for the future, because I am confident that monetary policymakers will not forget the lessons of the 1970s.[1]

The GFC of 2008, however, changed all these suppositions and hypotheses. The New Macroeconomists had to concede that their understanding of the economy was far from complete and the claim of the 'end of macroeconomics' was perhaps misconceived. Although a return to Keynes seemed inevitable, it was feeble and except for some half-hearted fiscal measures taken in the US in the immediate aftermath of the crisis, the neoliberal agenda remained fairly intact. In fact, austerity (fiscal restraint) is rearing its head back as governments make way for the market system wherein the private sector—in its pursuit of profit—maximizes 'social welfare',[2] macroeconomic growth and even development.

Short-term stabilization is, however, only one facet of the macroeconomic paradigm, the other two being growth and development. How does the new macroeconomics perceive growth and development? Let me begin with growth. Economic growth refers to increasing per capita incomes, the output per worker or productivity of labour. This is possible through the accumulation of capital, both physical and human. Think about it; if you were able to generate an output of ten pages per day working on an old typewriter, how could you increase your output to say fifty pages per day? One way would be to invest in a computer and a printer (physical capital) while also acquiring computer skills (human capital). But these investments are possible only if you or someone else (from whom you would borrow) saved. This was the basis for the earliest model of economic growth proposed by Roy Harrod and Evsey Domar. The main constraints to growth are capital stock, which in turn depended on the nation's marginal propensity to save or its ability to attract external funds as well as capital-output ratio. The latter furthermore depended on technology. But for how long can growth be sustained? Returning to our example, once you have invested in the computer and training, working additional hours could increase output but this will be subject to the law of diminishing marginal returns. As additional productivity gains slow down, economic growth stagnates and a fresh impetus to growth is only possible through further technological progress and innovation. You will need a better word processor with improved software and a faster printer. Technology and innovation were the keys to sustained growth in Robert Solow's thesis. In the neo-Keynesian view, the state was seen as an important 'exogenous' player in propagating technological progress; state-run R&D labs, university research and education, nurturing specialized institutions, both in industry as well as agriculture. Technologies could then be disseminated at a subsidized price to industry.

However, just as neo-Keynesianism fell out of favour in its short-term stabilization role, so did exogenous growth theories. A new *laissez-faire* world view took shape as 'endogenous' growth theories. While this paradigm acknowledged the importance of physical and human capital as well as innovation and knowledge, it reasoned that these could be generated endogenously through the working of the market system (and not exogenously through state interventions). Technological change is a response to economic incentives in the market. What is critical for this process to be forthcoming and sustainable are competitive markets and well-defined property rights.

Neoliberalism does not mean that the government does not spend or that it has no role in a modern economy. From street lighting to defence, from primary education to safety regulations, the government is crucial for the smooth functioning of the market system. However, the intervention must be limited to only those instances where market failure is an acknowledged fact (as in the case of public goods like primary education and health care, skills training, risk and uncertainty in R&D, enforcement of patent laws, etc.). It should be of no surprise when we find that neoliberal economies like Germany spend more than 9 per cent of GDP on health (India spends just 4 per cent) and USA spends 5.5 per cent of its GDP on education (India spends less than 3 per cent). Many advanced nations that are the main proponents of neoliberalism have the most stringent regulations on pollution, effluent treatment, worker safety and working hours. Nonetheless, here too, there was a consensus that governments should not be profligate in their spending; expenditures ideally should not exceed the government's earnings or revenue collections. A balanced budget is what governments must aspire for.

Martin Anderson at the Hoover Institution clearly hoped that neoliberal economic policies would result in this ideal condition in the US: '. . . both political parties [Democrats and Republicans] are committed to a balanced budget—at least by the year 2002—and the current debate is over whether or not we should include a balanced budget requirement in our Constitution.'[3]

THE NEOLIBERAL PARADIGM

The new macroeconomics now had a composite paradigm that included *laissez-faire* stabilization policies along with endogenous growth models. The final facet of macroeconomics, development, was easily subsumed within the stabilization and growth narrative. Low inflation and competitive markets would propel the economy on a high growth path, yielding higher tax revenues for the state, enabling greater social sector spending—the trickle-down effect. There was also a demand for countries to engage in structural reform; since most of the third world had begun their post-colonial phase on a wrong footing with high levels of state involvement in the economy, these had to be undone. Structural adjustment programmes essentially argue in favour of *laissez-faire* principles (free market supply-side policies); lesser state involvement, roll back on blanket subsidies, financial sector reforms and exchange rate depreciation. To reiterate, this does not mean that the state plays no role in social development; additional resources through taxation would enable the state to provide for the social sector (here too interventionist supply-side measures are recommended) which may otherwise be excluded from development due to market failure.

The European Commission articulates the neoliberal focus on structural reforms:

> Structural reforms address impediments to the fundamental drivers of growth by unshackling labour, product and service markets to foster job creation, investment, and productivity. Moreover, they aim to enhance an economy's competitiveness, growth potential and adjustment capacity.[4]

Structural reform is an integral part of a three-part strategy that begins with fiscal responsibility and encourages private investment. Figure 6.2 shows the three pillars of the economic policy priorities of the European Union.

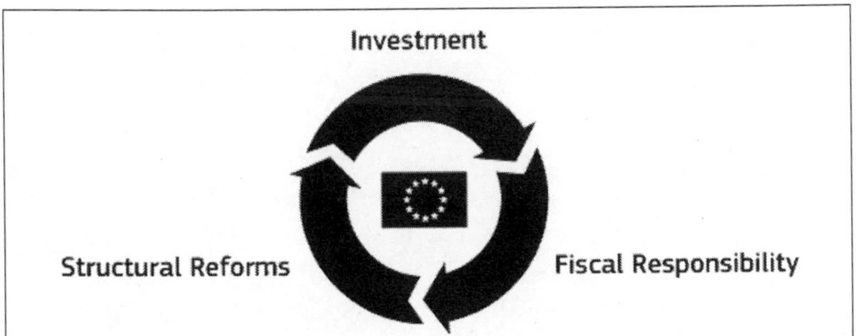

Source: https://ec.europa.eu/info/business-economy-euro/growth-and-investment/structural-reforms/structural-reforms-economic-growth_en

Figure 6.2: Economic Policy Priorities of the European Union

The Washington Consensus (Williamson 1990)[5] was perhaps the most celebrated document outlining neoliberal policies. It too begins with the need for fiscal discipline and advocates the need for prioritizing government expenditure away from *non-merit* goods and services, tax reform, greater liberalization of foreign direct investment, a floating exchange rate regime, privatization and deregulation. Today the Washington Consensus has become synonymous with programmes for structural reforms.

The Washington Consensus also encouraged infrastructure spending while spending on subsidies was discouraged. Subsidies, if they are used at all, should be targeted and wherever possible be delivered through cash transfers rather than in-kind. Only those who deserve the subsidies should receive it, not everyone. Blanket subsidies and transfers not only distort incentives but are also the primary cause of inflation, which then acts as a regressive tax. On the external front too, market forces needed to be unleashed. The removal of non-tariffs barriers, gradual lowering of tariffs, freely floating exchange rates and unrestricted movement of capital are seen as essentials for enhancing global productivity and economic growth. These changes in the international arena require a unified effort among nations and cannot happen in a few countries only.

A conspicuous absence in these documents is the purposeful targeting of unemployment through macroeconomic policy. In fact, a search of Williamson's 2004 paper[6] on the Washington Consensus for the word 'unemployment' yielded only one result but that was in the references, not the main body of the paper. Ignoring unemployment as an objective of policy in the new macroeconomic paradigm should hardly come as a surprise. The belief is that if all other policy prescriptions are indeed implemented, the need to target unemployment becomes redundant. *Laissez-faire* policies will ensure that the market system will always gravitate towards full employment. Although frictional unemployment cannot be ruled out, these occur primarily due to changes in technology and mismatching of skills; it is not a structural problem. Short-term safety nets may be necessary but wage flexibility will ensure that full employment is restored.

The pillars of the new macroeconomics were simultaneously articulated in terms of privatization, liberalization and globalization. Privatization ensures that the government is not in the business of business—business must be driven by the profit motive or maximization of shareholder value. It is the pursuit of profits that makes firms responsive to price signals. If firms are driven by other motives, for instance providing employment, it leads to inefficiencies like surplus output or lower per capita productivity of workers. Liberalization refers to the deregulation of markets; state intervention either through price floors (minimum support prices and minimum wages) as well as price ceilings (rent controls, drug price controls) has a distortionary impact. Quantitative restrictions, rationing or quotas also promote corruption. Excessive regulation also acts as a barrier to entry, limiting competition. Finally, globalization views the world functioning as one market. As barriers to trade, capital flows and ultimately labour flows are dismantled, resources will be optimally allocated across nations. For instance, without artificial wage floors, low wages will initially attract labour-intensive industries in the labour-abundant countries that slowly raises real wages and standards of living. The idea is that once such *laissez-faire* policies are adopted at the micro-level through privatization-liberalization-globalization, the state's role would be restricted to certain essential sectors like provision of public goods and welfare of the poorest of the poor only. As growth realizes additional tax revenues for increased and sustainable developmental activities, governments would be able to control their deficits resulting in macro-level stability in terms of stable and low inflation and consequently, high economic growth.

NOTES

1. Ben Bernanke, 'The Great Moderation', http://www.federalreserve.gov/BOARDDOCS/speechES/2004/20040220/default.htm
2. In economics, social welfare (the sum of consumer and producer surplus) maximization implies allocative efficiency.
3. Martin Anderson, 'The Ten Causes of the Reagan Boom: 1982-97', Hoover Institution, 1 October 1997, http://www.hoover.org/research/ten-causes-reagan-boom-1982-1997.

4. European Commission, 'Structural reforms for economic growth', https://ec.europa.eu/info/business-economy-euro/growth-and-investment/structural-reforms/structural-reforms-economic-growth_en
5. John Williamson, 1990, 'Latin American Adjustment: How Much Has Happened?' (Washington: Institute for International Economics.)
6. John Williamson, 'The Washington Consensus as Policy Prescription for Development, 1990', https://www.piie.com/publications/papers/williamson0204.pdf

CHAPTER 7

A Summary of Neoliberal Macroeconomics

MINIMUM GOVERNMENT

Let me summarize some of the basic tenets of neoliberal macroeconomics:

1. 'Minimum government', low fiscal deficits with low and stable inflation.
2. The primary target of monetary policy should be low and stable inflation. This task must be relegated to an independent central bank, which sets the overnight interest rate in the money market.
3. Government spending—fiscal policy—should be restricted to what is available within their means only, i.e. collected as taxes. Spending beyond their means implies the need to borrow in the market and/or 'printing' new money (borrowing from the central bank). The former 'crowds out' private sector investment spending as the government and firms compete for the same pool of private sector household and firm savings. The demand by the government for the supply of savings drives up the interest rate and reduces private investment because of increases in cost of borrowing.
4. The option of 'printing' money is inflationary and of no longer-term benefit in mitigating unemployment. It is, therefore, ruled-out as a policy option.
5. Let the markets work freely without interventions by the state in the goods and services markets, labour markets, capital markets (for savings and investment) and foreign exchange markets. This is done through free-market supply side policy initiatives including tax policies that are non-distortionary, i.e. they should not affect incentives for incomes and profits.

6. Foreign trade should be free and without quantitative restrictions.
7. To counteract the possibility of profligate government spending, independent central banks have the autonomy to set interest rates and achieve low and stable inflation.
8. An unfettered private sector in a macroeconomic environment of low and stable inflation rates will take the economy towards full employment.

Neoliberalism *centralizes fiscal deficit as the most critical policy variable* that affects the final target of macroeconomic stabilization policy, inflation, rather than output and employment as envisaged by Keynes and the Keynesians. If inflation is indeed so important then the key issue in macroeconomics is to contain the root cause of inflation: fiscal deficits. As long as a government continues profligate spending, the central bank would have to temper demand in the economy by raising (or maintaining) interest rates, making it more expensive for the private sector to borrow from banks and other financial institutions. Herein lies the basis for the rise of fiscal deficit targets as a key parameter in macroeconomic policy; it embodies the essence of macroeconomic debate spanning a period of almost a hundred years.

At the same time, with *laissez-faire* or 'let it (the free market) be' market-determined prices including those for goods and services, wages and interest rates (the price for loanable funds) will ensure that the economy operates at full employment. State intervention in markets at the micro level distorts the working of the market system, resulting in surpluses and shortages in demand and supply. Examples include minimum wage laws, agricultural support prices, export incentives, food and fuel subsidies, and so on. High and progressive taxes do the same by distorting incentives and disincentives to work, save and spend that are critical to the efficient working of the market system.

A FINANCIALLY CONSTRAINED SYSTEM

At the core of neoliberal ideas lies a simple, seemingly commonsensical idea; the economy is financially constrained—savings constrains investment and the state cannot spend beyond its means. This is the power of economic theory—however abstruse a theory may be, over time what remains are the 'simple' takeaways that can be transmitted to a large audience *as if it were obvious.* It would not be out-of-place to quote Keynes here:

> The ideas of economists and political philosophers, both when they are right and when they are wrong are more powerful than is commonly understood. Indeed, the world is ruled by little else. Practical men, who believe themselves to be quite exempt from any intellectual influences, are usually slaves of some defunct economist.

Concerns over the impact of neoliberal policies have, however, been growing across the world over the last three decades. The dismantling of the welfare state has not only relegated issues pertaining to poverty, unemployment and inequality to the private (personal) domain—rather than to structural causes—but have also made the working class more vulnerable and insecure to economic shocks. The rise of multinational corporations and weakening of trade unions has reduced the ability for wage negotiations resulting in the increasing divergence of real wage growth and productivity growth. This is evident from Figure 7.1.

With little room for economic interventions by the government and too much resting with independent central banks and monetary policy, the growing frustration with neoliberalism became palpable in the aftermath of the 2008 crisis. The strong reaction to neoliberal macroeconomics from people and nationalist-populist leaders across the world was therefore not entirely surprising. But policy and popular discourse need an anchor; for a while a return to Keynes seemed inevitable but neoliberal ideas so deeply entrenched have held forth.

Macroeconomics has played a critical role in shaping the discourse on the role of the state in a capitalist market economy. From embedded liberalism to neoliberalism, the world has undergone drastic changes over just a few generations. The stagflation episode of the 1970s led to dismantling of embedded capitalism. While neoliberalism with its emphasis on the efficiency of market forces did raise living standards across the world, it must be ques-

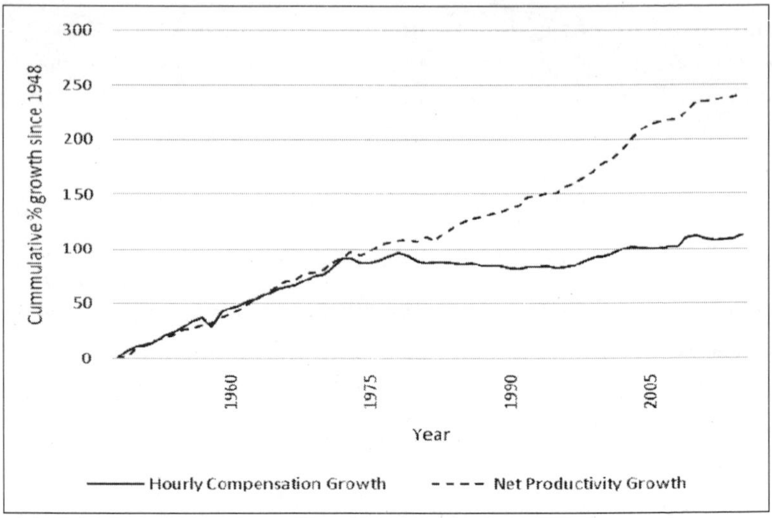

Source: The Productivity-Pay Gap, Economic Policy Institute, http://www.epi.org/productivity-pay-gap/

Note: Data are for average hourly compensation of production/non-supervisory workers in the private sector and net productivity of the total economy. 'Net productivity' is the growth of output of goods and services minus depreciation per hour worked.

Figure 7.1: Divergence in Real Wage and Productivity Growth in the US, 1948-2015

tioned on some its fundamental premises and failures, in particular, unemployment and rising inequalities. Given that a return to Keynesianism failed in the aftermath of the 2008 GFC, a fresh perspective and a fresh narrative to counter neoliberalism is now crucial.

PART II

POPULAR MACROECONOMIC DISCOURSE IN INDIA

CHAPTER 8

Putting India's Current Macroeconomic Policies in Perspective

FALL OF THE UPA GOVERNMENT'S MACROECONOMIC APPROACH

As India assimilated with the world economy under colonial rule, particularly since the mid-nineteenth century, it has been drawn into the vortex of global economic debates. The rise of neo-Keynesianism and the welfare state in the West and consolidation of socialism in the erstwhile USSR in the post-Second World War period coincided with India's independence from colonial rule, tempting it to experiment with *dirigisme* but without adequate success—at least in terms of economic growth and raising standards of living—for it to be sustainable. As the world made a structural break in the 1980s towards neoliberalism, embodied in the privatization-liberalization-globalization mantra, India found itself unable to swim against the tide.

The seeds of change through the adoption of pro-national business (and not necessarily pro-market) policies were planted by Prime Minister Indira Gandhi in the early 1980s on her return to power from the defeat she suffered after the Emergency. It was, however, in 1991 that India embraced full-fledged pro-market neoliberal economic policies, accepting the structural adjustment programme that accompanied the terms of an emergency bailout package from the IMF. Except for bouts of political instability and the inevitability of a thick icing of populist programmes in competitive electoral politics, successive governments continued on the path of pro-market reforms. This was until 2004 when the BJP-led coalition, the NDA unexpectely lost the elections. Its campaign slogan 'India Shining' had been rejected by the masses simply because, as the veteran BJP leader L.K. Advani put it, 'the fruits of development did not equitably reach all sections of our society'.[1]

The then newly-elected Congress-led UPA government, perhaps for the first time since the 1980s made a clear-cut shift in economic policies, from right-of-centre to left-of-centre by adopting a rights-based approach to development. The re-election of the UPA in 2009 was interpreted as an endorsement of this approach to development by the people. However, soon after this achievement, the UPA began floundering both in terms of implementation of programmes and a murky lack of governance that was apparent from several outrageous scams[2] that manifested itself in accelerating inflation, policy paralysis and sagging economic growth rates. Even before the 2014 election, the outcome was apparent—a victory for the NDA under the leadership of the BJP's Narendra Modi. What was shocking was not just the strength of their triumph but the almost total annihilation of the UPA. While the rejection of the UPA's administration was obvious it was not so clear whether or not the electorate had also rejected their approach to development. Nonetheless it seemed as if the BJP's election slogan 'Minimum Government, Maximum Governance' captured the aspirations of the restless India's masses especially its youth for improved opportunities and economic development.

India provides fertile ground to support a range of macroeconomic world views. For sake of completeness, let me once again dispense with the Left or Marxist perspective. As a mainstream political and economic alternative the communist parties are on the wane. This is especially true in large cities and urban areas where there is even less support for these parties, partly because the nature of the industrial working class has undergone major changes in the post-liberalized and globalized world. At the same time urban voters are looking for solutions to their immediate problems like employment, electricity, water, transport, housing and security. Visions of a proletariat revolution and the emergence of a classless society are not the aspiration of the masses especially when the state itself is regarded as corrupt and inefficient. While it would have seemed that the global financial crisis of 2008, de-globalization, agricultural distress, frustration of people over jobless growth, unemployment and inequality, would have been the ideal ground for a revival of the left, it seems to have completely lost the plot in India.[3]

In the present context, pragmatically speaking, the topical left is now rather left-of-centre, which more or less stands for a return to embedded liberalism and a rights-based approach to development that is openly pro-poor by larger allocations of resources to subsidies and social security, a stronger public sector, greater amount of state regulation including that of the financial sector, a heightened focus and a greater role of the state in education and health care, addressing concerns over growing regional, income and wealth inequalities, secularism, women's rights, rights of indigenous (tribal) communities over natural resources, higher minimum wages and agricultural support prices, employment guarantee schemes and strengthening of labour unions. In the second phase of its rule at the centre (2009-14), the UPA adopted such a left-of-centre posture with its entitlements approach, introducing and reinforcing programmes and legislations like the Mahatma Gandhi National Rural Employment Guarantee Act (MGNREGA), Right to Information (RTI), Right to Education (RTE), the rights of indigenous communities over forest resources as embodied in the Indian Forest (Amendment) Act and the Right to Food (National Food Security Act). It even took an overtly anti-business posture in its 2012-13 budget with the introduction of retrospective taxes. However, as mentioned above, the lack of governance, policy paralysis and widespread corruption—after it was re-elected to power in 2008, especially towards the end of its 10-year rule—reduced the approach of the UPA to profligacy, inflation and stagnation.

How do we interpret these policy choices made by different governments from the standpoint of the analysis developed in the previous chapter? In the real-world it is impossible to separate a government's policies into watertight compartments that conform strictly to neoliberal or Keynesian approaches; elements of both are inevitable at any point of time. However, broadly speaking, the BJP has always been considered as India's right or right-of-centre party (not just politically but also economically) with its pro-market, pro-reform and pro-business tilt. This does not mean that it is anti-poor; rather it is a belief that the issue of poverty and unemployment can be solved through rapid economic growth led by the private sector without overwhelming state intervention in the economic sphere. More recently, the demonetization exercise and passing of the Goods and Services Tax regime is seen by the present government as a means of transforming the informal sector and bringing it into the ambit of the formal sector.[4] This *formalization* of the economy will not only widen the tax base (an important element of neoliberalism) but also means that the strategy is not merely privatization but also corporatization of business.[5]

THE RETURN OF NEOLIBERAL MACROECONOMICS

The hope for massive supply-side reforms was definitely expected from the present government in 2014; the 'Gujarat Model of Development' with its business and trade friendly approach seemed in sync with the people's aspirations rather than the UPA's 'freebies'.[6] These hopes were reflected in the popular narrative at that time; for instance, soon after the victory of the NDA, the *Livemint* reported that Modi emphasized the need for poverty alleviation and employment generation 'through policies that *unleash* rapid growth' rather than 'large-scale, redistributive welfare schemes' that resulted in 'merely transitory income in the hands of the poor'.[7]

The *Wall Street Journal* published an article in the same vein, 'Modi Turns to the Supply Side'[8] in which it lists the various steps the new government was taking in order to bring the country out of stagflation (5 per cent growth with 10 per cent inflation):

- Remove disincentives to invest, barriers to hiring and regulatory bottlenecks.
- Rationalization and simplification of the tax regime to make it non-adversarial and conducive to investment, enterprise and growth.
- Deregulation including streamlining bureaucracy and merger of ministries.
- Speeding up of clearances by the Environmental Ministry.
- Amendments to the Land Acquisition Act and Industrial Disputes Act.

- Distortionary subsidies in the agricultural sector that disincentivize the drive to enhanced productivity.
- Lack of stable power supply, quality roads and ports.
- Embracing foreign investment and free trade.
- Reducing bureaucrats discretion and corruption.

These measures along with a series of others including Skill India, Stand Up and Start Up India was seen as nothing short of supply-side revolution. The popular macroeconomic narrative in India has favoured structural reforms. Perhaps one of the clearest remarks I have found on this appeared many years ago in a national daily:

> Are we [India] not a supply-constrained economy rather than a demand-constrained one? While others need to stimulate demand, we need to stimulate supply. . . . Say's Law will thereafter automatically come into play, as supply will create its own demand.[9]

Another key supply-side reform that Indian industry has been hankering for is the removal of interventions in the labour market. The CEO of a leading pharmaceutical company in India put across the objectives of labour reforms:

> If the country needs to create quality jobs, it needs to ensure a minimalist labour regime in the country. . . . Labour reforms must be framed in such a manner that it ensures the ease of doing business and simultaneously leads to jobs creation. India's labour laws are extremely rigid and discourage industrial employers to hire. . . . Besides, the laws should also focus on easing the compliance burden on small and medium enterprises.[10]

There is no doubt that excessive state regulation and interventions do affect the efficient working of the market system and that de-regulation does bring efficiency, growth and jobs. This was certainly the case in India since the 1991 reforms. However, the danger is that such an argument is subtly generalized to mean that the state intervention is *never* necessary like; for instance, these remarks from *Time* are indicative of this predisposition: 'We've all known that India's growth has come not because of its government, but in spite of it. India's IT entrepreneurs joke that they've been successful because the government didn't understand their newfangled industry and thus left it alone. They are right.'[11]

The first departure in the NDA government's policy preferences came in 2016, after its defeat in the Bihar elections. Commentators noticed perceptible pro-rural, pro-farmer, pro-welfare and pro-agriculture policy shifts by the government, with a change from its focus on infrastructure spending and market reforms.[12] In spite of the political successes of the BJP in state elections, the government has also becoming increasingly aware of its greatest challenge on which it still has to emphatically deliver results: employment.[13] Soon after its completion of three years in office, the GDP growth rates estimate slipped to just 6.1 per cent in the January quarter of 2017 and then further down to 5.7 per cent in the June quarter before showing a marginal increase in the September quarter of 2017. Abysmal figures were flashed predominantly in the news almost every other day, putting the government under intense pressure to prove its performance on the economic growth and employment front. The 2017 election campaign in Gujarat of the Congress further brought the unemployment issue into sharper focus. This remains contentious issue as India heads for the general elections in 2019.

To me it seems like the present NDA government is caught between two stools—its prior commitment to the neoliberal agenda (minimum government, maximum governance) of big bang structural reforms anchored by the pillars of privatization-liberalization-globalization and the more recent inward-looking, interventionist and statist positioning perhaps to shake off the tag of being pro-industry or pro-business while also pandering to its nationalist ideology. Moreover, the changes in the global context with the rise of illiberal leaders like Theresa May, Donald Trump, Recep Tayyip Erdogan, Vladimir Putin and Marine Le Pen may have induced a change in the present government's strategy. However, at the same time, there seems to be an underlying fear of neoliberal warnings; fiscal profligacy and destabilizing inflation, and instead relying on the effectiveness of monetary policy through interest rate cuts[14] in triggering private sector investment to kickstart the economy.

The government's response to this predicament will exert a huge influence on India's economic path in the coming years.

NOTES

1. BBC News, BJP admits 'India Shining' error, 28 May 2004, http://news.bbc.co.uk/2/hi/south_asia/3756387.stm
2. However, it must be mentioned that the verdict on the 2G scam in December 2017 has shown that there may have been no scam as made out to be.
3. In the more advanced countries it seems that the left-of-centre is making a resurgence, albeit tentative; Bernie Sanders in the US, Jeremy Corbyn in England and Moon Jae-In in South Korea.
4. R.S. Sharma, 'GST will transform the economy: Piyush Goyal', *Business Line*, 21 June 2017, http://www.thehindubusinessline.com/economy/gst-will-transform-indian-economy-piyush-goyal/article9731996.ece
5. Ken Allen, 'Say "corporatization" not "privatization"', *Huffpost*, 8 November 2011, https://www.huffingtonpost.com/ken-allen/say-corporatization-not-p_b_922892.html
6. Swaminomics by Swaminathan S. Anklesaria Aiyar, Can't buy me an election with budget freebies, 3 March 2013, http://swaminomics.org/cant-buy-me-an-election-with-budget-freebies/
7. Vivek Dehejia, 'Making a "Supply Side" Revolution', *Livemint*, 23 June 2017, http://www.livemint.com/Opinion/l5U2kGQ2hw24QZxXSRCjUJ/Making-a-supply-side-revolution.html
8. 'Modi Turns to the Supply Side', *Wall Street Journal*, 11 June 2014, http://www.wsj.com/articles/modi-turns-to-the-supply-side-1402419886
9. H. Nemkumar and Ashutosh Datar, 'An Open Letter to the Finance Minister', *Wed*, 15 July 2009, Mumbai , DNA, http://www.dnaindia.com/money/comment-an-open-letter-to-the-finance-minister-1274109
10. Habil Khorakiwala, 'Agenda for Education and Labour Reforms', *Business Line*, 11 January 2017, http://www.thehindubusinessline.com/opinion/india-labour-reforms-perspective/article9474121.ece
11. Michael Schuman, 'Is India's Government Killing its Economic Miracle?', *Time*, 18 January 2012, http://business.time.com/2012/01/18/is-indias-government-killing-its-economic-miracle/
12. 'Modi's Budget, in Policy Shift, to Focus on Rural India', CNBC, 28 February 2016, http://www.cnbc.com/2016/02/28/modis-budget-in-policy-shift-to-focus-on-rural-india-officials.html
13. See, for instance, M.K. Venu, 'Modi Government is in Deep Denial over India's "Jobless Growth" Crisis', *The Wire*, 19 May 2017, https://thewire.in/137092/denial-jobless-growth-unemployment-modi-bjp/

14. This strategy is often thwarted by the 'independent' RBI—it is therefore not surprising that the Finance Ministry is trying to exert pressure on the RBI to tow its line. World over, illiberal leaders like Trump and May have expressed their displeasure over the neoliberal idea of an independent central bank.

CHAPTER 9

India's Neoliberal Policy Framework

THE PANACEA OF STRUCTURAL REFORMS

The rise of Keynesian macroeconomics was based on the premise that the economy could be stabilized through the active intervention of the state. Here stabilization was primarily that of output and employment and in this endeavour fiscal policies (government spending and taxes) played a key role. Fiscal policy is, however, only one alternative available in solving the problem of falling output and increasing unemployment. The other is monetary policy wherein central banks set the price at which liquidity[1] is made available to the banking sector, the latter being the principal source of credit to the business and household sectors. This price or interest rate influences the cost of borrowing and thereby private sector investment and spending. Keynes, however, argued that monetary policy may not work during a recession or depression. In such a situation, interest rate is not the only factor which influences the decision to borrow money. Gloomy expectations of future demand in the economy may be so overwhelming that a mere change in costs of borrowing proves inadequate.

Neoliberalism changed the narrative; fiscal policy is ineffective at best, and destabilizing at worst. Monetary policy is a better tool, which should be left to an independent central bank, whose objective is to maintain low and stable inflation rates through setting of short-term interest rates. For sustained growth, the writing on the neoliberal macroeconomic wall was clear; reforms, reforms, reforms. The fine print is even clearer; maintain low and stable inflation and strict fiscal discipline. As the head of an international bank put it; 'India has a huge opportunity ahead of itself . . . key is to increase the pace of structural reforms *and maintain fiscal discipline* . . . the government will have to accelerate the pace of structural reforms even faster.'[2]

While structural reforms could bring in greater efficiencies in the working of the market system and per se is not disputed, there are two critical questions that must be raised; first, are they sufficient to revive growth and employment and the second is why the appended phrase, 'and maintain fiscal discipline'. This is of course the crux of the neoliberal paradigm which requires deeper examination.

Meanwhile, in India, the government has used three 'excuses' to counter the sudden spate of popular discussion on unemployment: first, the data actually shows otherwise.[3] Second, in spite of several reforms, the failure of private sector investment spending yet to take off has led to lackluster growth and employment opportunities. Finally, being committed to fiscal responsibility and consolidation, the government has its hands tied financially.

As can be seen in Figure 9.1, India's private sector investment

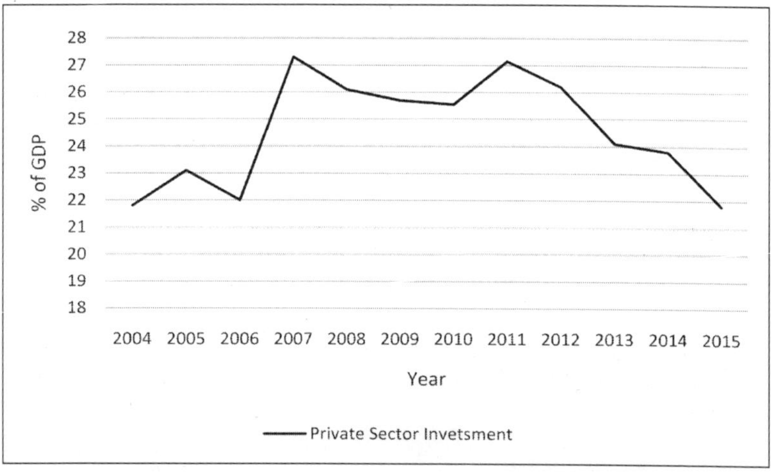

Source: https://tradingeconomics.com/india/gross-fixed-capital-formation-private-sector-percent-of-gdp-wb-data.html

Figure 9.1: India's Declining Private Sector Investment (Gross Fixed Capital Formation)

has been falling steadily since 2011 and the NDA government has not been able to reverse that trend. This growth in the economy has been sustained by higher government expenditure; nonetheless, the key to sustained growth is seen as a revival in private sector investment.

PRIVATE SECTOR INVESTMENT IS SAVINGS CONSTRAINED

But what ails private sector investment? Reasons for poor investment could be (i) aggregate demand related manifesting in poor capacity utilization rates and their non-performing liabilities (non-performing assets of banks) and (ii) investment financing remains supply constrained or in other words, investment is constrained by inadequate savings; the latter argument derived from the classical loanable funds model where savings (by households and firms) provide finance for investment.

As tersely argued by Buiter and Patel (present Reserve Bank of India Governor) in an earlier work, 'Capital formation is a key driver of the growth of potential output. With India's continuing widespread capital controls and persistently small inward foreign direct investment, the volume of capital formation in the country is constrained by domestic saving.'[4]

An increase in savings or an increase in supply of loanable funds would drive down interest rates and incentivize a greater amount of investment spending. This gives rise to an implicit corollary; the level of investment essentially is savings constrained and could be one of the reasons for India's private sector investment slowdown. As Raghuram Rajan articulated, the appropriate mainstream economics policy would be to raise the domestic savings rate, which can fund private-sector investment at a lower cost. '. . . those depositing money in the banks expect a high interest rate. Without the expectation of a high interest rate, people will not save and without savings there will be no investment and there will be inflation too. . . .'[5]

Ahead of the 2014 budget, the then RBI Governor Raghuram Rajan pitched for incentivization of domestic savings to boost investments in the country. 'The income tax benefits for an individual to save have been largely fixed in nominal terms till the recent budget, which means the real value of the benefits have eroded. Some budgetary incentives for household savings could help ensure that the country's investment is largely financed from domestic savings,' Rajan said.[6]

From Rajan's statements it seems that he made an implicit argument that at low interest rates there is an excess demand for loanable funds (for consumption and investment spending) given the low quantity supplied of loanable funds (savings). Could this also mean that the Reserve Bank sets interest rates at a level where the loanable funds market supposedly clears?[7] If savings could be increased (by, say, tax policies) the RBI would be able to set lower interest rates. Reading between the lines, to me, this possibly seems to be Rajan's view.

Jairam Ramesh, a minister in India's previous UPA government also made a similar argument; '. . . for a higher rate of investment we need a higher rate of savings . . . domestic savings will be the major determinant of investment even as we take steps to increase the contribution of foreign savings.'[8]

Although Ramesh goes on to clarify that it may be the other way round (as Keynesians would argue), that growth (investment) determines savings, he still concludes by reiterating; 'Even so, savings rate has to go up . . . the total savings rate has to be between 32 and 36 per cent of the GDP in order to trigger an 8 per cent rate of economic growth and keep it going.'[9]

More recently, another piece in a business daily raises the same issue: 'Even if one discounts the policy problems that prevent a higher rate of investment, the fall in savings has undercut the very basis of growth in India'.[10]

A question that remains hotly debated in India is whether the Reserve Bank of India should drastically cut interest rates in order to kickstart private sector investment and consumption spending. While the economist and politician Subramanian Swamy believed that this is imperative, the former RBI Governor Raghuram Rajan was strongly against it although he sometimes hesitatingly obliged the government. Nonetheless, the basis for these opposing arguments does have one thing in common—the classical loanable funds model.

On one side of the debate private sector investment is seen as an (elastic) function of interest rate so that interest rate cuts could induce increased private sector investment spending. However, a cursory look at interest rates and credit growth between 2014 and 2016 (Figure 9.2) for the Indian economy questions the assumption whether interest rate cuts are a sufficient condition to raise investment and consumption spending. A Keynesian would argue that as long as *expected sales* are weak, firms simply do not investment no matter what measures are taken to reduce the costs of borrowing.

On the other side, Rajan too implicitly drew from the loanable funds model to counter the call for cutting rates; as seen above, investment in India is savings-constrained and cutting interest would only decrease supply (savings) further. The fundamental

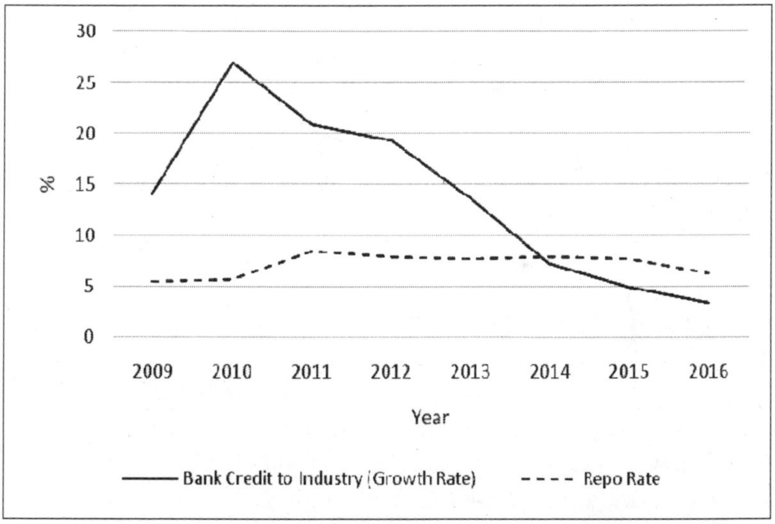

Source: https://rbi.org.in/Scripts/BS_PressReleaseDisplay.aspx?prid=39102# https://craytheon.com/charts/rbi_base_rate_repo_reverse_rate_crr_slr.php

Notes: Bank credit to Industry, Y-o-Y growth rate
Highest repo rates during the year has taken as the rate for each year

Figure 9.2: Credit Growth and Interest Rates, India, 2009-16

challenge was to raise India's savings rate, which responds positively to higher rates.

A possibility to relieve the (domestic) savings constraint for private sector investment is to allow net inflows of foreign capital, which in turn necessitates a current account deficit. Unfortunately, when combined with the current account deficit, the popular macroeconomic discourse on savings and investment is so badly conflated that one is left utterly confused on the cause and effect of a slowdown.

> The current account deficit (CAD), as a percentage of gross domestic product (GDP), is the difference between the investment rate and the savings rate . . . if GDP growth is as high as claimed in the official statistics, shouldn't the savings rate too be higher? . . . the low CAD we have now is the result of the investment drought in the economy, combined with a lower level of savings.[11]

Or consider the following remarks:

> The reflection of the high current account deficit is found in the widening domestic saving-investment gap . . . India's gross savings rate dropped to 30.8 per cent in the financial year ending March 2012. . . . More disturbing is the revelation that the financial savings of the households were down to 8 per cent of GDP in March 2012. . . . The Indian economy is thus, if I may be permitted to say, in a bit of a circular trap. If the current account deficit has to be reduced, then demand for gold needs to come off significantly, but this will not happen unless the real returns of domestic financial assets move higher.[12]

From this it seems that India's macroeconomic predicament is primarily because of its desire to save in physical (especially gold) rather than financial assets. This inadequacy of household (financial) savings is therefore the root cause for India's sluggish growth.

But how do buyers (firms) and sellers (households) come together in the loanable funds market? This brings neoliberal economists to construct their discourse on banking. The channelization of savings to investment takes place through banks (or more generally the financial sector).[13] The belief that banks are mere intermediaries has so deeply seeped into the mainstream macroeconomic discourse that it is now almost commonsensical—even the RBI exemplifies this view:

> Banks' primary purpose is to mobilize otherwise idle savings for the purpose of lending to productive investments. . . . The new paradigm of economic growth is that it is a function of savings rate, return on investment and cost of intermediation.[14]
>
> Savings are the backbone of investment, wherein higher savings lead to higher growth in an economy with conducive macroeconomic environment and a developed financial system . . . domestic investment is mostly financed by domestic savings. . . . According to the findings of the paper, there is a need for strengthening the financial system in order to effectively channelize household savings for enhancement of capital formation in India.[15]
>
> A well-designed financial system promotes growth through effective mobilisation of savings and their allocation to the most productive uses . . . banks have played a critical role in the financial intermediation process as they are able to deal more appropriately with transaction costs and information asymmetries in a financial system.[16]

Without financial intermediaries, households (savers) would have to search for firms (investors) with financing needs. The search and monitoring costs as well as asymmetric information between lenders and borrowers on the use of funds would be so prohibitive that savers would be compelled to hoard money, taking it out of circulation and causing a decline in output and income.

Such ideas from textbooks are now firmly entrenched in popular discourse. Haseeb Drabu, An economist who headed a nationalized bank and went on to become Finance Minister in the Jammu & Kashmir government puts forth ideas that emanate from the Say's Law and the loanable funds model:

> The new structure of public expenditure should be such that it recognizes the severity and seriousness of supply-side constraints that are holding growth. . . . Raising domestic household savings [is] a critical challenge for a future. This is also a systemic issue that needs to be addressed.[17]

In fact, this view is so strong in academic economics that as mere intermediaries, the NCM-DSGE models legitimized their disregard of banking and credit entirely. Should we then really be surprised that economists did not predict the crisis of 2008?

THE PARANOIA OF FISCAL DEFICITS

Broadly speaking, mainstream neoliberal economics essentially argued that the role of the state in management of the economy should be minimal. Fiscal activism of the government must be restricted. However, the government can play a role in eliminating market imperfections that arise especially in the labour and other factor markets as well as in the provision of public goods including infrastructure facilities that may not be provided by the private sector on account of their long gestation period or the non-excludable characteristic of the goods and services provided. To translate this ideological belief to the mundane level of policy, economists began targeting their attention on fiscal deficit numbers. India too succumbed to the neoliberal agenda.

Today, 24 × 7, from popular newspapers to business dailies and television channels, one economic issue that hits us hard and repeatedly is the dire need to contain the government's fiscal deficit. Every year, as the day of the government's budget announcement draws near, concerns over India's fiscal deficit only intensifies. For instance, prior to the 2015 budget presentation the first page of a leading business daily unequivocally declared. 'Current fiscal deficit level *unacceptable*[18]: Jaitley.'[19]

Let me quote a few lines from the same article because it succinctly captures the growing urgency and fear, desperation perhaps, over the fiscal deficit that takes the form of definitive numbers like 4.1 per cent, 3.6 per cent or 3 per cent of GDP.

> Government *will not stray* from plan *to slash* fiscal deficit to 3 per cent of gross domestic product, finance minister says.
>
> The Government *is scrambling to contain* the fiscal deficit at 4.1 per cent of GDP in the fiscal year ending March, after *a sharp downfall* in revenue that forced it to *rein in* spending (emphasis added).

I am quite sure that the Ministry of Finance or the Reserve Bank of India does not run some complex NCM-DSGE model that throws out a fiscal deficit of 4.1 per cent of GDP as the solution. Consider this; Bimal Jalan, ex-Governor of the Reserve Bank of India who then headed the Expenditure Management Commission recommended that the fiscal deficit be set at 3.6 per cent in 2015-16[20] while Arvind Panagariya, well-known liberal economist and former Vice-Chairman of the Niti Aayog stated rather casually that 'in an economy where you are trying to push up the growth rate, a fiscal deficit of 4.5 percent (of GDP) *is fine*.'[21] Do these targets not seem arbitrary?

It would be wrong to claim that fear over the fiscal deficit target is something limited to the present NDA government. Not too long ago, P. Chidambaram, Finance Minister of the UPA government said: '. . . fiscal deficit target of 4.8 per cent is a 'red line' that 'will not be crossed'.[22]

The race against a challenging fiscal deficit target is an ongoing one reported in the newspapers and TV channels like a thriller, unfolding over several months:

India's fiscal deficit in H1 *almost 83 pct* of full-year target.[23]
Fiscal deficit *hits 99* per cent of FY15 target at Nov-end.[24]
Modi's *pledge tested* with India deficit at 99 per cent of target.[25]

And then finally the moment of triumph!

Government *beats* its own fiscal deficit target[26]
Union Budget 2017: Salutary fiscal rectitude[27]
Modi government, best for fiscal discipline: Budget 2016-17 should be regarded as one of the best, perhaps the best, since 1996. . . . On deeper investigation, the path of fiscal consolidation for the current fiscal year is even more impressive than credited by experts.[28]
Market shoots up on fiscal discipline, tax clarity.[29]

Not only was the task achieved but there was an additional reason for celebration; all this was achieved *despite* previous governments. The Finance Minister Arun Jaitley said he had taken this as a 'challenge' to meet an ambitious and 'daunting target' set up by his predecessor P. Chidambaram.[30]

While any upward estimate of fiscal deficit puts the government in defensive, a reduction is not only seen as a victory but also as a mark of confidence that the deficit can be further lowered in future.

The Finance Ministry further said that the government is *firmly committed* to the path of fiscal consolidation and this is a *stepforward*.[31]

The discussion of the fiscal deficit is not limited to government officials from the Ministry of Finance. The Reserve Bank of India whose task is to check inflation is obviously concerned over the government's excessive spending and the need to reach a deficit target. Years ago, before becoming the Governor of the RBI, in an interview given to the IMF, Raghuram Rajan clearly articulated his position in so far as fiscal deficits were concerned: 'I'd say that it should be *a priority* to control the deficit. If nothing else, we know from the experience of many countries, that eventually it comes back to haunt you.'[32]

Rajan maintained this view as Governor of the RBI. His remarks in 2015 made it obvious that he had not outgrown this opinion: '*Finally*, the government has reiterated its commitment to adhering to its fiscal deficit target.'[33]

The popular media is all for fiscal consolidation, warning the government not to err; '. . . a view is emerging that the government should give a demand push to the economy by delaying fiscal consolidation . . . there is near unanimity in the government over the need for fiscal stimulus. The government *would be well advised* to avoid taking such a decision. . . .'[34] (emphasis added)

International rating agencies are perhaps the strongest arm-twisters, their language, threatening; 'Standard & Poor's, the credit rating agency, *warned* on Wednesday that it would *downgrade* India's sovereign debt rating *unless* the government moved *swiftly* to bring the country's widening fiscal deficit under control.'[35] (emphasis added)

To which even the then formidable Finance Minister, Pranab Mukherjee of the UPA government had to react cautiously; 'The situation may be difficult, but we will surely be able to *overcome* [the deficit].'[36]

In 2017 India received a Moody's rating upgrade. But it came with a caveat:

Getting a rating upgrade is impressive. But given the importance that the assessment places on fiscal improvement, Moody's indirect warning to the government is to refrain from having a populist Budget next year, and stay away from the temptation of undoing its fiscal consolidation in an effort to boost growth. To quote one of the early Spiderman movies: with great power comes great responsibility.[37]

Even domestic rating agencies tow the same line: 'Domestic rating agency Crisil said the 3.9 per cent fiscal deficit target is realistic, but *warned* of *slippage.*'[38] (emphasis added)

Supporting the views of these rating agencies are international institutions like the IMF. Just before the presentation of the NDA government's first (interim) budget, Thomas J. Richardson, the IMF's Senior Resident Representative in India categorically stated: 'It is *important* to continue the gradual process of bringing the fiscal deficit from relatively high levels to lower levels.'[39]

Alas, in spite of all the efforts, the rating agencies can sometimes be harsh: '3.2 per cent fiscal deficit not enough! Rating agencies say do more for rating upgrade'.[40]

Despite such decisive posturing by the government and pressure from the Reserve Bank as well as other institutions, the government struggles to find some space for manoeuvre to increase spending but taking care that they do not even seem that they want to rock the boat.

Prime Minister Narendra Modi and then [Finance Minister] Jaitley seem determined to spend more on roads and railways but, despite the views of their advisers, without breaking deficit commitments. The three top credit ratings agencies place India on the lowest rung of investment grade for its debt.[41]

Some, however, dare to test the waters and propose that the deficit target can be relaxed: 'the government's top two economic advisers, Arvind Panagariya and Arvind Subramanian, have both advocated loosening deficit targets to allow public spending on infrastructure to jumpstart economic growth.'[42]

Only to be immediately and brutally shot down. In response to the comments of the government's advisors, one of India's leading economic commentators, Swaminathan Aiyar cautioned the government of harbouring any such hopes:

Jaitley must stick to the path of consolidation . . . reducing the fiscal deficit to

3.6 per cent and 3 per cent of GDP in the next two years . . . Arvind Panagariya . . . made the case for living with higher fiscal deficits to finance urgently needed infrastructure. Sorry, but that would seriously dent Jaitley's fiscal credibility. To establish a tall reputation, he absolutely must stick to his fiscal reduction schedule.[43]

I have also seen those calling for increased spending due to recessionary trends always add a word of caution: '. . . when monetary policy is seemingly constrained by exchange rate considerations, fiscal fundamentalism may have to be abandoned. . . . Of course, like any other economic entity, our government also cannot perennially borrow and live beyond its means.'[44]

These remarks and reports I have collated and presented are just the tip of the iceberg but should make us a little more conscious of the emphasis placed on the fiscal deficit by politicians, economic experts and institutions. Repeated day-after-day simply as matter of fact and drilled into us by the media, the need for continually lower fiscal deficit targets has become an obsession although not just an Indian one. It engulfs the entire world and here is some evidence of this.

In typical American style, Barack Obama, before becoming the US President had remarked with reference to the growing budget deficit under President Bush: 'That's irresponsible. It's unpatriotic'.[45]

Of course, soon after Obama had made this comment, the US economy came under the grip of the Great Recession of 2008. Budget deficits had then to be increased multifold. The European Union is another, perhaps the best example of deficit authoritarianism with no guesses here for who is in command. 'German Chancellor Angela Merkel insisted on Thursday that there can be no exceptions to European Union rules on national deficit targets, a clear message to France after it backed off promises to bring down its budget overspend.'[46]

By now you would be getting the general drift of what I want to say. For those unconvinced, a Google search of the country followed by the keywords fiscal deficit and danger will help in overcoming their doubts. From Brazil to Australia, Russia to South Africa, it seems that every country in the world is under the fiscal deficit scanner.

In India, the unequivocal mention of the fiscal deficit problem, in its own right, first appears in the Economic Survey of 1991-2, months after an economic crisis had forced it to seek a bailout package in 1991 from the IMF that brought with it severe conditions for structural reforms.

The fiscal situation, which was large throughout the 1980s, reached a critical stage in 1990-1 with a sharp deterioration in the revenue deficit. Fiscal deficits generate pressures on inflation as well as the balance of payments. The gross fiscal deficit of the central government, which measures the total resource gap, had been more that 8 per cent of the GDP since 1985-6, as compared with 6 per cent at the beginning of the 1980s and 4 per cent in the 1970s. Such fiscal deficits were considered unsustainable and would have lead the country into a debt-trap.[47]

From hereon we find fiscal deficits taking a prominent, perhaps primary place in the budgetary exercise of the government. A little more than a decade later, the Fiscal Responsibility and Budget Management (FRBM) Act, 2003 was passed, imposing stringent fiscal discipline on the central government, stipulating that the fiscal deficit be brought down to 3 per cent of GDP by the year 2008. Although these restrictions were lifted during the Great Recession of 2008, the stage had been set for centering fiscal deficit targets in the macroeconomic debate even as the return to the FRBM target of 3 per cent of GDP still remains elusive and as mentioned above, the government struggles to find some policy space. Meanwhile, fear of failure to meet targets unleashing the wrath of rating agencies hangs overhead like the sword of Damocles 'Standard & Poor's (S&P) on Friday handed down a shocker, threatening to downgrade the country's sovereign rating to "junk" status if the government failed to keep pace with the global rating agency's expectation on reforms and containment of the twin deficits International credit rating agency.'[48]

The warning did not come just once, but repeatedly:

> Standard & Poor's (S&P) on Friday failed to enhance the credit rating on India's sovereign debt, currently just one level above '*junk* bond' status . . . What's more, S&P once again *warned* of a possible ratings downgrade . . . the agency said the main drag on India's rating is a high fiscal deficit and heavy Government borrowing.[49]

But the Indian government's (subservient) response was even more dismal:

> It is disappointing that S&P *has not seen it fit* to improve its outlook for India, especially given that it acknowledges the important steps taken by the Indian Government in recent months. International institutional investors, who have invested over $17 billion into India so far this year, do seem to have a different view. The Government will continue to do what is necessary to keep India on a stable, sustainable and strengthening growth path.[50]

However, with such reports constantly bombarding us, there seems to be little room for debate over this fixation on a fiscal deficit target. Moreover, why are economists, and consequently politicians, so anxious about the number, 3 per cent? Numbers like 3 per cent, 3.6 per cent or 15 per cent (US fiscal deficit in 2010) do not arise from macroeconomic theory; in fact one wonders where they come from. A little-known fact may help: the number was supposedly 'invented' by Guy Abeille, an official in the French finance ministry, and adopted by the Stability and Growth Pact agreement between EU member states. In an interview, Abeille supposedly said, '. . . we came up with this number in less than an hour. It was born on the corner of a table, without any theoretical reflection.'[51] Even as an obituary for the EU is being written by many, the 3 per cent deficit target number seems as robust as ever. If the figure is not spewed out by some complex dynamic stochastic general equilibrium model and was instead an (arbitrary) invention to ensure stability of the European Monetary Union, why is a country like India besieged by this enigmatic target number? The fiscal deficit target number of 3 per cent of GDP has now come to be taken for granted; dangerously so because when we reach this point in economic analysis, we stop questioning its basis.

More recently, the FRBM Review Committee suggested that the fiscal deficit target may adhere to a range rather than a fixed number. This notional flexibility in the deficit target has, however, been replaced by a preferred anchor: public debt (or the stock of accumulated deficits) at 60 per cent of GDP. One critical factor taken into consideration while arriving at the debt target as articulated by N.K. Singh, chairman of the committee, is 'the standard government solvency constraints'.[52] This is line with the IMF's position that 'prudence dictates that countries target a debt level well below the limit, the limit delineates the point at which fiscal solvency is called into question'.[53] To the general public, words like 'budget', 'deficit' and 'debt' are symbolically loaded, conjuring up images of a limit, a constraint, a 'red line', insolvency, bankruptcy, unsustainable indebtedness and countries going broke or simply falling off a (fiscal) cliff.

Debts must also be repaid. And who bears the burden of debt at the time of repayment? The obvious answer is that future generations will have to take the tab by paying additional taxes to the government in their lifetime. Although economists have a rather archaic term for this, 'Ricardian equivalence', it often finds expression in more poignant phrases: 'risking our future prosperity by sticking our children with the bill', 'stealing from future generations by running fiscal deficits', 'you don't want to take from your children's pocket' or 'the unborn must share higher fiscal burden'. From such economic imagery arises the widespread belief that all deficits and debt—including those of the government—are equally undesirable and the necessity to rein them is unequivocal. Short-term deviations may be acceptable but in the longer term, these simply cannot be endured. And if this is true for you and me, then it must be true for the government too.

The hype over fiscal deficits is becoming like an examination that the government must pass every year, year-after-year, to please rating agencies and to perhaps tell the local electorate that the world is happy with its economic policies. In a world where the state has overcome the crippling limitations of the gold standard, it is unfortunate that modern governments are unable to break out of the neoliberal macroeconomic paradigm. To an extent unless the popular discourse changes, the government will be unable to free itself from self-imposed constrains. The need for reframing macroeconomic discourse is therefore imperative and urgent.

As we have discussed earlier, there is, however, one category of government spending that is usually supported wholeheartedly in the popular macroeconomic discourse: capital expenditure or infrastructure spending.

Further, in a scenario of deflationary pressures being faced by the economy, the government should not shy away from recalibrating the fiscal deficit target in order to push public investments with a view to add productive capacity to the economy. It should be ensured that the spending stimulus is directed towards fruitful capital expenditure, especially in infrastructure,

said A. Didar Singh, Secretary General, FICCI [Federation of Indian Chambers of Commerce and Industry].[54]

The following excerpt from an interview with a global portfolio strategist also articulates the present disposition towards capital expenditure—not wasteful revenue expenditures—by the government:

It is ok to run a deficit . . . what is really a big problem is . . . when the deficit is being driven by a lot of social spending that doesn't really seem to have a big payoff in the future. . . . The ideal budget would be one in which they hit the deficit target of 3.6 per cent and where it shows a real emphasis on trying to improve the infrastructure of India. . . .[55]

But here too caution must be exercised; infrastructure spending may be increased not by raising the deficit but by cutting down revenue expenditures.

Let me quote at length from an article by Manas Chakravarthy, a popular commentator and an expert in his own right, that summarized a speech by the RBI Governor, Urjit Patel, succinctly capturing most of the points we have raised so far on fiscal policy:

He went on to hammer home the point that 'Borrowing even more and pre-empting resources from future generations by governments cannot be a short-cut to long lasting higher growth. Instead, structural reforms and reorienting government expenditure towards public infrastructure are key for durable gains on the Indian growth front'.

Patel is not known for making speeches. His remarks on the fiscal deficit should, therefore, be taken very seriously, particularly when there is much talk of relaxing the deficit in the budget. . . .

. . . the efficacy of government expenditure needs to be looked into. It is these factors that need looking into, not quick fixes such as pausing in our road to fiscal consolidation.

There are other things about which Urjit Patel may be wrong, but he's right about the dangers of a high fiscal deficit.[56]

Finally, as discussed in Chapter 2, another insight initially drawn from neo-Keynesian economics but now a favourite with neoliberals is the crowding out effect, which also arises from the savings-constraint. Let me put down a few comments on the crowding-out effect that I have collated from articles appearing in Indian newspapers.

Theoretically, it is not difficult to see why excessive borrowing by the public sector should result in the crowding-out of private expenditure. For a given level of money supply in the economy, more public sector borrowing would leave less funds for the private sector, thereby raising interest rates. A rise in interest rates would naturally discourage private expenditure. This link should be stronger for India given most government borrowing is domestic. The crowding-out theory is supported by some of India's leading economists.[57]

> . . . It leads to crowding-out of private borrowers as high government borrowing tends to (impose) an increasing cost of borrowing for others, [Urjit] Patel.[58]
>
> Higher government borrowing is considered bad for corporate India, as it tends to crowd out funds for the private sector.[59]
>
> The finance minister, last Thursday, argued that a lower fiscal deficit will not only avert a rating downgrade threat but also bolster economic growth prospects as borrowing costs for private investors will fall, helping lift capital investment growth from a five-year low.[60]

The crowding-out effect is even endorsed by the Reserve Bank of India:

> The Report of the Economic Advisory Council (EAC, 2001) stresses that high fiscal deficits, by raising real interest rates, crowd out private investment, especially in the context of the government borrowing being predominantly used to finance revenue deficits.[61]

All these explanations add up to a simple macroeconomic narrative; the government is doing all the right (neoliberal) things to keep growth buoyant—maintaining low and stable inflation rate and carrying out extensive structural reforms. It could do some more too; cut interest rates further (but at the cost of savings contracting) and of course, carry out even more reforms. But the results are not showing; India is stuck on a 7 per cent growth trajectory (that has declined sharply[62] to 6.1 per cent in the second quarter of 2017[63]) and is unable to raise the bar. And the media has now begun exerting pressure on the government pointing out its failure in creating adequate job opportunities as promised to the masses. Unfortunately, the private sector is constrained by finances.

But, as mainstream economists argue, so is the government. Arvind Panagariya highlighted the economist's concern on breaking away from the path of fiscal consolidation: 'For economists, fiscal consolidation is important. So when anything that stresses the [government's] finances is something that the economists worry about.'[64]

As Vivek Kaul reiterated:

> At the end of the day the government has a limited amount of money at its disposal. If India has to continue growing at greater than 7 per cent, then private sector investment needs to pick up and that doesn't seem to be happening currently due to various reasons.[65]

With its hands tied financially, what are the options for the government?

INDIA'S MONETARY POLICY FRAMEWORK

While fiscal austerity is one pillar of neoliberal macroeconomics, monetary policy—under the control of an independent central bank—is the other. State control over setting of interest rates was transferred to 'independent' central banks, which were in turn mandated to ensure a 'low and stable' inflation rate. This would act as an effective check against errant government behaviour of high deficits and low interest rates to boost the economy (but resulting in high inflation). An independent central bank could effectively counter the government's fiscal profligacy by raising interest rates to achieve the stipulated inflation target and furthermore, inflation expectations. In many advanced countries, in response to the Great Recession of 2008, monetary policy—low interest rates and quantitative easing[66]—took centre stage while the use of fiscal stimulus was comparatively restrained. With inflation in check, an efficient market system would supposedly propel an economy onto a path of long-term growth in an environment of competition and innovation. Short-term stability in price levels is considered a prerequisite for longer-term growth and development. This is what Raghuram Rajan said to the media and analysts after the bi-monthly monetary policy review in June 2015: 'Our job is to give people confidence in the value of the rupee, in prospects of inflation and having established that confidence, create longer-term framework to take good decisions. . . .'[67]

The institutional transition to central bank independence was neither smooth nor accepted at the same time by all countries. It is interesting to note that Margaret Thatcher, an epitome of neo-liberalism, had refused to grant autonomy to the Bank of England (BoE); it was as late as 1997, under Tony Blair, that the BoE was ultimately given the power to set interest rates. In India, neoliberal macroeconomics—as reflected in the centrality of inflation and adherence to fiscal deficit targets—took root post-1991. By institutionalizing a cap on the fiscal deficit with the FRBM Act of 2003,[68] governments have repeatedly signaled monetary policy and supply-side structural reforms as the key to stable growth in which the private sector would take the lead role. As described above, every year, as the day of the budget announcement draws near, the media is replete with warnings for the government on the need to adhere to its fiscal deficit target. Any failure to live up to its deficit commitments unleashes the wrath of international and national rating agencies. It is no wonder then that in his 2015 budget presentation, India's finance minister underscored the present government's commitment to reaching the 3 per cent of GDP fiscal target by 2017-18 as per the FRBM Act.

India's monetary policy framework has become clearer after the revised draft of the Indian Financial Code (IFC)[69] was proposed in July 2015. It initially set off debate on the simmering tensions between the government and the RBI over the setting of interest rates. The reformed code proposed to vest the decision on rates from the sole purview of the central bank with a seven-member monetary policy committee (MPC), four of whom were to be appointees of the central government, while three would be from the RBI. This legislation would have not only taken away veto power of the RBI governor in setting key interest rates but in effect, with the majority of appointees being of the central government, neither would the RBI governor nor even the RBI be the final authority over the primary instrument of monetary policy. Even though the proposal was amended to a six-member panel with an equal number of members elected by the government and the RBI, and the veto power of the governor restored in case of a tie, the majority of opinion in the press and media reacted adversely on the proposed MPC that seemed to be an assault on central bank autonomy. However, with Rajan, the then RBI governor, supporting the MPC and reiterating confidence that the RBI would continue to wield *de facto* power over monetary policy, resentment towards the MPC gradually receded.

The underlying implications of the revised IFC can, however, only be understood when seen in conjunction with the inflation targeting agreement reached between the Ministry of Finance and the RBI in early 2015, wherein it was decided that the inflation target would be pegged at less than 6 per cent by January 2016 and further reduced to 4 per cent plus or minus 2 per cent for subsequent financial years. At the time of this agreement, control over interest rates was unequivocally with the RBI governor. This after all was the instrument that he could use to achieve the inflation target agreed upon. In case of failure to reach the target over three successive quarters, he had to explain to the government reasons for failure and the corrective action proposed. The government accepted the validity of the RBI's (Urjit Patel Committee) recommendations in favour of a 'low and stable' inflation target. The essence of neoliberal macroeconomics—inflation targeting—was actually institutionalized in India at the eve of its decay in the West.

By accepting the inflation target, the Indian government had imposed a constraint on itself in leveraging its fiscal space for broader growth and developmental objectives including infrastructure building, social sector spending and employment generation. As long as its commitment to a low and stable inflation target remains intact, interest rate per se is not critical; in case it turns out inadequate in achieving the inflation target, the onus would instead fall on fiscal policy. Consider, for argument sake, what happens when the inflation target remains in place but the government appointees to the MPC decide to cut rates sharply? How can the RBI be then held answerable for its failure to achieve the inflation target? I see only one way out of this dilemma and perhaps the one that neoliberal economists anticipate: the government will have to ensure fiscal policy, in particular the fiscal deficit, is in sync with its inflation target.

The Indian government was not happy with the RBI over high interest rates and its unwillingness to cut rates and kick start private investment. This may have been one reason why Rajan's term may not have been extended; however, by getting the government to agree upon a low and stable inflation target, Rajan had won the war (for neoliberalism) even if he lost the battle (an extension of his term as RBI governor). If the demonetization exercise was reflective of the RBI's loss of autonomy, it will not be surprising to find the RBI obliging the government with interest rate cuts in future. But will 'pushing on a string' be sufficient to put the economy on a higher growth trajectory? This is far from certain.

While the disagreement between central banks and governments often seems to be over (low or high) interest rates it will at some point of time become obvious that the actual contention is over a low and unmalleable inflation target. And it is not the interest rate but just the possibility of higher inflation which severely constrains the fiscal deficit. Relegating their commitment to a specific inflation target could give governments a degree of freedom to not only increase spending and the fiscal deficit, but also set interest rates at a level they consider appropriate. Greater discretion on inflation rate will, however, mean the abrogation of neoliberal macroeconomics and with it, of central bank autonomy as well.

In the future we are likely to see heightened arguments and conflict over these questions. In fact, just weeks after I had written a piece for *The Wire*[70] incorporating some of these ideas, the MPC's independence was under attack by the government when it summoned the MPC members prior to their meeting to discuss government views on interest rate policy.[71]

Meanwhile, with its short-term successes, neoliberal macroeconomics has lost sight of what was the *raison d'être* of macroeconomic policy—full employment. Not only has this objective been left to the private sector but more importantly, unemployment has been transformed into a 'buffer stock' to meet the inflation target. Under emerging regimes across the world, it may well be the turn of (low and stable) inflation targeting to take a back seat (and with it central banks too), while populist-nationalist governments exert greater control over interest rates and trade policy to address the restlessness of their citizens over stagnation and persistent unemployment. The process has already begun even as the outcome is awaited with uncertainty and, for some, with fear.

The focus on the savings constraint, inflation and fiscal deficit target numbers has distracted economists from discussing other critical objectives of macroeconomic policy—reduction of unemployment, poverty and inequalities. These objectives have somehow been subsumed under the growth narrative, which assumes that once low and stable inflation is achieved in the short-run, growth rates will be maximized in the longer-term thereby solving these issues in a sustainable way. A few stylized (order of magnitude) facts on unemployment in India starkly indicate the enormity of the problem facing the country. In 2012 India's population was 1.25 billion, the second highest in the world. The labour force participation rate was about 50 per cent. The organized sector (both private and public sector) employed about 30 million people or just about 5 per cent of the labour force. Unemployment rate (persons registered at employment exchanges looking for assistance), although stated at 3.2 per cent of the total population, stood at some 44 million persons which exceeded the total employment in the organized sector. Youth unemployment rate stood at an alarming 18 per cent. The remaining portion of India's labour force works in the unorganized sector where employment is characterized by migrant workers, low subsistence level wages, gender discrimination, seasonal employment, lack of social security, and poor living conditions. Providing secured full-time and decent employment to hundreds of millions of people remains the greatest challenge for Indian policymakers.

The direct counterpart of the employment problem in India is poverty; the C. Rangarajan Committee reported in 2014 that approximately 38 per cent of India lived below the poverty line. Moreover, the poverty line itself has been fixed at levels which are probably at the margin of survival—a daily expenditure of Rs. 32 ($0.5) in rural areas and Rs. 47 in towns and cities. What is also disturbing is that real wages in India have fallen between 2010 and 2014; the overall average daily wage rate (at 1960 prices[72]) fell from Rs. 5.47 to 4.83 and in manufacturing from Rs. 6.97 to 6.25.

Getting people *employable* in modern sectors of the economy requires massive state expenditure let alone getting them actual employment. In an atmosphere where fear of inflation and fiscal deficits are overwhelming, how can the state rise to the occasion? Moreover, although higher GDP growth rate is a necessary condition for creation of productive employment opportunities it is no longer a sufficient one. The phenomenon of jobless growth and job displacement due to high technology is already raising concerns across the world and is no longer confined to advanced countries. Furthermore, structural reforms by themselves may not be adequate to create sufficient number of jobs. A study by Pal and Ghosh (2007)[73] shows that annual employment growth rates actually fell in the 1990s (1993-2000) to just 0.67 per cent (rural) and 1.34 per cent (urban) as compared to the 1980s (1988-93) when growth rates were significantly higher at 2.03 per cent (rural) and 3.39 per cent (urban). Mazumdar and Sarkar (2007),[74] in their study of the manufacturing sector, also found that although employment elasticity in the reform period (1986-96) was about 0.33, it slumped drastically to –1.39 in the subsequent years (1996-2002). Given that the adoption of modern technology cannot be rejected in a globally competitive world, growth in the manufacturing sector cannot be a solution to the problem of unemployment in India, at least on the scale required.

Despite these pressing problems in India, fiscal austerity remains the buzzword. How can a government confront television discussions, newspaper columns and even national and international institutions that unequivocally argue that governments must do all they can to contain the deficit beast? How do governments reconcile the obsession with fiscal deficit target numbers and the imperative need for social sector spending? How can it answer the premonitions of international rating agencies and simultaneously meet its objective of providing gainful employment to the masses?

The answer unfortunately requires nothing less than a paradigm shift. Given the level of acceptance that mainstream neoliberal macroeconomic views continue to hold, it is imperative that alternatives are at least proposed and debated. One such line of heterodox thinking that I find of particular relevance to the issues raised is Modern Money Theory or MMT. While the originality of MMT is sometimes questioned, I think the (re)interpretation of Keynesian views to the post-Bretton Woods era makes it relevant to our present context. Moreover, the simplicity of MMT, without sacrificing depth and consistency, has made many Keynesian and post-Keynesian ideas more accessible and understandable even to the non-economist. Most importantly, for a country like India, MMT provides policy space for the government to pursue vital developmental objectives that cannot be postponed to the longer-run, after the unlikely event that inflation is tamed 'once and for all'.

NOTES

1. Liquidity is a term that needs elaboration and will be dealt with in due course.
2. M.C. Govardhana Rangan and Joel Rebello, 'Structural Reforms to Keep India an Outperformer: Gunit Chadha, Deutsche Bank', *Economic Times*, 9 March 2016, http://economictimes.indiatimes.com/opinion/interviews/structural-reforms-to-keep-india-an-outperformer-gunit-chadha-deutsche-bank/articleshow/51319797.cms
3. Devanik Saha, 'BJP Claims Unemployment Rate Falls: Data Contradictory, Unreliable', *Hindustan Times*, 9 March 2017, http://www.hindustantimes.com/india-news/fact-check-bjp-claims-unemployment-rate-falls-data-contradictory-unreliable/story-7qfd6zuNrM73gorYGMVOwO.html
4. W.H. Buiter and U.R. Patel, 'Excessive Budget Deficits, a Government Abused Financial System, and Fiscal Rules', India Policy Forum 2006, https://

www.brookings.edu/wp-content/uploads/2016/07/2005_buiter_patel.pdf, p. 1.

5. 'Banking sector set for massive transformation', says Rajan, *Business Line*, 14 February 2016, http://www.thehindubusinessline.com/money-and-banking/banking-sector-set-for-massive-transformation-says-rajan/article8237564.ece
6. *Deccan Chronicle*, 12 December 2014, http://www.deccanchronicle.com/141212/business-latest/article/raghuram-rajan-incentivising-domestic-savings
7. This corresponds to Wicksell's notion of the natural rate of interest.
8. Jairam Ramesh, 'Save more, grow more', *India Today*, 19 June 2000, http://indiatoday.intoday.in/story/higher-rate-of-economic-growth-will-be-constrained-by-the-rate-of-home-savings/1/244348.html
9. Ibid
10. Improving India's saving rate, *Livemint*, 16 February 2014, http://www.livemint.com/Opinion/ZDgCdU87oxU6cPnClpc2yN/Improving-Indias-savings-rate.html
11. Current account numbers imply lower savings rate in the economy, *Livemint*, 23 March 2016, http://www.livemint.com/Money/vxxJOKFKJClGrRAIIbTHuJ/Current-account-numbers-imply-lower-savings-rate-in-economy.html
12. Indranil Pan, 'India's Current Account Deficit Limits Scope for More Rate Cuts', 1 February 2013, http://blogs.ft.com/beyond-brics/2013/02/01/guest-post-indias-big-current-account-deficit-limits-scope-for-more-rate-cuts/
13. This simple but powerful imagery of the working of the macroeconomy (that is almost always presented in standard macro textbooks) leaves not only a lot unsaid but is also fundamentally erroneous at least for a modern economy with fiat currency rather than one operating with a constrained gold standard.
14. R. Gandhi, 'Indian Banking Sector: Role in Triggering Future Growth', 14 June 2014, https://rbi.org.in/scripts/BS_SpeechesView.aspx?Id=899
15. Bichitrananda Seth, 'Long Run and Short Run Saving-Investment Relationship in India', RBI Working Paper Series No. 13, September 2011, https://www.rbi.org.in/scripts/BS_PressReleaseDisplay.aspx?prid=25217
16. 'Managing Resource Mobilsation', Reserve Bank of India, September 2008, https://rbi.org.in/scripts/PublicationsView.aspx?id=10488
17. Haseeb A. Drabu, 'Brewing a Budget', *Livemint*, 4 July 2014, http://www.livemint.com/Opinion/VlOeWN8wdbaNRIFOxYw2jN/Brewing-a-budget.html

18. Italics used throughout this chapter, unless otherwise stated, are mine for emphasis.
19. Ben Hirschler and Manoj Kumar, 'Current Level of Fiscal Deficit is Unacceptable', says Jaitley, *Livemint*, 23 January 2015, http://www.livemint.com/Politics/hVTwZgs5n5j8nJSoSRQGXM/Current-level-of-fiscal-deficit-is-unacceptable-says-Jaitle.html
20. K. Paramanandan, 'Budget 2015: Relax Fiscal Deficit Target, Go For Growth', Says Bimal Jalan, *International Business Times*, 21 February 2015, http://www.ibtimes.co.in/budget-2015-relax-fiscal-deficit-target-go-growth-says-bimal-jalan-624149
21. Rajesh Kumar Singh, 'Arvind Panagariya backs higher deficit for India revival', *Reuters*, 25 May 2014, http://in.reuters.com/article/panagariya-modi-economy-deficit-idINKBN0E505520140525
22. Won't cross red line on fiscal deficit: P. Chidambaram, *Economic Times*, 6 September 2013, http://economictimes.indiatimes.com/news/economy/policy/wont-cross-red-line-on-fiscal-deficit-p-chidambaram/articleshow/22351516.cms
23. Manoj Kumar, *Reuters*, 31 October 2014, http://in.reuters.com/article/india-fiscal-deficit-idINKBN0IK0TQ20141031
24. *Times of India*, 1 January 2015, http://timesofindia.indiatimes.com/business/india-business/Fiscal-deficit-hits-99-of-FY15-target-at-Nov-end/articleshow/45712601.cms
25. Anoop Agrawal, *Livemint*, 2 February 2015, http://www.livemint.com/Politics/LYmIyqU6QWRxMAc5BFtzvM/Modis-pledge-tested-as-deficit-at-99-of-target.html
26. VCCircle, 19 May 2015, https://www.vccircle.com/government-beats-its-own-fiscal-deficit-target-makes-room-rate-cut/
27. http://www.livemint.com/Opinion/dcC66p7hBH3BdK0EoQjEQN/Union-Budget-2017-Salutary-fiscal-rectitude.html
28. Surjit Bhalla, 'Modi Govt, Best for Fiscal Discipline', *Financial Express*, 12 March 2016, http://www.financialexpress.com/budget-2016/column-modi-govt-best-for-fiscal-discipline/224078/
29. George Mathew, *Indian Express*, 2 February 2017, http://indianexpress.com/article/business/budget/budget-2017-market-shoots-up-on-fiscal-discipline-tax-clarity-4503438/
30. Government contains fiscal deficit at 4 per cent; beats its own target, *Deccan Chronicle*, 17 May 2015, http://www.deccanchronicle.com/amp/150517/business-economics/article/government-contains-fiscal-deficit-4-cent-beats-its-own-target
31. Ibid.

32. The Fiscal Deficit Will Come Back To Haunt India, An Interview with Raghuram Rajan, International Monetary Funds, Views and Commentaries, 15 December 2003, https://www.imf.org/en/News/Articles/2015/09/28/04/54/vc121503
33. Joanna Sugden, 'Rajan Tells Economists Surprise Rate Cut is No Surprise', *The Wall Street Journal*, 15 January 2015, https://blogs.wsj.com/indiarealtime/2015/01/15/rajan-tells-economists-surprise-rbi-rate-cut-is-no-surprise/
34. Budget 2017: Government should stick to fiscal targets, http://www.livemint.com/Opinion/d5kH45JJOAEKGunqtOtmPK/Government-should-stick-to-fiscal-targets.html
35. James Fontanella-Khan, 'S&P Warns over India's Fiscal Deficit', *Financial Times*, 25 April 2012, https://www.ft.com/content/06bcf01e-8ebc-11e1-ac13-00144feab49a
36. Ibid.
37. Aurodeep, 'Moody's Just Warned GoI not to Undo Fiscal Consolidation to Boost Growth', *The Economic Times*, 17 November 2017, https://blogs.economictimes.indiatimes.com/et-commentary/moodys-just-warned-goi-not-to-undo-fiscal-consolidation-to-boost-growth/
38. Fiscal Deficit: Rating Agencies Frown at Fine-print, DNA, 1 March 2015, http://www.dnaindia.com/money/report-fiscal-deficit-rating-agencies-frown-at-fine-print-2065278
39. 'India Should Gradually Reduce Fiscal Deficit: IMF', *The Indian Express*, 11 June 2014, http://indianexpress.com/article/business/economy/india-should-gradually-reduce-fiscal-deficit-imf/
40. Amit Mudgill, *Economic Times*, 2 February 2017, http://economictimes.indiatimes.com/markets/stocks/news/3-2-fiscal-deficit-not-enough-rating-agencies-say-do-more-for-rating-upgrade/articleshow/56934531.cms
41. Ben Hirschler and Manoj Kumar, 'Current Level of Fiscal Deficit is Unacceptable', Says Jaitley, *Livemint*, 23 January 2015, http://www.livemint.com/Politics/hVTwZgs5n5j8nJSoSRQGXM/Current-level-of-fiscal-deficit-is-unacceptable-says-Jaitle.html
42. Ibid.
43. S.A. Aiyar, 'Ideas for a Dream Budget from Jaitley', *Times of India*, 1 February 2015, http://blogs.timesofindia.indiatimes.com/Swaminomics/ideas-for-a-dream-budget-from-jaitley/
44. S. Adikesavan, 'Much Ado about the Fiscal Deficit', *Business Line*, 30 January 2017, http://www.thehindubusinessline.com/opinion/budget-2017-should-create-more-demand/article9509974.ece
45. Barack Obama, At a campaign event in Fargo, ND, 3 July 2008, Left of the

Mark, http://leftofthemark.com/quote/barack-obama-bushs-deficit-spending-is-unpatriotic

46. Mail Online, Germany's Merkel Warns France over Fiscal Deficit, 16 October 2014, http://www.dailymail.co.uk/wires/ap/article-2795231/German-leader-warns-France-budget-deficit.html
47. Government of India, Ministry of Finance, Economic Survey 1991-92, http://indiabudget.nic.in/es1991-92_A/esmain.htm
48. S&P warns of rating downgrade, *The Hindu*, 17 May 2013, http://www.thehindu.com/business/Economy/sp-warns-of-rating-downgrade/article4724289.ece
49. 'High Fiscal Deficit Forces S&P to Affirm Negative Outlook on India', *Business Line*, 17 May 2015, http://www.thehindubusinessline.com/economy/high-fiscal-deficit-forces-sp-to-affirm-negative-outlook-on-india/article4724855.ece
50. Ibid.
51. Open Europe, From the archives: the story of the 3 per cent deficit limit, http://openeuropeblog.blogspot.in/2014/01/from-archives-story-of-3-deficit-limit.html
52. N.K. Singh, 'Budget 2017: Seeking Responsible Growth, *Livemint*, 2 February 2017, http://www.livemint.com/Opinion/hqKzM6ug 6P4Z CAdKD zv6NL/Budget-2017-Seeking-responsible-growth.html
53. N.K. Singh, 'Indian Economy: Combine Prudence with Growth', *Hindustan Times*, 29 March 2016, http://www.hindustantimes.com/analysis/indian-economy-combine-prudence-with-growth/story-fKgw6I2ruY1 HsadTe W7JRK.html
54. India Inc Seeks Measures to Stimulate Demand, Boost Investment', *The Tribune*, 19 February 2016, http://www.ficci.in/ficci-in-news-page.asp?nid=10959
55. Interview with Brain Jacobsen, 'Wells Fargo Funds Management', *Livemint*, 23 February 2015.
56. Manas Chakravarthy, 'How India's Government Finances Stacks up against Peers', *Livemint*, 17 January 2017, http://www.livemint.com/Opinion/V5mT2htUi8niVXWUEgrZxJ/How-Indias-government-finances-stack-up-against-peers.html
57. Prabhat Singh, 'Why We Should Learn to Stop Worrying and Love the Fiscal Deficit', *The Wire*, 28 February 2016, https://thewire.in/22849/we-should-learn-to-stop-worrying-and-love-the-fiscal-deficit/
58. Sahib Sharma, 'RBI Governor Urjit Patel says Farm Loan Waiver a "Moral Hazard"', *Livemint*, 7 April 2017, http://www.livemint.com/Politics/FLWzWep1Jdv8riZhMlNbtL/RBI-governor-Urjit-Patel-criticises-farm-loan-waiver-schemes.html

59. Bijoy Shankar Saikia, 'Budget 2016: Jaitley pulls off Revenant Act, puts Spotlight on Social Sector, but Fails to Win Oscar', *Economic Times*, 29 February 2016, http://economictimes.indiatimes.com/markets/stocks/news/budget-2016-jaitley-pulls-off-revenant-act-puts-spotlight-on-social-sector-but-fails-to-win-an-oscar/articleshow/51190711.cms
60. K. Vaidya Nathan, 'Austere Budget and "Crowding Out" Effect', *The Indian Express*, 28 February 2013, http://archive.indianexpress.com/news/austere-budget-and-crowding-out-effect/1081047/
61. 'The Role of Fiscal Policy in Invigorating Growth', Reserve Bank of India, 14 January 2002, https://www.rbi.org.in/scripts/PublicationReport Details.aspx?ID=270
62. This sharp fall may be due to the demonetization exercise carried out in November, 2016. However, it remains to be seen whether the economy will rebound soon or if the damage could be long-term.
63. Vijay R. Joshi, a renowned economist, thinks that the actual growth rate is closer to 5.5 per cent; 'India's National Accounts on Economic Growth Wrong', Vijay Joshi, *Hindustan Times*, 4 June 2017, http://www.hindustantimes. com/business-news/india-s-national-accounts-on-economic-growth-wrong-vijay-joshi/story-nYkGzK7eNoTCigdM03PQeK.html
64. 'Expect a more robust jobs measurement tool by end-2018', Arvind Panagariya, Moneycontrol, 22 June 2017, http://www.moneycontrol.com/news/economy/policy/expect-a-more-robust-jobs-measurement-tool-by-end-2018-arvind-panagariya-2310399.html
65. Vivek Kaul's Diary, 'The problem with India's economic growth is . . .', 12 January 2017, https://www.equitymaster.com/diary/detail.asp?date=01/12/2017&story=1&title=The-Problem-with-Indias-Economic-Growth-is
66. Unconventional monetary policy wherein central banks buy securities in the market to lower their yields.
67. RBI's job is to build confidence, not play cheerleader, *Business Line*, 2 June 2015, http://www.thehindubusinessline.com/money-and-banking/rbis-job-is-to-build-confidence-not-play-cheerleader-rajan/article7275505.ece
68. http://finmin.nic.in/law/frbmact2003.pdf
69. Indian Financial Code, http://www.prsindia.org/uploads/media//draft/Draft-%20Indian%20Financial%20Code,%202015.pdf
70. Sashi Sivramkrishna, 'Will the Rising Wave of Nationalist Leaders Sweep Away Central Bank Independence?', *The Wire*, 6 February 2017, https://thewire.in/105496/rbi-central-bank-autonomy/
71. 'An Early Attack on Independence of the RBI's Monetary Policy Committee', *Livemint*, 30 May 2017, http://www.livemint.com/Opinion/WbJLkm7

UxTm13LyVfn0kVJ/An-early-attack-on-independence-of-RBIs-monetary-policy-com.html

72. Re. 1 in 1960 would be worth approximately Rs. 40 today.
73. Parthapratim Pal and Jayati Ghosh (2007), 'Inequality in India: A Survey of Recent Trends', DESA Working Paper No. 45, ST/ESA/2007/DWP/45, July 2007.
74. Dipak Mazumdar and Sandip Sarkar (2007), 'Employment Elasticity in Organized Manufacturing in India', Munk Centre for International Studies, University of Toronto, Canada, April 2007.

PART III

MODERN MONEY THEORY

CHAPTER 10

Modern Money and Economic Sovereignty

UNDERSTANDING MONEY

The history of money is a long one. A digression here would take us on a winding and arduous road, away from the focus of this book. So let me cut across time and begin with 'modern money'; what it is and how it *differs fundamentally* from the pre-1971 fixed exchange rates era under the Bretton Woods system. Understanding the notion of modern money is the key to macroeconomics; unfortunately mainstream macroeconomics never quite delves into the essence of it. Consider how a popular textbook defines money: 'Money is the set of assets in the economy that people regularly use to buy goods and services from each other.'[1]

In fact, all money arises as debt, as someone's liability—a promise to pay—an 'I owe you' or IOU. And in a modern money economy, money is essentially the state's liability. The rupee note in your wallet is an IOU (a promise to pay the bearer), (personally) signed by the governor of the Reserve Bank of India.

Any market exchange gives rise to a claim or debt. If *A* sells *B* a kilo of rice then *B* owes *A* something worth a kilo of rice in return. How can she clear this debt without barter of a specific good in exchange? One possibility is with an IOU, a piece of paper on which *B* promises to pay A goods or services worth a kilo of rice. If rupees were the accepted unit of account, in terms of rupees then, *B* owes *A* (say) Rs. 50 for the kilo of rice. This debt can be settled when *B* hands over an IOU to *A* for Rs. 50. But will A accept it? Not unless he is sure that when he goes to market to buy something from *C* that *C* will accept it. But if *B* were to hand over a Rs. 50 currency note then A *will most probably*[2] accept it in discharge of debt. What does *A* holding a Rs. 50 note imply? It means that *A* has given *someone* in India (or where rupees are legal tender) Rs. 50 worth of goods and services and that *anyone* in India (or where rupees are legal tender) will give *A* Rs. 50 worth of goods and services in return on demand. Rupee currency is therefore an IOU that is acceptable anywhere and by everyone in India.

But what is in that Rs. 50 currency note issued by the Reserve Bank of India that makes it acceptable to everyone? In other words, why is it different from B's IOU? Presently, monetary systems across sovereign nations of the world are based on *fiat* currencies (currency by decree, regulation or law), which are deemed to be *legal tender*. Fiat currencies are different from currencies that are convertible into something else including precious metals like gold or silver. In other words, fiat currencies are not backed by precious metals or more precisely, not convertible into gold or silver at a fixed rate. Some fiat currencies may be convertible into foreign currencies where full capital account convertibility[3] is allowed. However, this is not usually at a fixed exchange rate, as it was in the Bretton Woods era. Fiat currencies also act as a common unit of account in terms of which the nominal value of all other goods and services produced and exchanged in the economy are expressed; the numéraire. In India the rupee is the unit of account as well as the money thing which corresponds to it.

The term legal tender is, however, much misunderstood. It is often taken to mean that any debt may be settled using state-issued notes and coins. This is simply not true; a private contract can specify any good which is acceptable in settlement of a debt, and as we know in many instances cash (currency issued by the state) may not be permissible or acceptable. Legal tender has more to do with the receipts and payments of the state; how it makes payments and receives payments due to it. A comprehensive definition given by Dror Goldberg is worth quoting at length:

> When the law confers legal tender status only on the government's currency, it implicitly allows the government to reject any other medium of payment. Indeed, the government almost always rejects anything other than its issued cash or financial instruments that are redeemable in this cash (i.e., checks and credit cards). By doing so, the government artificially creates a demand for the

> legal tender objects and makes them valuable. . . . Taxpayers must obtain legal tender objects in order to pay their taxes. While denominating a contract in foreign currency makes the legal tender law irrelevant for your contract, receiving your entire income in foreign currency will not exempt you from paying your taxes in dollars. Taxpayers are therefore willing to provide goods and services for the legal tender objects. This can result in their circulation as media of exchange. . . .[4]

Legal tender is then essentially deemed 'valid money'[5] which can be used to settle claims of the state on the private sector. MMTers too subscribe to the view elaborated by Goldberg or what is called the 'State Theory of Money' approach, whereby,

> . . . the State (or any other authority able to impose an obligation) imposes a liability in the form of a generalized, social or legal unit of account—a money—used for measuring the obligation. . . . Once the authorities can levy such obligations, they can name what fulfils this obligation by denominating those things that can be delivered. . . .[6]

The obligations that Randall Wray refers to in the above paragraph would typically include paying of taxes, fees for use of goods and services provided by the state as well as discharge of fines and penalties. Once people are obligated to settle claims of the state in a particular unit of account, they would require sufficient stock of this money so that if and when the need arises, they can use them to pay the government. Non-settlement of the government's claims in the designated unit would mean imprisonment (for non-payment of taxes, fines and penalties) or exclusion from access to state-provided goods and services like water supply, electricity or sanitation. This ensures the wide circulation and acceptance of state money.

Mainstream macroeconomics gives no importance to modern institutions that create money and instead base their theory on the idea of money as a medium of exchange—perhaps gold—'invented' by rational agents to minimize transaction costs that arise in barter. Money is reduced to a mere means of exchange that lubricates the wheel of commerce, enabling specialization to bring about dramatic improvements in standards of living. MMT dismisses this understanding of money as purely conjectural, having no historical or anthropological basis.[7] It is a naïve, simplistic and flawed notion of modern money. It is these shallow foundations on the notion of money that mainstream macroeconomic theory is built upon with disastrous policy implications that dominates macroeconomics discourse.

TAXES DRIVE MONEY

MMT instead adopts a 'chartalist' position on money where money is seen as a creature of the state, which through its sovereign power appropriates the right to define the unit of account as well as the money form or money thing that answers this definition.[8] From this perspective, money is a pre-market phenomenon; it arose from the state's desire to control production and only later did it gain widespread acceptance as a medium of exchange or a means of settling obligations between parties in the private sector. When the state makes it mandatory that taxes and other obligations to it have to be settled in a particular money form/thing, which it has defined and of which it is a monopoly issuer of, there will automatically be widespread demand for its currency. This demand for its money in turn enables the state to capture a share of resources and output produced in the private sector. The latter 'voluntarily' forego goods and services in exchange for state currency, the currency in which they must settle their dues to the state. The tax-driven money approach—also called the neochartalist or MMT approach—provides *a* (or *the*) logical *raison d'être* for the state to intervene in the monetary realm.

Warren Mosler, owner of a hedge fund and founder of MMT, explains the idea of 'taxes drive money' using a simple example. He pulls out his visiting card in a classroom and asks students whether they would be willing to buy them from him at a price of, say, one card for one hour's work that would be used to clean up the classroom. When no one accepts his offer, he tells them that to leave the classroom they would have to give a card to his henchman at the door who has a weapon on him and which he wouldn't mind using if they fail to surrender a card. He then asks the same question. Everyone now raises their hand; they are willing to work the necessary hours in exchange for his visiting card. He then goes on to explain that people become willing to hold his card because of the tax and the punishment imposed for non-compliance. Furthermore, unless Mosler distributes his cards first, he cannot ask students to submit cards at the door. In the same way, the state must first issue money (tokens) for them to be able to collect them back as taxes. This brings us to one of the most important tenets of MMT:

The state must first spend its tokens (currency) into existence and then collect them back as taxes. Expenditure precedes revenue. The state does not need the private sector's money to spend. It's the other way around; the private sector needs state money to settle its tax and other obligations to the state.

But what is the fundamental purpose of the state's exercise in using money? As Mosler mentions, it is to clean the classroom after the lecture or more generally, to transfer resources from the private sector to the public sector (state) for social purposes, including building infrastructure, providing water and health services, defence and policing, setting up courts and other institutions, and so on. Consider that the government decides to build a dam. How would it get workers to do the job? One way of course is, like in the past, use people as slaves. The other option is to impose a tax on people which has to be discharged in specific tokens that the state decides and is also the sole issuer of the token. In such a case we have people who are looking for paid work in order to obtain these tokens. The state employs these people to work for it and in return gives them the tokens that they want.

In this way, by exercising its authority over money, a state strives to control and direct economic activity 'since the state is the monopoly supplier of the currency, citizens must sell goods, services, and assets to the state in order to receive the necessary state tokens in order to pay taxes.'[9] Through taxation the state introduces its IOU or money—its debt—and is able to move resources from the private to the public sector. Moreover, since the state is the monopoly-issuer of state money, it can set price of its currency (in terms of what the private sector must give up to obtain a token as, for instance, one visiting card for one hour's work); the state is a price-setter, not a price-taker. Mosler, in fact, argues that all prices in the economy are consequently determined relative to this price set by the state to acquire its tokens.[10]

Continuing with Mosler's example, the question then arises as to why people would be willing to hold more tokens than the sum of their obligations to the state? The need to discharge obligations to the state may make the use of tokens, if there is sufficient number of them available, valid for a larger number of transactions. In Mosler's example if each person needed just one card each for payment of tax, then for a class of 60, the sum total of tokens demanded would also be 60. How can the government ensure that people accept more tokens so that they could increase state spending? One answer could be a kind of 'infinite regress'; if businesses must pay taxes in a particular token, they would insist on being paid for their goods and services in that token. Workers would therefore insist on being paid wages in these tokens. Businesses would also ask for loans from banks in these tokens and so on. In any modern economy, one cannot restrict the demand for state money to be only for payment of obligations to the state. With the state being an important participant in the economy, its currency must be accepted by those who sell goods and services to the state (legal tender). In a country with a large formal sector there is also a greater chance that people who you deal with would need currency to settle tax payments to the state and would therefore want state-issued currency. State-issued money therefore goes beyond being the accepted unit of account and the token that answers that definition; it becomes the token with which obligations to the state can be discharged and the basis for transactions in the cycle of production and consumption.

If, however, the state's tokens are still not readily accepted by the general public then it would be forced to reduce the price of each token or in other words, it would issue more tokens for each unit of goods or services offered against it. Suppose tax obligations are just 10 per cent of GDP. In such a situation, the government will be able to transfer only 10 per cent of GDP into the public sector. When the government increases spending in order to capture a greater share of the GDP, inflation might ensue as the people do not voluntarily surrender goods and services (as they already have enough to meet their tax obligations). The government may then have to offer more currency per unit of goods; such depreciation in the value of tokens could be interpreted as *inflation* in price of goods and services. Wray therefore cautions us that 'while it would be incorrect . . . to argue that taxes "pay for" government spending, it is true that inability to impose and enforce tax liabilities will limit the amount of resources government can command'.[11] Governments, especially in developing nations, therefore strive for widening their tax net or tax base as well as formalizing the informal sector. This would increase people's demands for government-issued tokens and their willingness to surrender the goods and services they produce to the government in exchange for the tokens. Using this logic in the case of India leads us to pose an interesting question; could widespread tax avoidance, the existence of a large informal sector, exemption of the agricultural sector from all forms of taxes and hoarding of gold as savings be important reasons for higher rates of inflation?

It is also important to see how the state, when it introduces taxes actually creates unemployment. At the first instance, when Mosler announced that each student had to submit a visiting card at the door, the students were willing to work for him, taking time out from other activities. With the tax students are willing to work at the going rate (one hour for one visiting card) but cannot find work, unless and until Mosler spends the card into existence. There is another possibility in Mosler's example; what if he issued only 50 tokens in his class of 60 students? There would be 10 students who were looking for paid work but would simply not be able to find it. They would remain unemployed. And it wouldn't matter to them whether the education system was changed or structural reforms undertaken. Insufficient spending by the state creates unemployment.[12]

THE MYTH OF TAXPAYER'S MONEY

The MMT view of money has important implications on the way we look at the state and its constraints; as monopoly issuer of state money the government[13] does not face a budget constraint like households or firms as is often assumed. Many economic commentators in the popular media wrongly make this assumption and then go out to draw prescriptions from their study.

For families, a budget is a statement of income and expenditure. Even though many do not draw up a budget, when they do it, it is just about tallying up income and expenditure items. . . . Most of these considerations apply to institutions, corporations *and to sovereigns.*[14] The first two, in most cases, have the ability to borrow more than individuals have. A sovereign state has the ability to levy taxes and hence, has more leeway on expenditure than households, corporations or institutions have.[15]

With headlines-after-headlines repeating the same language, it is difficult to think otherwise, and in fact most people don't.

How the government collects our money and where it is spent
Have you ever felt that you are paying ever larger amounts of your hard-earned money to the government in one form of taxation or another?[16]

Such an understanding of how the macroeconomy works actually finds wide publicity in the media. People begin to repeat the same argument without ever questioning where these ideas come from. The proposition that the government needs taxpayer's money to spend is incorrect, at the very core.

This is true even of mainstream economics where a government budget constraint (GBC) is incorporated into DSGE models. As Sims mentions in his model: '*Conceptually* [government's budget] the same as the household. . . . Government's budget must balance in an intertemporal present value sense, not period-by-period.'[17]

It is crucial that the reader appreciates the fundamental proposition of MMT and its argument against the mainstream; the state can decide the quantum of resources it wants to transfer from the private sector to itself[18] and can do so by issuing its IOUs—any amount of them—as long as people demand them for payment of taxes and other obligations imposed by and to the state. This, however, does not mean that an unlimited supply will not have (adverse) effects on an economy. As we will see later, inflation and depreciation of the domestic currency vis-à-vis foreign currencies could indeed be the outcomes of issuing 'too much' state money.

Nonetheless, these aspects should not be conflated by a government fiscal constraint, especially with target numbers like 3 or 3.5 per cent.

Returning to the example at the beginning of this chapter, the Rs. 50 that *B* gives *A* in discharge of the debt created when A sells B a kilogram of rice is an IOU—a debt—itself; an IOU of the Indian government or its note issuing agency, the Reserve Bank of India (or the country's central bank). Since it is not a promise to pay gold or silver worth Rs. 50 to the bearer of the note what does the Indian government actually promise to pay in return for the Rs. 50 note? Nothing actually. If you were to go to the Reserve Bank of India and ask for something in exchange of Rs. 50, what you will get in exchange may be another Rs. 50 note or perhaps five Rs.10 notes. The buck literally stops with the central bank. In countries where the central bank promises convertibility of the local currency into a foreign currency (full capital and financial account convertibility), the essence of fiat currency remains as long as the central bank does not promise that the conversion to any other currency (or any asset generally speaking) will take place at a fixed exchange rate. MMT characterizes its context as fiat currencies issued by sovereign nations in a flexible exchange rate regime —a modern economy.

The closure of the gold window in 1971 by the US President Richard Nixon marked the commencement of 'modern money' in the advanced nations of the world.[19] Until then countries had agreed to a fixed exchange rate of their currencies to the dollar, which in turn was fixed to gold at the rate of US $35 to an ounce of gold. In other words, the US was obliged to convert the reserves held by other countries into gold at a fixed price of $35 to an ounce of gold. State currencies from then on were no longer convertible to gold. Currencies therefore had no intrinsic value; they were worthless pieces of paper. Their value came from the fact that citizens were obliged to settle claims of the state in the currency it defined and issued. The modern money era had begun.

India, however, continued with a fixed exchange rate system over the next two decades. It was only in March 1993 that India adopted a managed floating exchange rate regime without any predetermined rate or band. This brought the Indian rupee close to the notion of 'modern money'; a fiat currency operating in a floating exchange rate system. Although a country adopts a *managed* float system we can consider this as essentially a floating exchange rate regime since there is no binding constraint imposed like, for instance, under a gold standard, a gold exchange standard or a currency exchange standard.

As a little aside a brief comment on the origin of money; although important the answer will never be unequivocal. What is less contentious though is the fact that 'the state has fought a long crusade to impose its sovereignty over money'.[20] Keynes's own argument that 'the age of chartalist or State money was reached when the State claimed the right to declare what thing should answer as money to the current money of account—when it claimed the right to enforce the dictionary but also to write the dictionary'[21] subtly indicates that state money has evolved and did not arise in the form we are now accustomed to. But we will not dig deeper into history; instead we accept Keynes' remark that 'to-day all civilized money is, beyond the possibility of dispute, chartalist'.[22] Keynes in fact said this in the 1930s, long before the end of the post-War Bretton Woods era. This is perhaps because the earlier wars and the Federal Reserve Act of 1933 had made it clear that by revoking the adherence to the gold standard, states could always issue currency to transfer resources from the private sector to itself.[23]

NOTES

1. G. Mankiw (2012), *Principles of Economics*, 6th edn., Cengage Learning, p. 620.
2. Technically speaking, *A* does not *have to* accept the note although she would most probably be willing to.
3. Full capital account convertibility refers to convertibility of domestic currency into a foreign one for all transactions on the capital account of the balance of payments.
4. Dror Goldberg, 'Legal Tender', Bar Ilan University, http://www.biu.ac.il/soc/ec/wp/2009-04.pdf (pp. 7-8).

5. Ibid., p. 622.
6. L. Randall Wray (2012), *Modern Money Theory: A Primer on Macro-economics for Sovereign Monetary Systems*, Palgrave Macmillan, Kindle version, Section 2.2 (page numbers not mentioned in Kindle version).
7. L. Randall Wray (2014), 'From the State Theory of Money to Modern Money Theory: An Alternative to Economic Orthodoxy', Levy Economics Institute of Bard College, Working Paper No. 792, p. 3.
8. Rochon, Louis-Philippe and Matias Vernengo (2003), 'State Money and the Real World: Or Chartalism and Its Discontents', *Journal of Post Keynesian Economics*, 26(1): 57-67.
9. Ibid., p. 60
10. Interview of Warren Mosler by Steve Grumbine of Real Progressives, https://www.youtube.com/watch?v=1RJP52bwmcw (~ minute 44)
11. Wray, 2012.
12. See Warren Mosler's (2013) lecture on Youtube at https://www.youtube.com/watch?v=Z1uWVj0YJ3M
13. Government here refers to the central government only, which can issue currency. State governments, municipal corporations, public sector enterprises are constrained like households and firms as they cannot issue their own currency. Similarly members of the European Monetary Union (like Greece and Spain) and are akin to an Indian state government—they are not monetarily sovereign.
14. Italics my own for emphasis.
15. Mukul Asher, V. Anantha Nageswaran and Narayan Ramachandran, 'Grasping the Nettle: Fiscal Consolidation is the Key to Economic Growth', Takshashila Institution, Discussion Document, 7 July 2014, http://takshashila.org.in/wp-content/uploads/2014/07/TDD-FiscalConsolidationKeytoGrowth-MVN-July2014.pdf
16. Headlines from *The Telegraph* (UK), 5 June 2017, http://www.telegraph.co.uk/finance/personalfinance/tax/9036295/How-the-Government-collects-our-money-and-where-it-is-spent.html
17. Eric Sims (2016), 'Fiscal Policy and Ricardian Equivalence, ECON 30020: Intermediate Macroeconomics', University of Notre Dame, https://www3.nd.edu/~esims1/fiscal_policy_slides.pdf. Italics my own for emphasis.
18. Again, we are not implying that the state should transfer everything to itself, nor would it want to. Modern states would want a healthy and efficient private sector but they may decide in public interest, say for instance, that more courts are required or perhaps more dams. Resources would then have to be transferred to the state.

19. It may be argued that the Gold Standard had effectively come to an end in 1933 with the Federal Reserve Act that ended free banking. This was followed by confiscation of gold from the private sector (except for industrial use and dental fillings) that effectively meant that currency was no longer convertible to gold within the US.
20. Rochon, Louis-Phillipe and M. Vernengo, 'State Money and Real World: or Chartalism and its Discontents', *Journal of Post Keynesian Economics*, Fall 2003, 26(1): 57-67, p. 58.
21. J.M. Keynes, *A Treatise on Money*, New York: Harcourt Brace, 1930: 5.
22. Ibid., pp. 4-5.
23. Sashi Sivramkrishna, 'Modern Money and the Obsession over Fiscal Deficits', *The Wire*, 4 April 2017, https://thewire.in/121017/modern-money-obsession-fiscal-consolidation/

CHAPTER 11

Fiscal Deficits in a Modern Money Economy

TAXES AS A DRAINAGE MECHANISM

From the previous chapter we have seen how taxes drive money in a modern money economy. The purpose of a tax is not revenue but making the private sector state money accept. In fact, the state does not need its own money; however, by making it compulsory for people to pay taxes[1] only in state money, the private sector is willing to give up resources to the state in order to earn that money. In this way, the government is able to move resources from the private to the public sector. Moreover, it is also able to put into circulation a money thing—an IOU—that is widely acceptable and available to the private sector as its medium of exchange.

To reiterate, it is important to realize that anyone can create money even within the private sector. If *A* buys something from B, she can give an IOU (debt) or perhaps *C*'s IOU to *B* in exchange for the good. But will *B* accept it? Although in some communities personal IOUs are accepted as money, such IOUs will not gain widespread acceptance. However, state IOUs (currency) are usually acceptable, at least within a country where it is fiat money and deemed to be legal tender. For this, as seen above, enforceable tax collection must prevail.

Taxes also serve another major purpose in a modern economy. It drains money spent into existence by the state out from the system. Money spent into existence to buy resources from the private sector becomes purchasing power within the private sector. If supply is not forthcoming at the required rate, this potential demand within the private sector will translate into rising price level or inflation. In order to prevent this, the government can drain the purchasing power through imposition and collection of taxes.

By way of illustration let us say the government wants to hire a person to dig a hole and procures this service from individual *A*. It will credit her bank account by Rs. 1,000. Now *A* could use this money to buy vegetables in the market. If the supply of real goods and services are not forthcoming, there is a possibility of this triggering inflation. The government may then want to tax the private sector; in our example, a tax of (say) Rs. 600 may be imposed on *A*. This will either mean her bank account is debited by Rs. 600 or her paying the amount in cash. In either case, she will now have only Rs. 400 worth of purchasing power in her hands. It is clear that the government first spends and then taxes. Moreover, the tax was not required for the government to spend (they could have forced her to work); instead, the tax drives state money (makes it acceptable) and also drains 'excess' purchasing power from the private sector.

This is the pure monetary aspect of taxes. Other purposes of taxes are, however, not unimportant—to influence the allocation of resources, behaviour of economic agents and mitigating inequalities in income and wealth. By taxing one product (say, thermal power) and subsidizing another (solar power), the government can affect the allocation of resources in favour of the latter given its less harmful impact on the environment or compensate for negative externalities accruing on account of thermal power that the market cannot otherwise factor in. Taxes on cigarettes or alcohol could discourage habits that affect the health of people. Progressive income taxes are also considered appropriate to deal with the issue of inequalities in incomes and wealth. These are some important 'real' objectives of taxes, and not the funding of government spending.

One pertinent issue for India is its low tax base. In such situations, the government has to drain out the excess money put into circulation through its spending from a relatively small percentage of the population. What happens then is that a few households and firms bear the brunt of high tax rates. This was the situation in the period after Independence in India; since government spending was large and the tax base limited, the government was compelled to impose very high taxes on relatively few people. Indirect taxes are an alternative; however, they are not only regressive but in an economy with a large informal sector, the base for indirect taxes may once again be limited. It was therefore not government spending that was the problem per se but the imperative for draining excess purchasing power from a small base of taxpayers to control inflation that had serious repercussions on incentives and growth, particularly on the most productive (private) sectors of the economy. The problem continues to this day in India. Only 2.7 per cent of the Indian population pays income taxes and just about 0.5 per cent of the population reports an income exceeding Rs. 500,000 (US $7,500). This has forced the government to depend on indirect taxes for almost 50 per cent of its revenues[2]—or more appropriately, its drainage mechanism. Widening the tax base, especially of income taxes, could reduce the distortionary effects of taxes in India. Another issue that often arises in India is the differential contributions by Indian states. Whereas Maharashtra, Tamil Nadu and Karnataka are net positive contributions to the central government, many other states are net users of tax collections. This is increasingly perceived as unfair and distortionary.[3]

To summarize; tax reform is essentially designing a better drainage system that must serve its dual objectives—'real' and 'monetary'—the latter being effective inflation control, and not a source of finance.

Keeping aside the 'real' effects of taxes, MMT focuses on its monetary significance. Fiscal policy, which refers to government spending and taxation, is usually announced in the government's annual budget. If one has observed the presentation of the central government budget, it begins with expenditures and then moves on to the *expected or estimated* 'revenue' through tax collections. This is why economists consider government spending (G) as autonomous whereas tax collections (T) as endogenous or a function of GDP (Y).

Fiscal deficit is then the difference between G and what it collects back in taxes (T) which are dependent on GDP (Y). Therefore,

$$FD = G - T(Y) \qquad (1)$$

If $FD > 0$ it implies a deficit, $FD < 0$ implies a surplus and $FD = 0$ implies a balanced budget.

Going back to our earlier example where the government fixes its expenditure at Rs. 1,000 by hiring *A* to dig a hole and then imposing Rs. 600 as a tax on her income, we can illustrate the monetary effect of fiscal deficits. The government runs a deficit of Rs. 400 ($G - T = 1{,}000 - 600$). What is usually not mentioned in macroeconomic discourse is that *A* (or more generally the private sector) is left with a surplus of Rs. 400 in cash or in her account because the government had decided to run this deficit. Implicitly, or sometimes even explicitly, we are made to feel how wonderful it would be if the government ran a balanced budget or perhaps even a surplus budget. Hilary Clinton, for instance, definitely thought so; 'We had a balanced budget and a surplus when my husband [Bill Clinton] left the White House. . . . I would hope, with sensible economic policy, we could get back moving toward balance'.[4]

But would this be prudent economics? Running a balanced budget would simply mean that the government takes back *all* it gave to *A* to dig that hole. That reduces to something worse than slavery; in the latter case she may have at least received some food and shelter. Now what about a surplus budget? The government actually takes away Rs. 1,100 from *A*, leaving her with a debt to the government of Rs. 100, which she may have to repay in kind (labour perhaps) in the next period. The government's surplus is *A*'s deficit! What would you prefer now; a government surplus/private sector deficit or vice-versa?

A balanced budget may be fine if everyone in the economy is fully employed but when unemployment exists, the situation could improve through government spending. Moreover, even under full employment conditions any growth in the economy would necessitate an increase in state money, just for transactions purposes. Unless the government runs a deficit, the private sector would have an insufficient quantum of money (state IOUs) in circulation for transactions purpose, inducing deflation. It is no surprise then that most countries in the world (we will see the exceptions later) perpetually run deficits; the USA, UK and India are cases in point. India, however, has never ever run a surplus since independence in 1947—and rightly so.

Mainstream macroeconomics with its naïve and vague definition of money as nothing but an asset fails to grasp these plain institutional truths about modern money. What we have presented above is not theory;[5] it's just simple accounting. Unfortunately, with little or no understanding of basic double entry accounting principles (but with a baggage of complex mathematics and physics perhaps) economists have committed fundamental blunders in their pursuit of modelling the market system.

There is something else important about the fiscal deficit that economists and the popular discourse fail to realize; the fiscal deficit is non-discretionary. While there is heated debate year-after-year on whether the deficit target should be 3.1 or 4.5 per cent, what is missed is that the government cannot determine the actual outcome at the start of the financial year. What it does in the budget exercise is to fix (autonomous) spending and tax rates. The actual tax collections (endogenous) depend on what the GDP turns out to be. The latter cannot be set by the government. This makes the fiscal deficit outcome, non-discretionary. In fact, if the economy were to boom (slowdown), then for a given level of *G*, the deficit would reduce (increase). The deficit, or rather fiscal policy, therefore, acts as an automatic stabilizer. This makes it futile to rave and rant over a basis point in the fiscal target and even make it the focus of policy. Isn't it interesting to note that so much discussion takes place over the deficit target whereas so little is known about the outcome? And does the government decide on the current year's expenditure based on what it collected in the previous year? Obviously not; it doesn't really matter.

Before continuing with the deficit, let me conclude by stating another important tenet of MMT; taxes act as a drain of money introduced through government spending to control inflation. It is not a source of funding to the government. The government does not need taxpayers' money. Deficit targets are self-imposed constraints by the government on itself. There is no upper bound on the deficit, although there may be economic repercussions.

DEMYSTIFYING FISCAL DEFICITS

Although war is an extreme event, it does illustrate some fundamental misconceptions about fiscal deficits and modern money which neoliberal macroeconomists continue to cling to. Issued just one day after Britain declared war on Germany, the Currency and Bank Act of 1914 'permitted the [British] Government to print notes as legal tender in place of gold sovereigns and half-sovereigns'.[6] The gold standard was *de facto* suspended. The notes or treasury currency were made legal tender so that obligations to the state (payment of taxes, duties, fees and fines) could be settled with these notes. But since printing of the currency would take time, the Act even allowed postal orders to 'temporarily be current and legal tender in the United Kingdom in the same manner and to the same extent and as fully as current coins'.[7] Free from the constraints of the gold standard (that required conversion of currency to gold at a fixed rate), the government was then able to procure resources from the private sector to fight the war. From a small fiscal surplus in 1913, Britain faced a fiscal deficit of almost 48 per cent of GDP in 1916-17 while the national debt to GDP ratio increased from 26 per cent in 1913-14 to more than 127 per cent in 1918-19 and monetary base ($M0$) more than doubled between 1913 and 1919.[8] But what were the economic consequences of such profligacy? First, Britain did eventually win the war and second, its economy did not collapse. There were repercussions on the economy, positive in terms of the real GDP growth rate, negative in terms of inflation.

Coming back to the fiscal deficit equation (1), what happens to the deficit in the mainstream narrative when the government imposes a constraint on itself that it cannot monetize the debt or 'print' more money? In other words, suppose the government decides it wants to spend Rs. 1,000 but its estimated revenues are only Rs. 600, then how does it get the remaining Rs. 400 to spend? The answer is that it must 'borrow' this money from the private sector.

The MMT argument is, however, wholly to the contrary. The government does not need to fund its expenditures for as we have seen it spends money into existence; in other words, it does not need to borrow money to finance expenditures. Nonetheless, borrowing actually serves two purposes; we will discuss the first here and the second later in the book in Chapter 14. Like taxation, borrowing also drains excess purchasing power accruing to the private sector on account of government spending. In our example, we saw how the government takes away Rs. 600 from *A* through taxes, leaving her with Rs. 400. Suppose the government wanted A's spending to be restricted to just Rs. 200 it could have simply raised taxes to Rs. 800. Instead, it could *choose to* sell *A* a bond for Rs. 200. In this way, purchasing power with *A* is restricted while, at the same time, *A* has accumulated a financial asset, which may also earn her an interest. And wouldn't she love holding a secured asset like a government bond that gives her an interest income? Don't we all want to hold safe and secure, income yielding, financial assets, preferably a government bond? The government need not run deficits or debts; they could simply have drained all their injections through taxation. Fortunately for us they decide to sell bonds instead of taxing us through the roof.

It is also important to realize that unless the government ran a fiscal deficit in the first place, how on earth could it have sold bonds to us? In other words, how could you (or banks) have bought the bonds since the government would accept (as in the case of taxes) only its own IOUs in exchange for the bonds? Just as expenditure by the government precedes taxes so does the sale of bonds. This simple MMT analysis brings out a major flaw in the mainstream NCM model, which fails to consider the desire of households to accumulate net financial assets (liabilities of the government).

Going a step further; the sum of bonds accumulated over the years is the public debt. This is some US $25,000,000,000,000 in the United States! India's public debt is somewhere around Rs. 62,000,000,000,000!! If you want to get psyched there is a site that gives you figures from around the world, real time.[9] But what do these figures tell you apart from it being public debt. By simple double entry book-keeping we know that someone's financial liability must be someone else's financial asset; in this case public debt is private sector assets. In fact, from the private sector's point of view, a more appropriate term for the national debt should be 'government-issued assets'.[10] Imagine if the government were to run surpluses, year-after-year accumulating assets—then these figures would be private sector debt. That's certainly bad for the economy because unlike the government, private sector debt cannot be rolled over for too long. Usually it must be paid back within a lifetime. At the same time, by running debt, the government allows the private sector to satiate their desire for safe and secure financial assets.

This brings us to yet another tenet of MMT; government borrowing is not 'borrowing'. Just like taxation, the sale of bonds (rather than borrowing) is a method to drain money spent into existence into the economy by way of government spending. It also allows the private sector to accumulate financial assets and earn a return on it. Accumulated public debt of the government is net asset accumulation of the private sector. The government selling its bonds is a policy choice.

Suppose the government decides to repay its 'debt'? What happens? Economists argue that the burden might fall on our (hopefully someone else's) helpless grandchildren. They are most likely to find the MMT answer unbelievable; the government will simply move its liabilities from bonds (securities account) to currency (reserve accounts[11]). This is like the bank moving money from your savings account to your current account. Nothing really changes in the size of its balance sheet. As Mosler categorically asserts:

> The debt is paid off by a simple debit and credit on the Fed's [central banks] books. There are no grandchildren or taxpayers in sight—they would only be getting in the way. There is no such thing as leaving our debt to our grandchildren![12]

To the contrary, our grandchildren would be twice blessed; they inherit the bond which now turns into cash and moreover, they also inherit the physical assets (a road, bridge or dam perhaps) that may have been created by the government spending.

Mosler draws another important analogy of how the modern money system actually works. The central bank is just a scorekeeper (as in a cricket match). There is no fixed quantity of runs to start with. Instead, when the government spends the central bank would increase the score of the private sector and when it pays taxes it reduces its score. The idea of money as a limited quantity of something physical is naive and arises from the way it is defined in mainstream macroeconomic textbooks.

It should now be clear to the reader that an economically sovereign government which issues its own currency can never go bankrupt in its own currency. Period. I am not talking about going debt repayable in a foreign currency but specifically in its own currency. What is most surprising is that even the present Governor of the Reserve Bank of India, Urjit Patel, in his earlier work has argued that insolvency is possible with Dirac-like mathematical (although not accounting) precision:

> Eventual insolvency will occur if at least one of the following conditions holds:
>
> 1. The roots of $1 - \hat{a}(L)$ do not all lie outside the unit circle.
> 2. $\acute{a}_1 > 0$, that is, there is a positive deterministic time trend.
> 3. $\acute{a}_0 > 0$, that is even though the $[PDV(B_t)]$ process is stationary, its unconditional expectation is positive.[13]

Given the difficulty for economists to accept simple accounting principles, it is critically important that at least the *popular* macroeconomic discourse stops equating the government to households and firms and applying the same principles (and emotions) of thrift and prudence to government liabilities. Only then can we begin reframing macroeconomic discourse in India.

NOTES

1. This would also include payment of fees, fines, settlement in courts, and other obligation to the state.
2. Aarti Krishnan and Mahima A. Jain, 'Infographic: The Narrow Tax Base', *Business Line*, 1 February 2017, http://www.thehindubusinessline.com/economy/budget/the-narrow-tax-base/article9514691.ece
3. Praveen Chakravarthy, 'Analysis: the protesting Tamil Farmer Pays for the UP Farmer's Loan Waiver', *The News Minute*, 8 June 2017, http://www.thenewsminute.com/article/analysis-protesting-tamil-farmer-pays-farmer-s-loan-waiver-63344
4. Jeff Spross, Hillary Clinton Loves to Trumpet Bill's Budget Surplus. She

shouldn't, *The Week*, 24 May 2016, http://theweek.com/articles/625515/hillary-clinton-loves-trumpet-bills-budget-surplus-shouldnt

5. My purpose here is not in any way to deride theory. At the same time economic theory cannot be inconsistent with plain (accounting) facts.
6. World Gold Council, *The Heyday of the Gold Standard, 1820-1930*, vol. II, https://www.gold.org/sites/default/files/documents/1914aug6.pdf
7. Ibid.
8. Stephen Broadberry and Peter Howlett, 'The United Kingdom During World War I: Business as Usual?', https://pdfs.semanticscholar.org/9a41/a1fe329508a87f92313396bc273ec4f75766.pdf
9. http://www.nationaldebtclocks.org/
10. Steve Roth, 'Isn't it time to stop calling it "The National Debt"'?, *Evonomics*, 15 May 2016, http://evonomics.com/isnt-time-stop-calling-national-debt/
11. More on reserve money in the next chapter.
12. Warren Mosler, 'MMT to Washington: There is no long-term deficit problem!', *Huffpost*, 11 May 2013, http://www.huffingtonpost.com/warren-mosler/mmt-to-washington-there_b_2822714.html
13. W.H. Buiter and U.R. Patel, 'Excessive Budget Deficits, a Government Abused Financial System, and Fiscal Rules', India Policy Forum 2006, https://www.brookings.edu/wp-content/uploads/2016/07/2005_buiter_patel.pdf, p. 10.

CHAPTER 12

The Hierarchy of Money

ALL MONEY IS NOT THE SAME

The basic tenets of MMT that we have presented so far are critical to understanding the essence of a modern money economy; however, we need to delve further into the present institutional and systemic complexities to fully comprehend modern money. As a first step in this direction, we introduce in this chapter the notion of the hierarchy of money.

Perhaps the single biggest criticism of orthodox or mainstream economics is that it fails to understand money fully. Money is brushed aside as simply a means of exchange that lubricates the wheels of commerce and trade that would otherwise be limited by barter. Money is a veil that must be lifted to truly appreciate the 'real' economy and the working of the market system. Banks and credit play no really significant role in such an economy except one; they act as an intermediary in bringing lenders (savers) and borrowers (investors) together which may otherwise have been impossible given asymmetric information and search costs in financial markets. This is also one of the greatest shortcomings of DSGE models which had ignored banking and credit; it is therefore not surprising that these models were more or less useless in predicting the global financial crisis (GFC) or in recommending policies to deal with it. Although efforts are being made to incorporate money and credit into these models, they remain ad hoc and tentative.

There is another issue that economists are not used to when discussing goods or services; hierarchy. To an economist all goods are on par—at the same level—be it apples or aircraft, labour or beer. This is probably why earlier day economists chose an imaginary good called 'widgets', which doesn't exist, probably to emphasize that goods used in illustrative examples per se does not really matter. Call it X or a widget. This logic is extended to money. Money is money; there is no hierarchy in money. But this is not true and the failure to understand the hierarchy of money is at the root of many financial crises.

As we have seen money is an IOU and can be created by any two people to record a debt. Suppose I ask you for a kilo of sugar and give you ten kilos of salt in exchange, there is no credit or debt created and therefore no money comes into existence. Suppose, however, that instead of the salt I give you an IOU signed by me on a piece of paper stating that I will repay you Rs. 50 at a future date in lieu of the kilo of sugar you gave me today; if you accept this IOU, money has been created. If you do not accept it, the IOU cannot be called money. This IOU records a social relation between us that would appear in our books of accounts or our balance sheets; as a financial asset for you and a financial liability for me.

The hierarchy of money, as we have already seen, arises because of the acceptability of the IOU. Suppose you wanted to buy half a kilo of tea worth Rs. 50 from the shop next door and you have in your possession an IOU drawn by me (which I had given you in exchange of goods you sold to me). Would the shopkeeper accept my IOU as settlement of the debt that arises when you express your intention to buy tea? Perhaps not. Would she accept a cheque issued by a bank? A good chance, yes. Would she accept a Rs. 50 note issued by the Reserve Bank of India? Quite certainly, yes. All IOUs are obviously not equally acceptable; some are more acceptable than others. This is in essence the hierarchy of money. As Perry Mehrling put it, 'always and everywhere monetary systems are hierarchical'.[1]

THE INSTRUMENT LAYERS OF MONEY

The hierarchy of money can be illustrated as a four-tiered pyramid (Figure 12.1). At its base is the IOUs of individuals and households, which will generally not be acceptable in the general

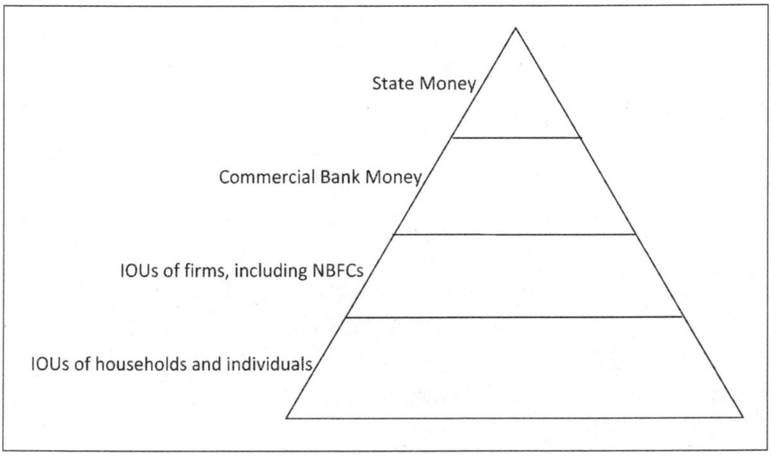

Figure 12.1: The Hierarchy of Money

economy; their use may be restricted to a specific community of traders. However, they do serve as money—think of your credit line with a local grocery store. Next up in the hierarchy are the IOUs of firms including non-banking financial companies (NBFC). When a firm borrows money and promises to repay it at a later date, it's IOU (a bond or stock) becomes an asset for the holder and a liability of the firm. However, there is no guarantee that the nominal value will be repaid—there are default risks. The bond or stock may also be illiquid so that its holder may not be able to convert it into other IOUs as and when she desires to do so. Nonetheless the IOUs of firms are considered superior to those of households for there are markets (for example, bond markets and stock markets) where such securities can be traded at market-determined prices.

Above this tier come banks and bank money; their IOUs are widely accepted in a modern economy. Banks are really economic agents that issue their own IOUs against IOUs issued by other agents to settle claims upon each other. Returning to the example above where you give me sugar against my IOU but the shop does not accept my IOU for the tea you wanted to buy; a bank could make this trade possible by first loaning you a sum of Rs. 50 (say, against my IOU in your possession as collateral) and at the same stroke create a deposit account in your favour for the same amount. You then issue a cheque (an IOU of the bank) in favour of the shopkeeper. The likelihood of the shop accepting a cheque (bank's IOU) from you is much greater than accepting my IOU. The bank has therefore validated your IOU and transformed it into their IOU thereby making it acceptable to a larger population. But why do we 'trust' a bank more than individuals or firms? We will return to this question a little later, once we complete the hierarchy.

At the top of the hierarchy is state money or currency issued by the central bank. As we have seen, if this is fiat currency there is no promise made on its convertibility to gold or a precious metal. In case convertibility of the currency into a foreign currency is permitted then this may pose a problem especially if the exchange rate is fixed. Where a floating exchange rate and/or only limited capital account convertibility is permitted there is really nothing above national currency in the hierarchy.

In a modern money system, state money is definitive money. This, as we have seen, is because it is legal tender—it can be used for the settlement of obligations due to the state including taxes, fees and fines. The state, *by design*, also accepts bank IOUs in settlement of its dues[2] and this is what makes bank money definitive money. In fact, it for this reason that bank money too has found wide acceptance in a modern economy. Even if convertibility of bank money into state money were to be suspended indefinitely, the acceptance by the state to settle obligations to it in bank money would make the latter an acceptable means of payment in an economy.[3]

While the hierarchy of money emphasizes the *qualitative* difference in instruments, the existence of different types of money does provide a great deal of elasticity in the system. During good times, when business and expectations about the future are positive, all instruments seem almost as good as each other. There is a thriving market for securities (shares and bonds), cheques are accepted in settlement of claims and there may be no great demand for cash or state money. Credit expands quickly in the system. But then when a crisis arrives, things change rapidly. Everyone wants to hold the more definitive monetary instruments; deposits are preferred to bonds or stocks and cash might even be preferred to bank accounts, especially in an economy where banks can easily go bankrupt and shut down. The element of discipline enforced by the hierarchy of money sets in and the qualitative difference between monetary instruments is exposed. As Mehrling puts it, these swings in credit expansion and contraction not only explain the business cycles that get transmitted through the system but may even explain the rise and fall of civilizations.

INSTITUTIONAL LAYERS OF MONEY

There also exists a hierarchy of monetary institutions corresponding to the hierarchy of instruments. The money at the top of the pyramid, state money, in reality consists not only of cash/currency held by the public and in bank vaults but also 'reserve money'. Reserve money (*M*0) takes on different names like base money, high-powered money (HPM), narrow money or liquidity. But who creates this reserve money? The answer—the central bank; in India, it is the Reserve Bank of India.

When can we consider HPM or *M*0 to be at the top of the hierarchy? If a currency is backed by gold, then the stock of gold would lie at the apex because domestic or foreign citizens could demand conversion of currency into gold at mint parity (fixed rate). It would be the task of the central bank to ensure that it is able to convert such demands into gold at the stipulated rate. However, for a sovereign country that issues its own fiat currency a promise of conversion to gold does not exist and fiat currency is at the apex of the pyramid. As we have seen, according to MMT, people will demand this currency since they are obliged to pay their taxes and meet other claims of the state in this money only. Moreover, payments made out by the state in this currency have to be accepted by people as it is legal tender.

Below the central bank come commercial banks. The banking system comprising of these commercial banks provide much needed credit to the private sector. Without credit it would be impossible for a modern capitalist system to function; finance precedes production, followed by sales and revenues. Banks are therefore responsive to the needs of the system and can expand or contract the amount of available credit to private enterprises and individuals. In other words, they provide elasticity to the system by ensuring a supply of (bank) IOUs as and when needed.

The only catch, however, is that banks are also required to convert their IOUs into state money (currency) on demand; for instance, when an individual draws cash from her account or to put it differently, commercial banks trade (or swap) deposits for state money and vice versa. There is another constraint on commercial banks; interbank transactions can only be settled in state money (reserves) and not bank IOUs. For these reserves as well as currency, commercial banks have to depend on the central bank. The central bank of a country provides currency and reserves to banks depending on the quantum of IOUs they have issued, which determines their demand for reserves. Although the central bank cannot deny a bank's demand for reserves, it does control the price at which it supplies it (much more on this later). This could then affect the price at which banks are able to leverage reserves and issue their IOUs or provide credit to economic agents.

In many countries (though not all[4]), commercial banks are mandatorily required to hold a fraction of their deposits as reserves at the central bank. But unlike as portrayed in orthodox economics, there is no constraint on the amount of HPM that will be provided by the central bank as and when banks need reserves. Usually banks with deficit reserves obtain such reserves from surplus banks in the interbank money market. However, when there is an expansion of credit by the banking system as a whole, a systemic shortfall in reserves would result making it necessary for the central bank to provide the necessary quantum of reserves. Although the central bank would oblige it would do so at a price—the interest rate, which in turn influences the cost of borrowing for the private non-banking sector. Therefore, as we will see in the next chapter, it is not reserves which constrain credit expansion; rather it is the availability of credible borrowers in the market and prudential banking norms that restrict the expansion of credit by the commercial banking sector in the economy.

This brings to another important tenet of MMT; at the macroeconomic level, credit and consequently investment is not supply constrained, it is demand constrained.

Sliding down the pyramid, at the base of the hierarchy of money are firms (including NBFCs) and households that trade in securities/IOUs of all types including debt, equity and derivative securities.

As Mehrling puts it, these institutions also straddle the instrument-layers and in the process create markets for each monetary instrument. As seen above, banks bridge the hierarchy of money between private IOUs and state money. The NBFCs trade securities for deposit accounts in banks; if you want to buy (sell) a stock for a reduction (increase) in your deposit account with a bank, a security dealer (NBFC) will do it for you. If you then want to trade a deposit account for state money (cash) or vice versa, a bank will do that. And if you want to exchange a national currency for foreign currency dollars, the central bank can do that.

It is important to note the difference between an NBFC and a bank. Usually, we simply assert that the former is not given a license to accept deposits from the public while banks are allowed to do so. This is at best a superficial understanding of monetary institutions. Banks and banks only, have reserve accounts at the central bank. Most NBFCs do not have reserve accounts at the central bank;[5] the access to reserve accounts at the central bank is the key differentiator between banks and other institutions, which gives them a superior position in the hierarchy of money. NBFCs cannot exchange securities for state currency (money) but only for a deposit in a bank. The bank is, however, permitted to promise and to exchange deposits for state money. The banking system today consists of a network of banks that freely accept each other's IOUs which, however, must be settled through a centralized payment system of the central bank in reserve money.

This further brings us to the price at which these securities trade. The rate between securities and deposits depend on the forces of market demand and supply. You will therefore get a price for your equity shares depending on the market conditions prevailing at that point of time. The NBFC does not assure you of a guaranteed price. Banks which occupy a higher position in the hierarchy are allowed to exchange deposits for money (currency issued by the central bank). However, the bank's IOUs are not only expected to be converted into state IOUs *on demand* but also *at par.* In other words, as a deposit holder I take it for granted that I will always be able to convert my Rs. 100 deposit into Rs. 100 cash (state money) on demand. Unlike, equity shares or property there is no possibility of a capital gain or loss. It is, however, possible that this assumption could become weak during a crisis[6] or a bank run. It is at this point we realize that conversion of bank deposit to state money below par is also a real possibility.[7] Finally, if a central bank has promised conversion of a currency into gold or a foreign currency at a fixed rate, they too might have to go back on it during a crisis. However, for modern fiat currency systems, as we have seen, the buck stops at the central bank with the national currency.

Matthew Berg[8] argues that a modern economy must necessarily have a hierarchy of money where not all money are equally acceptable; state money is universally acceptable but not all bank money. Only a part of bank money is actually validated by state money. Neither are all households and firm debts (IOUs) validated into bank money—only some of it is. In fact, it is the possibility of default which ensures that a hierarchy exists. If private IOUs did not run the risk of default, there would be no difference between these IOUs and those of a bank. The hierarchy of money therefore imposes an element of discipline in a modern monetary economy. Similarly if banks did not face the risk of bankruptcy or solvency, there would be no reason for state money to be higher up in the hierarchy. In fact, in a modern economy with the growing security provided to the commercial banking sector, there is a danger that banks may engage in reckless lending and Ponzi schemes since there is little fear of default; what economists refer to as the 'too big to fail' issue.

It is truly astonishing, to say the least, how mainstream macroeconomics fails to consider the hierarchy of money, monetary institutions and instruments as relevant in the modern world. The purpose of macroeconomics or, in other words, the study of market failure on a grand scale, is circumvented—either by indifference, ignorance or deception—rather than explained by mainstream economists.

NOTES

1. Perry Mehrling (2012), 'The Inherent Hierarchy of Money', prepared for Duncan Foley festschrift volume, and conference 20-1 April 2012, http://ieor.columbia.edu/files/seasdepts/industrial-engineering-operations-research/pdf-files/Mehrling_P_FESeminar_Sp12-02.pdf p. 1.
2. Individuals and firms in the private sector can also issue bank cheques in favour of the government to settle claims of the latter.
3. Kelton, 2001, p. 159.
4. This includes the Bank of England and Bank of Canada.
5. Some primary dealers (PDs), however, are registered NBFCs, who may have reserve account with the central bank.
6. This would especially be true when banks are run entirely as other enterprises in an economy and do not receive state support in times of crisis.
7. The Financial Resolution and Deposit Insurance (FRDI) Bill 2017 supposedly incorporates a bail-in clause whereby NPAs of banks may be set off against deposit accounts. The bill has, however, been withdrawn from the Lok Sabha in August 2018.
8. Matthew Berg, 'Essays in Monetary Theory and Policy: On the Nature of Money', 21 December 2013, New Economic Perspectives, http://neweconomicperspectives.org/2013/12/essays-monetary-theory-policy-nature-money-2.html

CHAPTER 13

Banking and Endogenous Money Theory

THE MONEY MULTIPLIER MODEL

We have seen the position of banks in the hierarchy of monetary instruments and institutions. Although they may be placed below the central bank (institutionally) and deposits may be considered lower than currency (instrumentally), we must understand that more than 95 per cent of money in circulation in most of the advanced countries of the world consists of bank IOUs (deposit), only a mere 5 per cent consists of currency. We have already delved into the process of money creation by banks from the mainstream point of view. Unfortunately, conventional macroeconomics is not only woefully inadequate in this respect but as contested by many heterodox economists they may also be incorrect in their construction of how bank money is created in an economy. This has significant implications for macroeconomic theory as well as monetary policy.

Mainstream macroeconomics usually articulates that a central bank effectively controls bank credit expansion by injecting new state money into the system or altering the reserve requirement. Almost every student of economics would have studied the money multiplier—it is actually quite likely that this is the only thing they may remember (though vaguely) from their macroeconomics courses. The story begins with a person depositing money in her bank account, say, Rs. 1,000. The bank has to keep a small portion of this (say, 10 per cent = Rs. 100 in this case) as reserves with the central bank (implicitly, this reserve is considered necessary as a matter of prudence) and can lend the remaining Rs. 900 to a borrower. When the borrower spends the money by writing a cheque it will be deposited by the receiver in his bank account. The second bank now has deposits of Rs. 900 from which it can once again lend Rs. 810 after keeping aside 10 per cent (= Rs. 90) as reserves. The process goes on, until there is (almost) nothing[1] for the last bank to lend. When we look at the total money created by banks from the initial deposit of Rs. 1,000 it works out to be:

$$1{,}000 + 900 + 810 + 729 + \dots = \text{Rs. } 10{,}000 \quad (1)$$

In general, this is the sum of an infinite series where:

$$\Delta TD = \frac{1}{r}(\Delta D) \quad (2)$$

Where ΔTD = change in total deposits (Rs. 10,000), ΔD = initial new deposit (Rs. 1,000) and r = % reserve requirement (= 10 % = 0.1). The money multiplier[2], m is given as:

$$\text{m} = 1/r$$

In our example banks can, therefore, create 10 times the money supply from the initial deposit of Rs. 1,000.[3] We call these deposits as money because they allow exchange of goods and services, which add to economic activity and GDP. All this would not have been possible if banks had not created their IOUs or bank money. There are three important points that must be noted from this model: first, it is based on the idea that banks lend after receiving deposits. The basis for this understanding is once again the loanable funds model. Deposits drive lending (investment); banks are intermediaries, channelizing savings into investment. And as discussed in an earlier chapter, this view is accepted even by central bankers:

> The role of the financial system is to intermediate between lenders and borrowers and provide avenues for saving and help investors find their financing needs. The financial markets impact growth by channelling saving to firms and improving the allocation of capital. (Speech delivered by R. Gandhi, Dy. Governor of the Reserve Bank of India, 2014)

Second, the initial deposit of Rs. 1,000 must accrue from a *net* deposit or injection of reserve money (state money) into the system—not merely the transfer from one bank account to another.

How do these net deposits increase? This can happen either from new government spending or the purchase of bonds from the private sector by the central bank. In either case, the central bank will inject new reserve money into the banking system, after which the money multiplier process takes over. Third, the central bank can also affect total money supply in the economy by changing the reserve requirement. In our example if the central bank changes the reserve requirement to 5 per cent then the first bank would have Rs. 950 to lend out, the second bank would have Rs. 902.50 and so. The money multiplier would be 20 (= 1/0.05) and total change in money supply would have been Rs. 20,000. This happens without a change in the quantum of initial net deposit.

BANKS CREATE MONEY

Endogenous Money Theory and MMT (or EMT-MMT) considers this whole story as nothing but fiction, propagated and sustained by mainstream macroeconomics even though it has been accepted by none other than the Bank of England as being an incorrect depiction of the modern money system.[4] Imagine physicists claiming that the world is a cube and writing textbooks based on such a premise! Once again, this can happen only in economics.

How really does the modern commercial banking system function? I will keep the narrative simple and intuitive, abstracting from accounting details. Let's say Bank *A* gets a licence to commence operations. Unlike what mainstream economists propose Bank *A* does not have to wait for someone to deposit (reserve) money before it lends out money. Instead, if Bank *A* finds a credible person or firm (*X*) who wants to borrow money it will lend it. When *X* borrows the money, Bank *A* has an asset (the loan) and a liability (deposit account) created in one stroke, out of thin air. It has now expanded its balance sheet from 0 to, say, Rs. 1000 (the loan and deposit). Bank *A* gives *X* a cheque book with authority to draw up to Rs. 1,000 worth of cheques. Now let's say *X* signs a cheque in favour of *Y* for Rs. 1,000 in exchange for some iron supplies.[5] What does *Y* do with the cheque? She will deposit it in her bank, Bank *B*. When she does that, Bank *A* has to transfer

Rs. 1,000 to Bank *B*. Here's where reserve (state) money steps in. Bank *A* cannot sign its own cheque in favour of Bank *B*; instead, it *must transfer only reserve money*, the transfer being cleared through the payments system of the central bank.

The payments or settlement system is a key operation of central banks. Millions and millions of transactions take place each day between banks. At the end of the day, net positions have to be computed and banks would know how much they owe and are owed by other banks. Banks do not deal with each other directly for settlements; all transactions pass through the payments system of the central bank and moreover, interbank transactions must be in reserve (state) money only.

Returning to our example, at this point Bank *A* is kind of stuck. It has to transfer reserve money to the central bank (which will send the reserve money to Bank *B*) in order to clear the cheque. Where does Bank *A* get the reserve money from? There are three possibilities; first, it will try and attract deposits from new customers. Suppose Bank *A* is able to get a new depositor who transfers money from another bank, Bank *C*. In this way Bank *A* now has reserve money to transfer to Bank *B* via the central bank's settlement system. Since current accounts and savings accounts (CASA) are a cheap source of reserve money (interest payments are lower than other sources) banks compete with each other to attract new deposits by setting up new branches and offering a multitude of services. Second, Bank *A* could go to the interbank money market to borrow reserve money from other banks. In the commercial banking system, there may be banks who have lent more money than they have got in deposits, while there may be others who have managed to attract more deposits but few borrowers. In such a situation the latter could lend reserve money to the former in the money market at the going rate. Finally, if the commercial banking system as a whole has increased lending but deposits have not come in, then there would be a net shortage of reserve money available in the system. In such a situation the entire payments system could stall causing havoc across the economy. Here's where the lender of last resort—the central bank steps in—to lend reserve money to commercial banks. The central bank would always lend reserve money to commercial banks as and when the need arises; however, the rate at which it lends—the repo rate[6]—could be changed 'at will' by the central bank (which would then subsequently affect the bank's lending rate and demand by the private sector for loans).

A question may arise as to how does the central bank create reserve money? Once again, the answer is unequivocal; out of thin air. The central bank swaps reserve money for securities held by commercial banks; this collateral given by a commercial bank to the central bank (securities) become assets of the central bank whereas the reserve money given in exchange to the commercial bank are the central bank's liabilities. This is how the central bank expands its balance sheet. At the same time, the balance sheet of the commercial banks would see a substitution of one asset (securities) with another (reserve money or deposits held at the central bank). The changes in balance sheets (or in assets and liabilities) of the central bank and commercial banks are shown by what is called T-accounts.

Central Bank		Commercial Bank	
Assets	*Liabilities*	*Assets*	*Liabilities*
Securities +	Reserve Money +	Securities (-)	
		Reserve Money (+)	

EMT-MMT completely changes the tenets of banking in a modern monetary system. Banks are not intermediaries between savers and investors in the sense that they do not collect deposits of savers (loanable funds) and *then* go looking for borrowers. Most importantly, EMT-MMT points out what has been missing from orthodox economics; credit is not generated from savings. Instead, credit drives investment, production and output that then generates income and savings. The business cycle begins with an expansion of credit and investment and ends with savings, rather than the other way around. And in a strictly theoretical sense, there is no limit on the banking system ability to create credit. Put differently, credit is not supply constrained; only demand constrained.

As Figure 13.1 illustrates, loans (or bank credit) never cease in the aggregate and can be sustained over an infinite time horizon. There is no start or end date for aggregate credit. Furthermore, an increasing amount of credit cannot be taken to mean a corresponding amount of 'accumulating pain tomorrow'. When a construction company takes a loan to build an apartment complex (which a bank creates endogenously) and you take a loan to buy an apartment (also created by a bank endogenously), the process of investment and production is set in motion. As economic growth happens, incomes and savings accrue so that the net worth of firms and individuals too increases even as credit and debt in the economy increases. Individuals and firms will repay their loans over a finite horizon but only to be replaced by even more credit by which the economy once again grows. Of course, this is sustainable only when the financial sector has ever-increasing viable opportunities. A crisis, however, happens when large amounts of credit created by banks

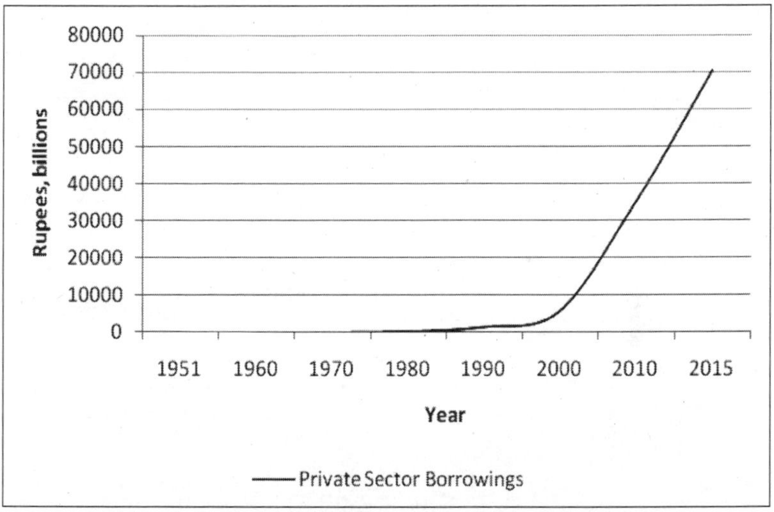

Source: Bank for International Settlements, Credit to the non-financial sector, http://www.bis.org/statistics/totcredit.htm

Note: Private non-financial sector borrowings from banks

Figure 13.1: Credit Expansion in a Growing Economy, India, 1951-2016

is not repaid—non-performing assets pile up, the chain is broken, new incomes and savings are not being created in adequate measure thereby causing economic disruption.

The expansion of credit by banks also necessitates the expansion of reserve money by the central bank. Table 13.1 shows expansion of the Reserve Bank of India's balance sheet between 1950 and 2016. There should be nothing alarming about this; as the Indian economy has grown so have the number of transactions and consequently the scorecard too. Imagine a game of monopoly played between more and more players, with many more properties. Obviously we would need more currency to play with. The banker's balance sheet would have to expand to meet the growth in volume of transactions in the extended game. As Mosler advices, it is better to think of the monetary system as an ever changing—expanding and contracting—scorecard rather than thinking of money as something physical and limited by nature.

TABLE 13.1: BALANCE SHEET OF THE RESERVE BANK OF INDIA 1949 AND 2015-16, SELECT ENTRIES

(*in billions of rupees*)

Liabilities	1949	2015-16	Assets	1949	2015-16
Notes in circulation	12	17,077	Sterling securities	11	
Deposits		5,065	Government of India securities	5	
Other Liabilities		10,220	Investment-Domestic		7,022
			Investment-Foreign		23,062

Source: D.K. Malhotra, *History and Problems of Indian Currency: 1835-1949*, Minerva Book Shop, Simla, 1949, p. 90 and Reserve Bank of India, Annual Report, 2016, https://www.rbi.org.in/scriptsAnnualReport Publications.aspx?Id=1184

SOME FURTHER REVELATIONS OF ENDOGENOUS MONEY THEORY

There are several other nuances of modern banking, which can be grasped from the EMT-MMT perspective. Reserves, which are a part of *M*0, can only be transacted by banks, not by individuals.

Banks cannot lend out reserves; reserves can only be lent or transferred between banks since consumers like *X* and *Y* cannot have reserve accounts at the central bank. As consumers we can deal only in deposits although banks give us guaranteed access to state money at par. This includes currency as well as money to settle obligations to the government, including taxes. When a person issues a cheque in favour of the government for payment of taxes, the bank converts its IOUs to reserve money. Payment of taxes, therefore, drains reserve money from the banking system just as government spending injects reserve money into the system. Mainstream macroeconomics completely ignores these crucial subtleties.

As Wray puts it, 'privately created credit money can thus be thought of as a horizontal 'leveraging' of reserves (or, better, High Powered Money), although there is no fixed ratio.'[7] Horizontal transactions are those between private sector agents (households, firms, NBFCs, banks). Figure 13.2 shows the hierarchy of money;

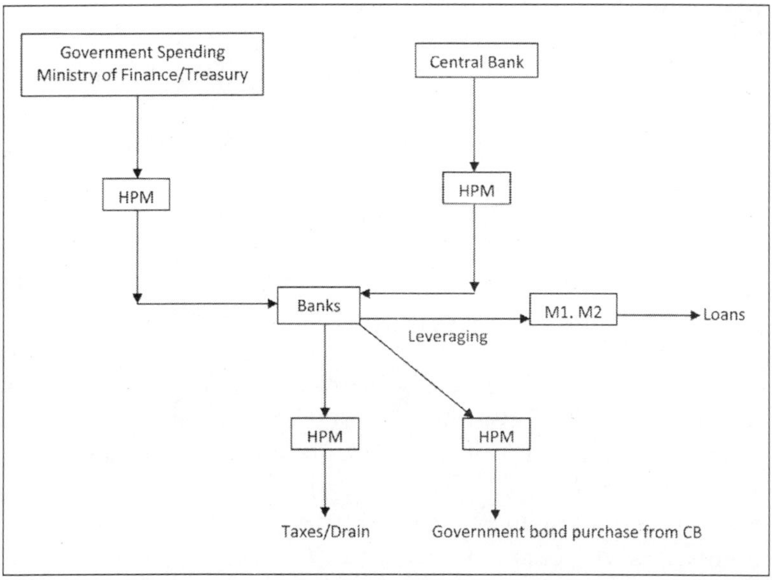

Source: Randall Wray, How to frame and teach money, pp. 32-5, http://www.econo-monitor.com/lrwray/files/2013/02/Mexico-how-to-teach-money-pdf.pdf

Figure 13.2: Vertical and Horizontal Aspects of Money

the vertical hierarchy of money can now be looked at as transaction between the government and private sector or in terms of HPM (*M*0) and the horizontal hierarchy as the banking sector's role at leveraging it. The Figure also shows how HPM can be drained out of the system, by the government through taxes and by the central bank through the sale of bonds. This is again something we will return to later.

It might seem that banks have the power to create an infinite quantum of money since they would always have recourse to reserves from the central bank. But in reality there are limits to this. First, while new money is constantly created in an economy, money is also being destroyed as consumers and firms repay their loans. Second, if the government pumps money into the economy through the central bank, banks might actually find that the increased availability of money leads to repayment of loans and deleveraging of bank money, i.e. they might actually find a paradoxical situation of deposit money contraction. Third; the most important constraint upon banks is the interest rate target of the central bank. By influencing the cost of banks borrowing reserves and thereby the cost of other non-government players in raising loans and consequently the demand for credit, the central bank can ensure that monetary growth is consistent with their inflation and/or exchange rate target.

The pursuit of profits in a competitive economic environment also acts as a natural check on the temptation for banks to expand credit imprudently. The business model of a bank is to give loans at a higher interest than that paid on deposits made into the bank. The spread between these rates are used to cover operating costs and make a profit. We have seen why banks have to attract or retain new deposits else they will simply run out reserves. In a competitive market this would exert pressure on banks into lower lending rates (to attract borrowers) and higher rates offered to deposit holders (to induce them to retain or open new deposit accounts with the bank). This reduces the spread available to the bank and thereby its profitability. The type of deposits made into banks also matters. For example, current accounts can be withdrawn on short notice that can put a bank into a liquidity crisis.

Banks therefore need an adequate amount of longer term deposits like savings bank accounts and/or fixed deposits. These, however, require a higher interest to be paid and squeeze the bank's interest spread.

Private sector banks also seek new borrowers but here they have to carefully assess the risk of non-repayment or what are commonly referred to as bad debts or non-performing assets (NPAs). This is called credit risk; to safeguard against such risks banks require an adequate amount of capital to absorb losses arising from NPAs. All loans have risks associated with them. As a bank expands its lending activities, the quality of loans would fall and credit risk increases. To factor this, banks would charge a higher lending rate which in a competitive market may mean loss of customers or lending to more risky borrowers. Competitive forces could actually drive banks into undervaluing risks to generate business in this direction that develops into systemic risk. Regulation is then required to ensure that banks follow prudential norms that include capital and liquidity adequacy as well as ensuring that banks do not make high-risk loans.

ORTHODOX *VS.* HETERODOX APPROACHES TO BANKING

Having outlined the tenets of EMT-MMT, we summarize the differences between this heterodox and the mainstream-orthodox approach to modern banking. Recall that orthodox economics views money as merely a veil over the real economy; it plays no part in the real economy except as a medium of exchange. In a simple one sector economy with no government and foreign sector, savings must be compensated by an exact amount of investment in real goods so that the circular flow of income is complete. For equilibrium all that is produced must be consumed either by households or by firms. In such a situation, credit can be ignored because all debt is cancelled out by credit, the assets of lenders is equal to the liabilities of borrowers so that savers and investors cancel out each other without any net effect on the economy (except perhaps when their propensities to consume differ).

Even a neo-Keynesian like Paul Krugman cannot accept the fact that banks can create money out of thin air. In a rather vicious debate between him and the heterodox economist, Steve Keen, he argues:

> [Steven] Keen then goes on to assert that lending is, by definition (at least as I understand it), an addition to aggregate demand. I guess I don't get that at all. If I decide to cut back on my spending and stash the funds in a bank, which lends them out to someone else, this doesn't have to represent a net increase in demand. Yes, in some (many) cases lending is associated with higher demand, because resources are being transferred to people with a higher propensity to spend; but Keen seems to be saying something else, and I'm not sure what. I think it has something to do with the notion that creating money = creating demand, but again that isn't right in any model I understand.[8]

However, with EMT there is a possibility of leverage (the essence of finance) where net claims in an economy can in fact exceed the value of current output. Even Bernanke, although he had acknowledged a possible role for credit in the early 1980s, had, by the mid-1990s returned to a mainstream view of credit, highlighting several problems that arise in the intermediation process like asymmetric information, and so on, although the basic idea was clear: 'By credit creation process I mean the process by which the . . . savings of individuals or firms are made available for the use of other individuals or firms (for example, to make capital investments or simply to consume).'[9]

In the more sophisticated DSGE models, finance appears only as an external shock which then affects the real sector. The financial sector is perceived as a zero sum game; one individual's profit is another's debt. For the real economy, growth in credit should be synonymous to the growth in the real GDP—credit is needed to support the real economy. Mainstream or orthodox theory of exogenous money supply argues that newly created money by the central bank leads to multiple expansion of credit (money multiplier), predicting that changes in broad monetary aggregates will follow the change in *M*0 (HPM). Suggestions by monetarists led by Milton Friedman in the 1970s that central banks should control inflation through changes in money supply had led to disastrous effects—ultimately resulting in their rejection as a confirmed policy failure.[10] Even staunch neoliberal economists, Kydland and Prescott (1990) found that:

> There is no evidence that either the monetary base or M1 leads the [credit cycle], although some economists still believe this monetary myth. Both the monetary base and M1 series are generally pro-cyclical and, if anything, the monetary base lags the [credit cycle] slightly.[11]

Moreover, in the aftermath of the GFC of 2008, the money multiplier in the US fell from approximately 1.5 to less than 0.5 indicating that reserve money in the system was expanding at a faster rate than credit.[12] The reason for this is clear to the heterodox economist; money supply is endogenous (demand driven) and does not follow $M0$. It is no surprise that central banks now implement inflation targeting using interest rate setting policies rather than control money supply. In fact, many heterodox economists view the extensive discussion on monetary aggregates like $M1$, $M2$, etc., in macroeconomics textbooks as a futile exercise.

While orthodox economists consistently failed to predict the crisis of 2008, many heterodox economists anticipated the crisis. To them, credit expansion and consequent debt build-up by households was unsustainable and were quick to realize that at some point of time they would have to deleverage their debt by either defaulting on debt and/or cutting back on consumption. As Malcolm Knight, then General Manager of the Bank for International Settlements noted,

> . . . the prevailing mainstream theoretical paradigms . . . typically have limited —or no—room for an active role for liquidity. . . . They see the economy as being quickly self-equilibrating, which can hardly allow for the cumulative build-up of financial imbalances and the corresponding distortions in real expenditures and capital accumulation.[13]

The heterodox approach to macroeconomics is not rooted in equilibrium analysis but in double entry accounting relationships. Moreover, all money arises as debt—money must be distinguished from physical assets. Debt is a counterpart of credit. Banks can create credit *ex nihilo*, which means a corresponding amount of debt in the economy. This process can go on *ad infinitum*, constrained only by prudential banking norms. However, as articulated by Bezemer, 'The financial sector can support growth but it can also cause crisis'.[14] Credit also inflates markets for financial assets and property (speculation). Excessive credit that leads to asset bubbles have an effect on rising inequality, falling capital formation, rising uncertainty and even fraud and corruption. Credit fuels the FIRE (finance-insurance-real estate) sector and financialization. Many nineteenth and early twentieth-century economists were concerned by the impacts of credit on economic stability; that concern vanished with the advent of mainstream macroeconomics.

The orthodox or exogenous money theory takes the view that money supply determines interest rates, the price level and/or the level of real output. This idea is built from the Quantity Theory of Money which states that the quantity of money in circulation would increase real output but after full employment would lead to a rise in the price level (assuming that the velocity of circulation of money is fixed). EMT takes the opposite view; it is the economic environment which determines the demand for loans and thereby the supply of credit.

EMT-MMT stresses the need to understand the need to understand how money is linked to production and exchange. As the economy grows banks increase their loans so that firms can make payment towards factor costs and/or towards rollover of debt in advance of realization of proceeds from sales or more precisely, anticipated sales. A downward trend in anticipated sales could become a self-fulfilling prophecy as banks begin restricting the amount of new credit injected into the economy.

The uninhibited endogeneity of money became a possibility only when the central bank became the lender of last resort, which in turn is possible only under a fiat currency system. Until then money supply was by and large exogenous. Rochon summarizes five propositions of EMT-MMT:

- The causality between money and income in the Quantity Theory of Money is reversed. The supply of money is a function of profit expectation. The causality runs from profit expectation

(*PE*)—the expected (or desired) income of firms—to the demand for credit (*DC*). It is the demand for credit that leads to the creation of money (*MC*). The creation of money through loans leads to the creation of effective demand (*ED*). The flow of causality can then be summarized as follows:
$PE \rightarrow DC \rightarrow MC \rightarrow ED$

- The causality between reserves (*R*), deposits (*D*) and loans (*L*) is reversed:
$L \rightarrow D \rightarrow R$
- Being endogenous, bank reserves have no causal influence on loans. This suggests the rejection of the money multiplier model.[15]
- The causality between savings and investment is reversed. In other words, savings cannot cause investment. Investment cannot be financed by savings because in a world of endogenous money it is the creation of income resulting from an increase in investment that creates savings.
- The rate of interest is exogenous. Interest rate is not determined by the market mechanism—it is determined neither by the supply of and the demand for savings nor the supply of and the demand for money. The nominal interest rate is exogenous because it is set by the central bank. Interest rate is exogenously determined according to internal and external economic objectives of the government and central bank. Keynes' approach to money was not singular; he was rather contradictory in his view and this has led to various types of 'Keynesian' theories including the Liquidity Preference model discussed in Chapter 2.
- The money supply is 'demand-determined and credit driven'. Money which is primarily a flow exists as a result of the demand for credit that allows firms to fulfil their expenditure plans. Being endogenous, the supply of credit is determined by decision of commercial banks.[16]

The EMT-MMT perspective exposes the fundamental flaws in mainstream macroeconomics; the latter, however, continues to dominate popular discourse and opinion by elevating finance or the lack of savings, rather than factors determining demand for credit, as the biggest constraint on private sector investment.

THE ROLE OF SAVINGS IN A MODERN ECONOMY

EMT-MMT may be misinterpreted to mean that private (household) savings play no role in a modern economy. This is simply not true. From a household's point of view, savings are critical for high-value consumption expenditures as well the future security. From a macroeconomic perspective, savings act as a drain from the circular flow of money which lowers expenditure, thereby dampening inflationary pressures in the economy that may arise from higher government spending and expansion of bank credit. To the extent that investment is financed from savings, growth will be non-inflationary as injections (investment) are matched by leakages or withdrawals (savings) from the circular flow of income and output. NBFCs, banks and financial markets play an important role in the channelization of savings into investment. Without these institutions, households would be at a great loss as they would be forced to put their savings 'under the mattress' without safe returns. At the same time, savings provide a cheap source of finance for banks, which can their leverage their balance sheets by providing credit to industry. Encouraging savings is therefore important in keeping costs of lending low and at the same time, ensuring a non-inflationary source of finance to industry (and even the government). However, as pointed out by EMT-MMT, investment (and government) spending in a modern economy is not savings-constrained; there can be a net expansion of credit by banks (and government) even without the existence of adequate savings—it is this important aspect that mainstream economics fails to consider in its analysis.

NOTES

1. Mathematically this will never be 0 but will become infinitesimally small.
2. There are many fuller versions of the money multiplier but are not any different in essence.
3. The simple money multiplier model assumes that banks lend out all their excess reserves and that there exists demand from credible borrowers for

these reserves. Moreover, it also assumes that banks do not choose to use their reserves to buy securities.

4. Michael McLeay, Amar Radia and Ryland Thomas (2014), 'Money creation in the modern economy', Bank of England, Quarterly Bulletin, Q1.
5. Here, the bank cheque has functioned as money and made the real exchange of goods or services possible, adding to economic activity and GDP.
6. We will discuss this in more detail later in the book.
7. L. Randall Wray (2014), 'From the State Theory of Money to Modern Money Theory: An Alternative to Economic Orthodoxy', Levy Economics Institute of Bard College, Working Paper No. 792, p. 3.
8. Paul Krugman, 'Minsky and Methodology' (Wonkish), *New York Times*, 27 March 2017, https://krugman.blogs.nytimes.com/2012/03/27/minksy-and-methodology-wonkish/
9. Ben S. Bernanke, 'Credit in the Macroeconomy', *FRBNY Quarterly Review*, Spring 1992-93, p. 51, https://core.ac.uk/download/pdf/6290968.pdf
10. Richard Adams, 'Milton Friedman: A Study in Failure', *The Guardian*, 16 November 2017, https://www.theguardian.com/commentisfree/2006/nov/16/post650
11. F. Kydland and E. Prescott, 'Business Cycles: Real Facts and a Monetary Myth, Federal Reserve Bank of Minneapolis Quarterly Review', Spring 1990.
12. Vuc Vukovic, 'Graph of the week: money multiplier', 29 February 2012, http://im-an-economist.blogspot.in/2012/02/graph-of-week-money-multiplier.html
13. Speech by Malcolm Knight, General Manager of the BIS, for the ECB Colloquium, Otmar Issing's Festschrift 'Monetary Policy: A Journey from Theory to Practice', Frankfurt, 16-17 March 2006, 'Money, Credit and Asset Prices: (Re-)learning to Read their Message, Bank for International Settlements', http://www.bis.org/speeches/sp060317.htm
14. Dirk J. Bezemer, 'Finance and Growth: When Credit Helps, and When it Hinders', https://www.ineteconomics.org/uploads/papers/bezemer-dirk-berlin-paper.pdf p.1
15. MMTers also argued that Quantitative Easing would be ineffective because it merely injects reserves into the commercial banks (swapping them for securities). It, however, does not automatically create the demand for credit by the private sector and would therefore just remain with banks.
16. L.P. Rochon, 'Cambridge's Contribution to Endogenous Money: Robinson and Kohn on Credit and Money', *Review of Political Economy*, 13(3): 287-307.

CHAPTER 14

Monetary Policy in the MMT Framework

AN OVERVIEW OF MONETARY POLICY

The mainstream economic theories of interest rate determination, both the classical loanable funds and Keynesian liquidity preference models are perhaps the most distant from macroeconomic reality. And it is on these models that the entire configuration of monetary policy recommendations are designed and propagated.

Today, most central banks across the world are mandated to ensure price stability as their primary objective although some weight may also be assigned to full employment. The European Central Bank is, however, mandated to only maintain price stability, with an inflation target of +2 per cent. The instrument available to central banks to achieve their target is the overnight interest rate or what is commonly referred to as the repo rate in India. The transmission route of monetary policy is rather simple although its efficacy may be challenged;

Δ (change in) Repo rate → Δ Commercial banks' cost of borrowing reserves from the central bank → Δ Lending rates by commercial banks to firms and households → Δ quantum of borrowing demanded for investment and consumption spending → Δ GDP growth → Δ inflation rate.

We have already examined the operation of the commercial banking system. Banks create money *ex nihilo*; however, interbank transactions can only be settled with reserve money issued by the central bank. Moreover, commercial banks may be obliged to keep a certain portion of their reserve money with the central bank as a 'reserve requirement' as well as require some amounts of cash for customer withdrawals. When banks increase their lending activity to the non-banking sector, they would need additional quantities of reserve money for the reasons outlined above. They could borrow this from other commercial banks in the 'call money market'. If there is a surplus of reserve money available in the system, the excess supply of reserve money given a rather inelastic demand curve for reserves,[1] would drive the short-term money market rates to zero. At the same time, a shortage of reserve money in the system will lead to an increase in money markets rates steeply.[2] To prevent these wide fluctuations in interest rates in the money market which would in turn hamper the central bank's ability in realizing its inflation target, the central bank enters the money market by offering to 'lend' reserves to commercial banks at the repo rate and to 'borrow' excess reserves from commercial banks at the reverse repo rate. The repo rate acts as a ceiling on the money market rate; a commercial cannot offer to lend its excess reserve money to deficient banks at a rate above the repo rate as borrower-banks can instead borrow from the central bank at the repo rate. Similarly the reverse repo rate acts as a floor or lower bound on the money market rate, preventing interest falling to zero as it mops up the excess at the reverse repo rate.

Although it is common to refer to the central bank lending and borrowing money at the repo and reverse repo rate respectively, it is important to understand that reserve money is not an asset of the central bank or money that it has earned. Reserve money is in fact a liability of the central bank. This is because it is a 'promissory note' of the central bank (a credit into the bank's account held at the central bank) given in exchange for securities deposited with them by commercial banks. Since the commercial banking system needs the central bank's promissory notes (reserve money) for interbank transactions or for transfer of tax money collected from the firms and individuals to the government, it is willing to swap its assets (securities) for the liabilities of the central bank (reserve money) at an interest rate (repo rate). In fact, heterodox economists[3] argue that the term lending reserves is incorrect since the term 'lending' usually refers to the temporary lending of an asset—for example, you lend a car or a book to someone.

As lender of last resort, the central bank will always stand by commercial banks to provide *any* quantum of reserves they need. If there is a shortage of reserves in the system two problems will arise; first, there will repercussions on the payment settlement system as cheques cannot clear and second, the money market interest rate target will be breached and consequently, the central bank may not be able to achieve the mandated inflation target. By ensuring that supply of reserve money is infinitely elastic or to put it more precisely, supply is always be forthcoming from the central bank it can maintain its interest rate target.

Counter to the classical or loanable funds model, the interest rate per se does not reflect a scarcity or excess of reserve money in the system. The rate is a policy decision—based on its inflation target—which can be maintained by the monopoly issuer of reserve money, i.e. the central bank. It is like Oil and Petroleum Exporting Countries (OPEC) trying to maintain a certain price of oil by controlling its supply, except that OPEC is not a pure monopoly as much as a central bank is. As an aside; for all talk of a competitive free market system, the apex monetary institution—the central bank—is a pure monopoly issuer of definitive (reserve) money in most countries across the world.

CONDUCT OF MONETARY POLICY IN INDIA

Given this general understanding of monetary policy, let us briefly look at the conduct of monetary policy in India. The short-term money market for reserves usually for loans up to a week to meet the requirements of reserves of commercial banks—liquidity—is called the interbank call money market. This market is located at various centres across India including Mumbai, Kolkata, Chennai, Delhi and Ahmedabad. The interest rate for interbank lending of reserves is called the call rate. This market is also the focal point for interventions by the RBI.

Volatility in call rates and the possibility of deviation from the target rate is controlled by the RBI through the liquidity adjustment facility (LAF), which consists of two primary instruments;

the repo and reverse repo rate. The repo rate is the rate at which the RBI 'lends' (or rather, swaps) short-term reserves against collateral to commercial banks to meet their reserve requirements. The reserve money of the RBI is a liability, a promissory note of the RBI that commercial banks require for interbank settlements, cash withdrawals, payments to the government and maintenance of stipulated cash reserve requirement (CRR).[4] In exchange for these promissory notes, banks have to provide collateral—central government securities and treasury bills—to the RBI. The cap on the quantum of reserves that a bank can obtain from the RBI against the LAF is 0.5 per cent of net demand and time liabilities (NDTL).[5] In the RBI's balance sheet, reserves appear as a liability whereas securities held are the corresponding asset. For banks, securities given as collateral are a reduction of assets corresponding to the reserves received, which are an asset.

When liquidity dries up in the LAF or in other words, banks require more reserves than the cap on LAF, the RBI has set up a 'discount window' called the marginal standing facility (MSF). The banks can further borrow reserves from the RBI under MSF; however, the MSF rate is set at 1 per cent higher than the repo rate. Therefore, while liquidity is made available it comes at a higher rate. The MSF also provides reserve money to banks when banks do not have sufficient quantum of securities as Statutory Liquidity Requirements (SLR). MSF also provides convenience in terms of working hours.

When there are excess reserves with commercial banks it is likely that the call money rate will breach the lower bound required by the RBI to reach the inflation target. In such cases, the RBI would intervene in the call money market to drain excess reserves by offering to compensate banks by lending them securities in exchange for their own promissory notes. The rate at which this swap is made is called the reverse repo rate.

The repo (and MSF rate) and reverse repo rates acts as a ceiling and floor to call money market rates. Figure 14.1 illustrates India's monetary policy framework. By effectively controlling rates between this band, the RBI aims to reach its target inflation rate.

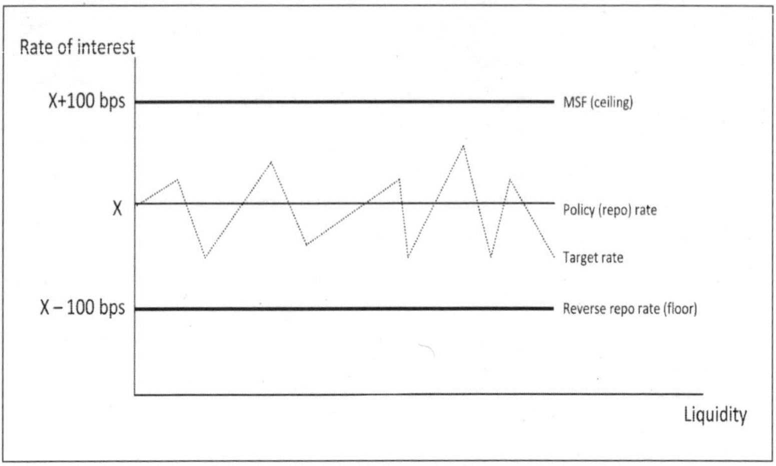

Source: Deepak Mohanty, 'Changing Contours of Monetary Policy in India', *RBI Bulletin*, 12 December 2011, https://www.rbi.org.in/scripts BS_View Bulletin.aspx?Id=12768

Note: MSF or marginal standing facility is available for up to 1 per cent of banks' NTDL (net time deposits liability) against collateral of government securities from required statutory liquidity requirement (SLR) securities. Liquidity in call money market is provided against excess SLR securities and export refinance facility for banks and liquidity facility for primary dealers (PD). At the floor, liquidity absorption by the RBI is carried out against government securities. Basis point (bps) is 0.01 per cent.

Figure 14.1: India's Liquidity Adjustment Facility (LAF) Framework

Figure 14.2 shows LAF and MSF corridor and the movement of the call money market rate in India between 2016 and 2017.

THE MMT APPROACH TO MONETARY POLICY

While these technicalities are widely discussed in the money and banking literature, there are certain nuances that MMT emphasizes that are critical to understand the working of a modern macroeconomy. As already mentioned and reiterated, the RBI does not lend an asset, it swaps its own promissory note (liability) for an asset (securities) at the repo rate. But how do banks come to

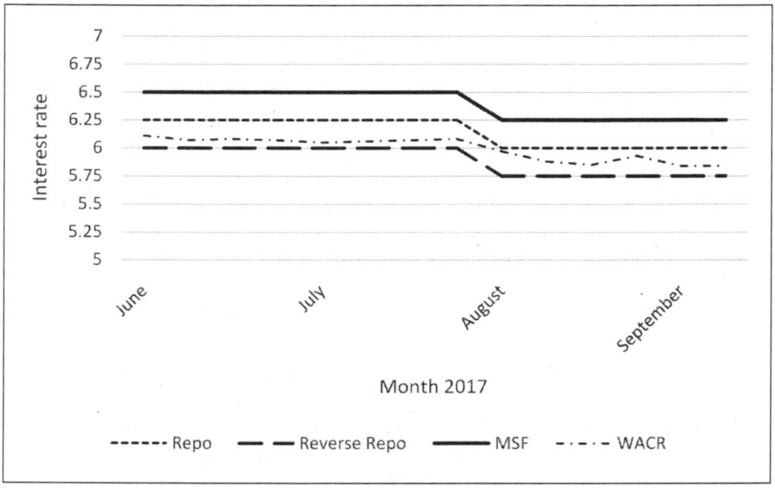

Source: RBI, Weekly Statistical Supplement, https://www.rbi.org.in/scripts/WSSViewDetail.aspx?PARAM1=4&TYPE=Section

Note: WACR = weighted average of call money market rate.

Figure 14.2: Actual Movement of Call Money Market Rates in India within the LAF Band, June-September 2017

possess such securities? The answer is simple; when the RBI sells government securities. But in exchange for what? Once again, banks must pay for these securities in reserve money or the central bank's promissory notes. But how do banks get the RBI's promissory notes? The answer; it is only possible when the government spends money. In other words, unless the government spends, banks cannot obtain reserve money to buy government securities from the central bank. This is similar to what we mentioned at the beginning of our discussion on MMT; taxes drive money. The government must first issue its tokens before it can ask people to settle their tax obligations in those specific tokens and those only.

MMT therefore views sale of government securities as a monetary operation so that central banks can maintain an interest rate target by intervening in the call money market. It is not a fiscal operation to raise money for government expenditure. Theoretically speaking, there is no need for a government to issue bonds–

it is not a financial operation to raise funds but a monetary operation to drain excess funds in the market that arises from government spending, maintain interest rates and prevent inflation. When the government spends money through commercial banks it injects reserves into the economy. This would drive the call money market rate towards zero. The central bank may therefore be unable to reach its inflation target when interest rates fall steeply. To stabilize the interest rate, the central bank drains excess reserve money (or liquidity) in the system by sale of securities in exchange for reserve money. Note that unless the central bank had first injected reserve money into the system, there is no way it can sell these securities in exchange for those reserves.

There is another MMT corollary that directly questions one of the main beliefs of neo-Keynesians and even neoliberal economist; the crowding out effect. Government spending injects reserve money into the system and actually drives down interest rates in call money markets, perhaps all the way to zero. It does not increase interest rates and crowd out private sector investment—this is just a myth based on a completely erroneous understanding on the essence of money and working of the modern money system.

Government securities are also required at the opposite end of the spectrum. When demand for liquidity is high, call money market rates could shoot up through the roof (given its inelastic nature in the short term) and drag the economy into a slowdown. The central bank must intervene to maintain interest rates within its stipulated band—the RBI, for instance, does so by buying securities and injecting reserves through the LAF and MSF; once again these operations would not be possible without the issuance of government securities. This is another critical reason for the sale of securities by central banks.

Monetary policy based on purchase and sale of securities became an acute problem in the aftermath of the 2016 demonetization exercise in India. When people deposited their cash with commercial banks, the latter were flush with currency (state money). Interest rates in the call market declined sharply. The RBI intervened by selling bonds to mop up the surplus liquidity; however, it soon faced a shortage of bonds available with it to mop up the excess liquidity in the system.[6] The RBI was therefore contemplating a Standing Deposit Facility where the excess liquidity could be parked at interest but without collateral of government securities.[7]

The central bank plays an important role in smoothing out reserve inflows and outflows from the system and their impact on interest rate and thereby on inflation rate. As seen above, when the government spends, the system is flush with reserves, driving down interest rates in the call money market. Similarly when the government taxes are due, there will be a massive outflow of reserve money from the banking system, driving up call money rates. Apart from using the reverse repo and repo to stabilize the call money market, the central bank also allows specified commercial banks to maintain government accounts to act as a buffer on reserve movements into and out of the system. In the US, these are called the Treasury Transfer & Loan (TT&L) accounts whereas in India,

> A network comprising the Public Accounts Departments of RBI and branches of Agency Banks appointed under Section 45 of the RBI Act carry out the Govt. transactions. At present all the public sector banks and three private sector banks, viz. ICICI Bank Ltd., HDFC Bank Ltd. and Axis Bank Ltd. act as RBI's agents. Only authorized branches of Agency banks can conduct Government business.[8]

To summarize, monetary policy consists of maintaining the money market interest rate within the targeted band using the LAF, MSF as well as allowing commercial banks to maintain government accounts. Security purchase and sales operations are not fiscal policy; they are a part of monetary policy, specifically LAF and MSF.

Apart from the importance of government securities for the conduct of monetary policy, they serve another critical purpose; the private sector in any country will always want their savings portfolio to comprise of financial assets, including interest-bearing, risk-free debt. Only the government can provide such an asset to the private sector, which are at the same time its own liabilities or public debt. As we will see later, the non-availability of sufficient quantum of public debt could result in the private sector increasing its proportion of savings to income[9] in order to fulfil its savings desire thereby reducing consumption, forcing GDP down and causing the government's budget deficit to rise (G-T) as tax payments fall and spending (transfer payments increase). This vicious circle pulls the economy in a downward spiral. The fulfilment of the private sector savings desire in financial assets, particularly in government debt is almost altogether ignored in the mainstream narrative.

MMT has been subject to much criticism on one point; in reality today, governments across the world are constrained by their inability to sell securities to the central bank directly for fiscal expansion. It must, therefore, raise money in the market. MMTers have, however, argued convincingly against this criticism.[10] First and foremost, this constraint is self-imposed and not one which arises from the monetary system. Moreover, there are several institutional arrangements by which the government and central bank circumvent this constraint. Through the mechanism of auctions to primary dealers the central bank ensures that there is adequate response to government bond issues. These primary dealers are not only obligated to participate in these auctions but they are also assured of the availability of funds as the central bank will supply reserves through repos or outright purchase of existing treasuries held by the primary dealers. It is also important to appreciate that there is a huge demand for government securities from banks, financial institutions as well as firms and individuals so that sale of government debt is never a major issue.

However, the bottom line is that any constraint on financing of spending by the government is a self-imposed constraint and did not exist in the past. Moreover, in times of need, these constraints can be revoked by the government—war is a classic example of such a situation. The treatment of the central bank as if it were an independent institution is a creation of neoliberalism in many countries. In India it was the FRBM Act 2003 which imposed a constraint on the ability of the government to borrow directly from the RBI. However, here too, the Act specifically states that the constraint will not be binding in case of exceptional situations like national security, national calamity or other exceptional grounds that the central government may specify.

NOTES

1. Banks would be in need only a certain amount of reserve money to meet the stipulated reserve requirements; they do no demand reserve money just because money market rates fall.
2. In this case, banks absolutely need reserve money to meet the stipulated reserve requirements; there is no available alternative to reserve money.
3. Eric Tymoigne, *The Financial System and the Economy: Principles of Money and Banking*, 2016.
4. Even if CRR is not warranted by central banks—and many countries like England and Canada do not have CRR requirements—commercial banks will still demand reserve money to make interbank settlements.
5. NTDL = demand + time deposits of a bank – deposits held at other banks.
6. Anirban Nag and Subhadip Sircar, 'Modi's Demonetization Move Risks Bond Shortage for RBI', *Livemint*, 24 November 2016, http://www.livemint.com/Money/erY0FtbPGa4jb2RzZi7qxI/Modis-demonetisation-move-risks-bond-shortage-for-RBI.html
7. Gopika Gopakumar, 'RBI May Focus on Draining Excess Liquidity in the System', *Livemint*, 3 April 2017, http://www.livemint.com/Politics/Ua2IgVEkHU3gNbsbVYYC2N/RBI-may-focus-on-squeezing-excess-liquidity-in-the-system.html
8. RBI as banker to the government, https://www.rbi.org.in/scripts/FAQView.aspx?Id=61
9. The ratio of savings to income is called the average propensity to save (APS). An increase in APS would necessitate an increase in the marginal propensity to save (MPS).
10. See for instance, Éric Tymoigne (2014), 'Modern Money Theory and Interrelations between the Treasury and the Central Bank: The Case of the United States', Levy Economics Institute of Bard College, Working Paper No. 788, http://www.levyinstitute.org/pubs/wp_788.pdf and Scott T. Fullwiler (2008), Modern Central Bank Operations—The General Principles, http://www.cfeps.org/ss2008/ss08r/fulwiller/fullwiler%20modern%20cb%20operations.pdf

CHAPTER 15

The Sectoral Financial Balances Model

MACROECONOMIC ACCOUNTING

Macroeconomics entails a clear understanding of the interrelationship between several parameters—GDP growth, inflation, fiscal deficits, taxation and public debt, private sector investment and savings, exchange rates and balance of payments—to draw an aggregate picture of the economy, which at the same time, sheds light on the direction of policy responses to tackle market failure. A theoretical framework that allows us to incorporate a multitude of stylized facts and figures into a comprehensive whole is the much neglected Sectoral Financial Balances (SFB) model developed by the post-Keynesian economist, Wynne Godley. Before delving into an analysis of the Indian economy, we briefly present the SFB model which has unfortunately been kept outside the scope of mainstream macroeconomics.

The SFB model builds on the double entry accounting axiom that every debit has a corresponding credit or for every asset there must be a corresponding liability—a fundamental accounting axiom that must hold true. As one financial analyst commented:

> There is no short cut to head-on recognition of the importance of accounting to economics. There is no rationale for departing from the correct logic and method of double-entry bookkeeping as it exists—no reason to 'spice it up' with creative but anomalous departures from what it actually is. Double-entry bookkeeping is not 'a work in progress'. It is what it is. The neo-classical concepts of exogenous money and the money multiplier and loanable funds and IS-LM[1] and supply/demand equilibrium are part of the fog within which mainstream has constructed some economic imagery that is in fundamental

conflict with the facts of accounting logic and real world financial measurement.[2]

If an economy is divided into three sectors namely, the private domestic sector, the government sector and external sector (which consists of foreign private and foreign government sectors) then *net financial* asset accumulation across these sectors must add up to zero. In other words, for net financial asset accumulation in one or at most two sectors there must be a corresponding net accumulation of liabilities in at least one of the other sectors. Therefore,

$$(T - G) + (S - I) + (M - X) = 0 \quad (1)$$

Where G = government expenditure, T = tax revenues, S = private sector savings, I = private sector investment, M = imports and X = exports. Note that a current account surplus (deficit) where $X - M > 0$ ($X - M < 0$) implies outflow (inflow) of capital from (into) the domestic economy and accumulation of liabilities (assets) by foreigners. Rewriting equation (1) we get:

$$(S - I) = (G - T) + (X - M) \quad (2)$$

Post-Keynesian economics, in particular Modern Money Theory (MMT), has elaborately discussed the importance of this fundamental equation. Drawing from Wray,[3] I briefly explain its logic. In a one-sector economy with only a domestic private sector, financial assets by one person must be offset by financial liabilities of another; your account in a bank (asset) is offset by the bank's liability to you (deposit). When you take a housing loan, the asset of the finance company (loan to you) is matched by your liability to the company (loan taken by you). While financial assets are always equal to financial liabilities, real assets can still be accumulated. Such real assets are not the liability of another agent in the economy. Consider your decision to buy a car; when you buy a car from a company on loan your IOU is the company's asset while it is your financial liability. But the car is now an asset in your books of accounts that is not the liability of the company. While financial assets and liabilities cancel out each other, the car remains the real asset on your books; this is also called net worth, i.e. total assets (financial assets + real assets) minus financial liabilities. To accumulate net financial assets for the domestic private sector *as a whole* it is necessary that it earns more than it spends[4] (keeping aside real assets). But this is possible if and only if there is a sector 'outside' the domestic private sector which accumulates financial liabilities. In an open economy with three sectors (private domestic, government and foreign sectors) this could be either the government sector (which runs fiscal deficits) and/or foreigners—the latter in some sense 'allow' the domestic economy to run a current account surplus and thereby let foreigners accumulate liabilities in the domestic economy.[5]

This, however, does not answer another important question; why would the domestic private sector want to accumulate financial assets outside its own sector? Private sector assets like a car, house or even plant and machinery are inherently risky; house prices could fall, stocks are subject to wild swings, corporate bonds and securities are subject to credit risks. In other words, the private sector may wish to accumulate financial assets that are not backed by real assets of other domestic private sector entities because of their inherent risk. There are two possibilities then—hold foreign (external) financial assets (which may belong to the private and/or government sector) or hold promises of the domestic government. Usually government liabilities not backed by real assets, both domestic and foreign (like US, UK, Japanese or German treasuries and bonds) are considered the most risk-free.

The appetite of the domestic private sector for net financial asset accumulation may vary depending on the state of the economy and outlook of private sector stability. When an economy is booming, the domestic private sector may not be averse to holding other private sector financial liabilities, usually in expectation of high returns. On the other hand, in times of economic recessions and crisis, households and even private sector firms may prefer to hold their savings in government debt.

A necessity for domestic private sector to accumulate government liabilities may also arise when private sector investment plummets with savings remaining unchanged. In such situations, the government must accommodate the private sector's increased desire to net save through accumulation of financial liabilities, i.e. the government must run larger fiscal deficits. In an open economy, the foreign sector may also afford an opportunity for the domestic private sector to accumulate financial assets (or liabilities of foreigners); this, however, would happen only when the current account surplus (deficit) increases (decreases).

The SFB equation leads us to another basic tenet of MMT: In an economy with only two (domestic) sectors it is impossible for both sectors to accumulate positive net financial assets in a given period at the same time—if the private sector desires to accumulate net financial wealth it is necessary that the government runs a budget deficit. If instead the government were to run a budget surplus (tax > government expenditure), then the private sector must necessarily run a deficit in that period (dissave) thereby entailing a reduction in its net financial wealth.

To understand the sequence through which equilibrium is reached in a three sector economy, consider disequilibrium arising from a situation in which the domestic private sector increases its desire to accumulate net financial assets (say when I falls, all else constant) but where neither the government nor the foreign sector raises its financial liabilities. In other words,

$$(S - I) > (G - T) + (X - M) \tag{3}$$

As domestic savings rise and consumption falls, the economy contracts. Given that S, T and M are endogenous variables—and a direct function of income—the fall in income would induce a fall in levels of S, T and M until the new higher level of $(G - T)$ and $(X - M)$[6] for any given level of I, G and X readjusts to the new level of domestic private sector net financial asset accumulation $(S - I)$.[7] The danger, however, is when, due to contraction of GDP, the private sector raises its marginal propensity to save (MPS),[8] triggering off another bout of contraction thereby drawing the economy into a deflationary spiral.

What happens if the private sector, especially during good times, accumulates net financial liabilities ($I > S$)? Although this may be possible for a limited period of time, a linear build-up is unsustainable as the private sector would have to settle claims of a sector external to itself (government and/or foreign sector) within a finite time horizon. In other words, the private sector cannot leverage indefinitely and would sooner or later begin to deleverage to pare down its debt. This constraint does not apply to the government in a modern money economy, which as we know, can accumulate liabilities or debt indefinitely.

The SFB model also provides a number of important insights into the consequences of the budget on the economy. Let us now introduce some basic behavioural equations into the SFB model. We assume that the desired level of government spending, investment spending by firms and exports are exogenous and fixed at:

$$G_d = G_0;\ I_d = I_0;\ X_d = X_0$$

The desired level of taxes, savings and imports are, however, considered endogenous and positive functions of the level of income.

For a country like India which usually runs a current account deficit, i.e. $(M_d - X_0) > 0$, for positive net financial asset accumulation by the private domestic sector, $(S_d - I_0) > 0$, we must have a budget deficit, i.e. $(G_d - T_0) > 0$. In equation 4 we illustrate this argument with some hypothetical numbers that might be considered as percentages of GDP.

$$\begin{array}{ccccc} (G_0 - T_d) & = & (S_d - I_0) & + & (M_d - X_0) \\ 5 & = & 3 & & 2 \\ >0 & & >0 & & >0 \end{array} \tag{4}$$

What happens if the government changes its objective and cuts spending to G_1 attempting to force a lower fiscal deficit to 3 per cent of GDP? All else constant, this could result in something like equation (5):

$$\begin{array}{ccccc} (G_1 - T_d) & = & (S_d - I_0) & + & (M_d - X_0) \\ 3 & = & 2 & & 1 \\ >0 & & >0 & & >0 \end{array} \tag{5}$$

A cut in government spending causes income to fall. This in turn causes savings and imports to fall so as to bring about the adjustment seen in equation (5). Moreover, as income falls tax revenues will also begin to decline so that in order to achieve the budget deficit target of 3 per cent, further expenditure cuts would be necessary ultimately leading to a new equilibrium at a significantly lower level of GDP. There is a further danger here; if households are not satisfied with their level of savings there could be an increase in the marginal propensity to save implying a decrease in household marginal propensity to consumer thereby negatively impact business of firms as well as investment sentiment.

What happens if the government goes the whole hog and decides to run a fiscal surplus—a dream for austerity enthusiasts and international rating agencies? To achieve this end it cuts spending to G_2 attempting to force a fiscal surplus? All else constant, this could result in something like equation (6):

$$\begin{array}{ccccc} (G_2 - T_d) & = & (S_d - I_0) & + & (M_d - X_0) \\ -3 & = & -4 & & +1 \\ <0 & & <0 & & <0 \end{array} \tag{6}$$

Here for the government to accumulate positive financial assets, the domestic private sector must accumulate net financial liabilities even as the foreign sector continues to accumulate financial assets within the country. Recollect that this is a simple double-entry bookkeeping requirement and does not arise from high theory; when one sector accumulates financial assets the other sectors must (combined) accumulate liabilities. In other words, when the state is taking money out of the economy by taxing more than it spends, the non-government sector must be dissaving. In this case it is the households that bear the largest impact. This is not sustainable and must ultimately lead to an upward (downward) revision in the marginal propensity to save (and therefore to consume).

For sake of completeness, it is also possible, however, to have an outcome as in equation (7) in response to the government budget surplus;

$$\begin{array}{ccccc} (G_2 - T_d) & = & (S_d - I_0) & + & (M_d - X_0) \\ -3 & & +1 & & -4 \\ <0 & & <0 & & <0 \end{array} \tag{7}$$

As can be seen in Equation (7) in spite of a budget surplus the domestic private sector is accumulating net financial assets. This, however, requires the country to now run a massive current account surplus from its prior position of a current account deficit. With exports unlikely to increase drastically in a short span of time, this could happen because of a drastic fall in imports that may come about only with a massive contraction in GDP. Moreover, under a flexible exchange rate mechanism, the trade surplus would induce an appreciation of the domestic currency, causing exports to fall.[9] If we instead remain with equation (6), the government's budget surplus implies domestic private sector dissavings or rising private sector debt, which is unsustainable over a longer period. If the domestic private sector wants to reverse dissavings into net positive savings, it has to increase its marginal propensity to save thereby slowing down the economy. This would in turn have adverse repercussions on tax collections—the country would ultimately reach equilibrium but at the cost of a contraction in GDP.

A limitation of the SFB equation is that it does not establish cause and effect. However, since it is an identity that must hold true, desired or exogenously induced changes in a sector's financial balances will have cyclical repercussions on the economy; the feedback to the equation working through changes in income.

MAPPING THE SFB

One major issue that has to be dealt with in mapping the SFB equation for a country is the availability of data on domestic private sector savings and investment, namely S and I. Even in advanced countries like Japan, Germany and the US where flow of funds data is maintained, there remain 'so many estimation and sampling challenges' that it is better to compute $(S - I)$ from the government budget and balance of payments numbers. Koo justifies this approach 'because the data of these two sectors are relatively accurate. . . .'[10]

We first re-write equation (1) as:

$$(S - I) + (M - X) = (G - T) \quad (4)$$

This equation articulates that net financial asset accumulation by the domestic private sector and foreign sector (in the domestic economy) must equal net accumulation of financial liabilities by the domestic government.

Figure 15.1 maps SFB equation for India between 2012 and 2017 using the data presented in Table 15.1. For illustrative purposes we consider $(T - G)$ in the figures so that a negative $(T - G)$ value must be understood as a fiscal deficit (or $G > T$).

The US SFB data in Figure 15.2 illustrates the MMT argument. In 2000, President Clinton was able to run a budget surplus (a rare occasion in the history of any country); however, as can be seen in Figure 15.2, with a CAD ($M > X$) this came at the cost of the domestic private sector accumulating liabilities. This situa-

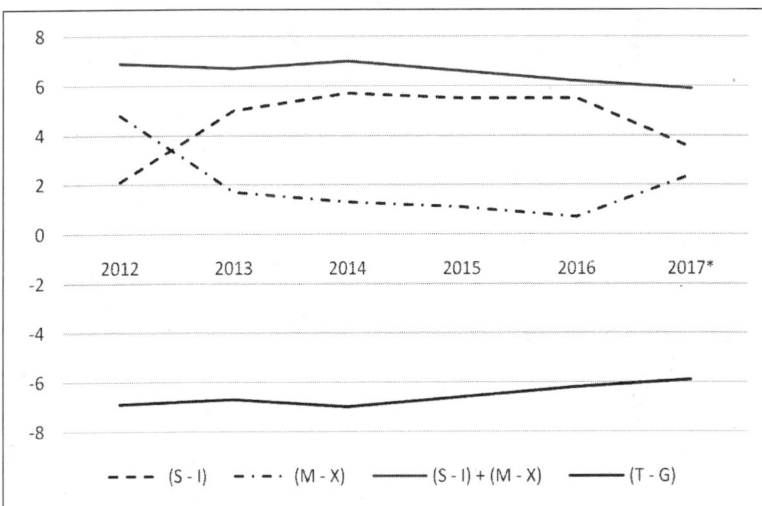

Source: Current account deficit from https://tradingeconomics.com/india/current-account-to-gdp Fiscal deficit: K. Muthukumar, 'How GST Could Tame Centre-states' Fiscal Deficit', *Business Line*, http://premium. thehindu-businessline.com/portfolio/news-analysis/how-gst-could-help-tame-centrestates-fiscal-deficit/article9719897.ece

Note: * Figures for 2017 are based on trends

Figure 15.1: India's Sectoral Financial Balances

TABLE 15.1: INDIA'S SECTORAL FINANCIAL BALANCES

Year	(G–T)	(S–I)	(M–X)	(S–I)+(M–X)
2012	6.9	2.1	4.8	6.9
2013	6.7	5.0	1.7	6.7
2014	7.0	5.7	1.3	7.0
2015	6.4	5.5	1.1	6.6
2016	6.2	5.5	0.7	6.2
2017*	5.9	3.5	2.4	5.9

Sources: Current account deficit from https://tradingeconomics.com/india/current-account-to-gdp Fiscal deficit: Muthukumar, K. 'How GST Could Tame Centre-states' Fiscal Deficit', *Business Line*, http://premium.thehindubusinessline.com/portfolio/news-analysis/how-gst-could-help-tame-centrestates-fiscal-deficit/article9719897.ece

Note: * Figures for 2017 are based on trends.

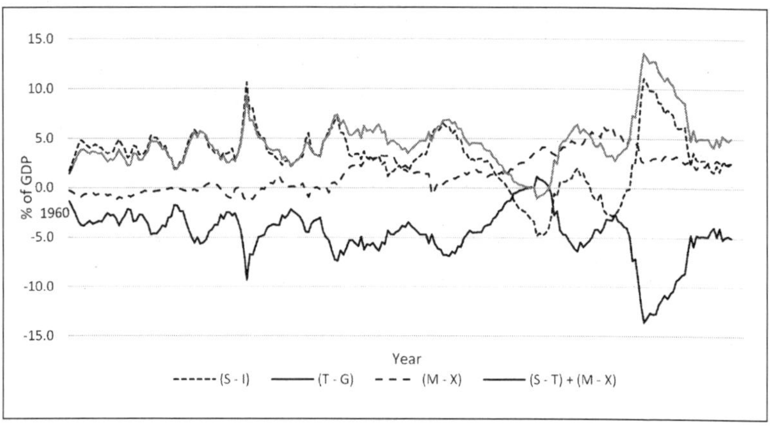

Source: https://fred.stlouisfed.org/graph/?g=ejty

Figure 15.2: US Sectoral Financial Balances

tion was not sustainable so that the Republican President George W. Bush Jr. had to revert back to a 5 per cent government deficit. However, the boom in the housing sector fuelled large household borrowings and debt that had to be matched by a growing US current account deficit that was driven by imports of Chinese goods. When the housing bubble finally burst or rather exploded in 2008,

US households had to increase their savings (reduce consumption), supported by way of close to 15 per cent fiscal deficits.

SECTORAL FINANCIAL BALANCE MODEL AND STABILIZATION POLICIES

In the previous section we have used a simple SFB model to demonstrate the importance of government budget deficits in sustaining the non-domestic government sector's (which includes the domestic private sector and foreign sector) net financial asset accumulation. We have also attempted to understand the present concerns over budget deficit targets as a possible outcome of the rise of neoliberalism, an ideological shift from a Keynesian or demand driven world view of economic development. However, the 2008 GFC and its aftermath reopened the debate on the possible countercyclical role of fiscal policy.

We illustrate this imperative for accommodative fiscal policy with a diagrammatic extension of the SFB model that maps equation (1) on to a 4-quadrant (*Q*-1 to *Q*-4) diagram as in Figure 15.3. The line SI_0 drawn at an angle of 45° through the origin is a set of points where $(S - I) = 0$. Consider point *A* on the *SI* line; if $(S - I) = 0$ then from equation 2, $(X - M) = -(G - T) = (T - G)$ or a fiscal surplus. If $(S - I) = 0$, a positive current account balance must be matched by an equal fiscal surplus; given that the domestic private sector is neither accumulating assets not liabilities, if foreigners are accumulating net financial liabilities then the domestic government must be accumulating an equal amount of financial assets.

Now consider a point such as *B* where $(X - M) > -(G - T) = (T - G)$. Put differently,

$$(X - M) - [-(G - T)] > 0, \quad \text{or}$$
$$(X - M) + (G - T) > 0$$

From equation (1) we therefore have $(S - I) > 0$ at point *B*. In general all points to the right (left) of the *SI* line are points where $S - I > 0$ ($S - I < 0$), i.e. the domestic private sector is accumulating a positive quantity of net financial assets (liabilities). Each of the

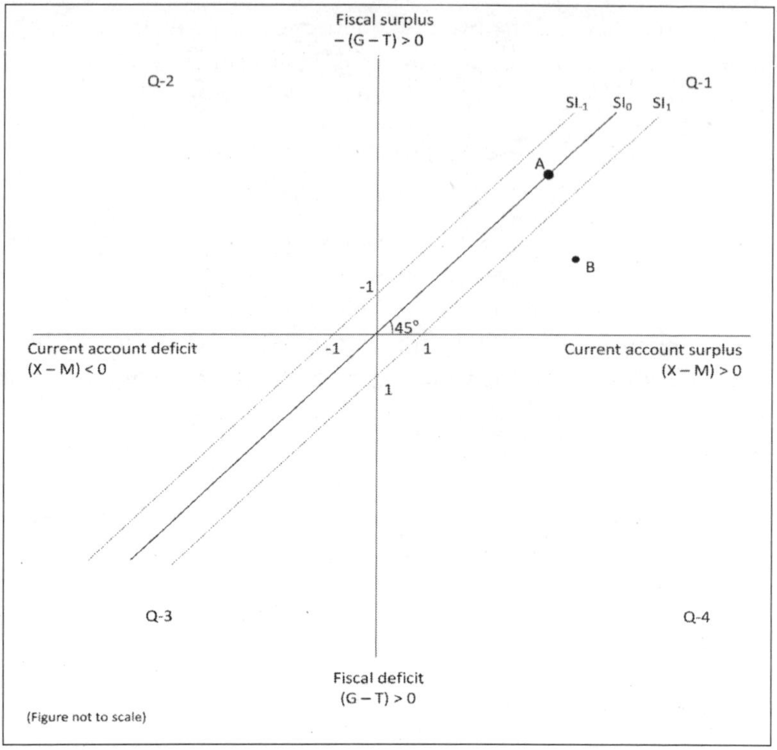

Figure 15.3: The SFB Template

dashed lines parallel to the *SI* line are possible combinations of fiscal and current account balances that yield a certain level of net financial asset accumulation by the domestic private sector; for example SI_1 yields one per cent net financial asset accumulation, while points on SI_{-1} imply a one per cent net financial accumulation of liabilities by the domestic private sector.

AN SFB PERSPECTIVE OF INDIA'S POLICY PREDICAMENT

The SFB equation model can provide useful insights into some of India's policy challenges. Let us begin in 2012 when India's current account deficit to GDP was at a high of 4.2 per cent followed by significant windfall that benefited India; the oil price crash since June 2014. With oil imports accounting for more than 30 per cent of India's total imports, India's import bill fell significantly between 2014 and 2016, from $45 billion to just about $25 billion.[11] On the other hand, depressed commodity prices and a slowdown in commodity-exporting countries also dampened India's exports although this decline was by a much smaller percentage. This allowed India's current account deficit to contract significantly from 4.8 per cent of GDP in 2012 to less than 1 per cent by 2016.[12] While exports had not fallen in comparison to imports there was concern that India's exports had not shown robust growth. This concern is apparent when we look at India's share in global exports (as opposed to the dollar value of exports and/or the current account deficit as percentage of GDP), which has remained at just about 1.5 per cent since 2011 while countries like China and Vietnam have managed to increase their share. The main (neoliberal) argument for India's poor export performance has been attributed amongst others to an overvalued exchange rate that keeps FII investment flows stable but at the cost of rendering exports uncompetitive.[13]

Given the level of fiscal deficit[14] we can compute $(S - I)$ using equation (2). Figure 15.4 shows the shifts in India's key macroeconomic variables using the SFB equation. The declining CAD and fiscal deficit was possible if the Indian private sector had significantly ramped up its net financial asset accumulation—a process that seems to be one of deleveraging—that was apparent until 2014. Since 2014 there, however, seems to have been a slowdown in this trend. A further decline in net financial asset accumulation $(S - I)$ will occur given the increase in current account deficit[15] and decrease in fiscal deficit to 3.2 per cent of GDP.

Let us examine the two components of private sector financial balance; investment and saving. The leveraging phase began in India like in other emerging markets around 2004 with significant growth in private sector investment spending. The statistics are alarming; between 2003-4 and 2015, private corporate debt has grown at a CAGR of more than 28 per cent, while public debt grew at just about 11 per cent.[16] India's debt-to-equity ratio at

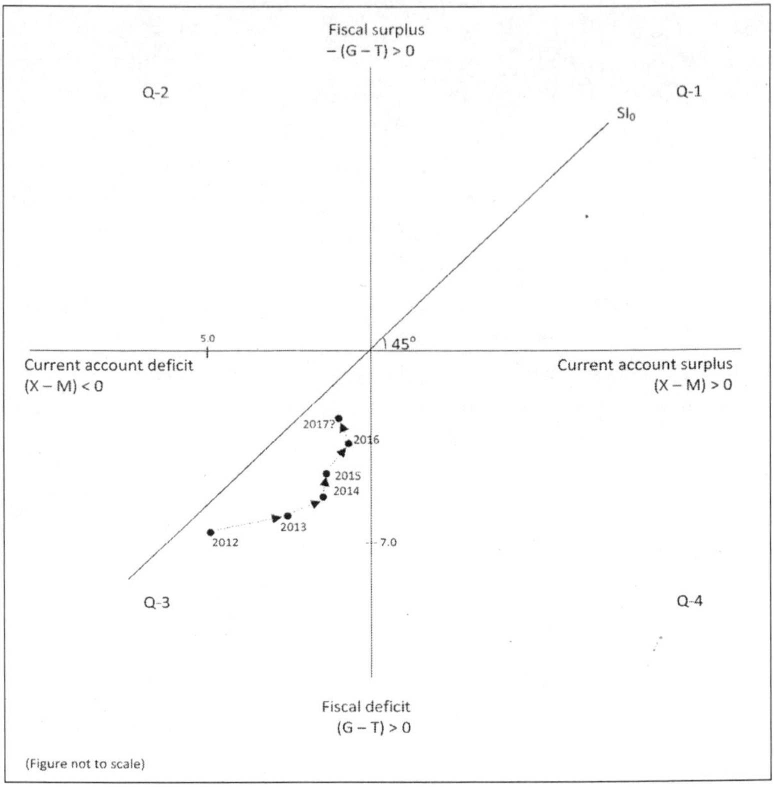

Source: Same as in Table 15.1.

Figure 15.4: Shifts in India's Sectoral Financial Balances, 2012-17

80 stood at the top amongst emerging markets followed by Brazil at about 78.[17] Corporate debt to GDP stood at above 40 per cent for India; although this is relatively less than China's ratio of 120 per cent, it still remains higher than other emerging markets including Brazil, Russia and Mexico.[18]

The trend, however, changed *c.* 2011-12. Investment (gross fixed capital formation) as a percentage of GDP has declined consistently by more than 5 per cent, from 35 per cent in 2011 to about 29 percent in 2015.[19] While this consists of both, private and public sector investment spending there is little doubt that investment spending by India's private corporate sector has slowed down. In a study by the RBI, it was found that: 'In the year 2014-15, altogether 830 companies intended to invest in projects with aggregate cost of Rs. 1,459 billion in comparison with an investment intention of Rs. 2,148 billion by 1,065 companies in 2013-14.'[20]

The study included capital expenditures financed from all sources (except retained profits, FDI and private placements), and therefore signalled a major contraction in investment. In another survey by a leading research firm, it was found that planned capital investments by the private sector had fallen continuously from a high of Rs. 1.4 trillion in 2012 to Rs. 800 billion in 2016.[21] The trend continued with gross fixed capital formation decreasing a further 2 per cent in 2016-17.[22] There are several other indicators which strengthened the claim of a 'crisis' in private sector investment demand; poor credit growth, stagnation in manufacturing and capacity utilization at suboptimal levels as well as an erratic trend in the Index of Industrial Production.

While the slowdown in investment is a cause of concern, the problem is accentuated by the growing non-performing liabilities of borrowers (or growing non-performing assets of lenders). Based on the IMF Stability Report of 2014 there was growing consensus that:

> Asset quality of Indian banks in terms of gross non-performing loans (NPL) is the worst among all Asian economies. Among [14] emerging markets, Poland and Russia rank lower than India. Gross NPLs in India are at 4 per cent. Stressed assets (which include restructured assets) are much higher at close to 10 per cent.[23]

The total non-performing assets of 39 listed banks was estimated to be Rs. 4.38 trillion (US $15 billion) in 2016.[24] Between 2008 and 2014, private sector external debt has increased from about 13 per cent of GDP to 19 per cent.[25] In the period 2005-14, external commercial borrowings (ECB) as a share of external borrowing has increased from 20 per cent to 33 per cent while ECB as a share of long-term debt has increased from 21 per cent to 43 per cent.[26] This is another major source of concern for the private sector. The danger of the rupee depreciating on account of a hike in interest rates by the Fed is a looming possibility with disastrous consequences for the private sector.

Reducing investment spending is only one way of deleveraging, the other being asset sales. At the ground-level, India is also witnessing an unprecedented sale of assets by large corporations:

> In the first decade of the existence of ARCs [Asset Reconstruction Companies], banks sold all of Rs. 87,049 crore of bad loans for Rs. 19,308 crore. But in the two years 2013-14, ARCs have bought bad assets worth Rs. 102,068 crore for Rs. 43,243 crore.[27]

A recent headline sums up the situation: 'Poor show by banks, private investors challenge for economy: Arun Jaitley.'[28]

While the investment crisis is an acknowledged fact, we must also look at the savings component of private sector's net financial asset accumulation. While private corporate sector savings have shown a steady upward trend between 2010 and 2015, household sector savings have declined from about 25 per cent of GDP to about 19.1 per cent of GDP 'resulting from elevated inflation and inflation expectations, and higher gold purchases' (IMF, 2015c: 30). Overall private sector savings increased marginally by about 1.5 per cent of GDP between 2010 and 2015. Putting S and I together, we have from Table 15.1 and Figure 15.4, a clear situation of a steady increase in net financial asset accumulation by the private sector, i.e. $(S - I)$ increasing until 2014. However, there were indications that savings as percentage of GDP began showing a steady downward trend from 2015;[29] the decrease in $(S - I)$ is shown as a leftward shift in the arrow in Figure 15.4. This could have been because the rate of savings fell at a faster rate than the decline in investment. With a declining fiscal deficit and a larger current account deficit, a further squeeze on private sector net financial asset accumulation was expected in 2017.

But is this desired level of net savings? If the private sector's savings desire for financial assets outside the sector increases[30] then it will have to be accommodated with either an increase in net exports and/or a larger government deficit. The current account situation remains volatile; however, as mentioned above based on

*Q*1 data there were indications that this would increase with rising oil prices. In such a situation, if the fiscal deficit does not accommodate the desire for an increase in $(S - I)$, then the only recourse to the private sector would be to increase its propensity to save resulting in a further slowdown in economic growth.

There are two additional insights that need to be highlighted about the fiscal deficit; first, as can be seen earlier, India has always run a budget deficit since Independence. For that matter, almost all sovereign nations of the world run budget deficits and not surpluses. The reason for this should be obvious now. Second, while there may be discussion and debate over fiscal deficit targets like 3.0 or 4.5 per cent, the basic fact is that the fiscal deficit outcome is non-discretionary. Once again we don't require sophisticated macroeconomic models to understand this. Given that tax collections depend on income, as GDP growth rates increase the deficit shrinks, when GDP growth slows down the deficit swells. In any budgetary process what is discretionary are quantum of government expenditures and tax rates while actual tax collections rise and fall with income and output. There may also be a non-discretionary component to expenditure like transfer payments (example, spending on rural employment guarantee scheme) during years of low growth. The prime concern over the fiscal deficit is its impact on inflation. Nonetheless making a non-discretionary outcome the target of macroeconomic policy seems a rather futile exercise.

Moreover, centring the fiscal deficit target in discussions on the budget is of serious concern because it deflects attention away from the key objectives of macroeconomic policy which includes full employment with low and stable inflation, high GDP growth, socio-economic development and the reduction of regional and income disparities. We need to focus on whether or not government expenditures achieve these objectives. Unfortunately, fiscal consolidation has become an end in itself and everyone seems think it is simple common sense. After all isn't the government just like you or me and spending more than it earns cannot be right? It resorts to borrowing, accumulating debt that's going to drive it to bankruptcy someday.

THE INDIAN GOVERNMENT CAN UTILIZE ITS FISCAL SPACE

Such thinking is flawed. India is a sovereign nation, issuing its own fiat currency under a floating exchange rate regime. The government does not face a solvency issue. As a monopoly issuer of currency, the government cannot be likened to a household or a firm. Such definitive numbers are not derived from macroeconomic theory; in fact one wonders where they come from. The government must steer the debate away from arbitrary deficit targets to efforts being made at raising the quality of spending and how governance can alleviate real constraints in the economy.

Over the years, the government appears to have yielded to pressure from international rating agencies to announce a fiscal target of less than 3 per cent. But why is India considering itself to be on par with Greece or Spain and calling for austerity measures? These European nations are not sovereign, economically speaking, because they surrendered their right to issue their own currencies and instead chose to become like a state government, municipal corporation, a firm or household. Their governments were forced to borrow money from markets because the European Central Bank did not support their needs for spending. And even worse, the troika (ECB, EU and IMF) decided that the right way out for Greece, Spain and others was severe austerity measures—cut spending, raise taxes. The first order effect of these measures was obviously a slowdown in growth, which as we have seen, leads to a non-discretionary fiscal outcome—increasing deficits. The response to this was greater austerity that ultimately led to disastrous conditions in many countries of the EU. How can 25 per cent unemployment and 50 per cent unemployment amongst youth ever be considered prudent macroeconomic policy or for that matter, socially just? It's an unequivocal waste of resources—there are able bodied people willing to work but cannot find jobs. There are firms wanting to increase sales but find no buyers for their products. This is a classic instance of market failure on a grand scale.

The Indian government must realize that it has enormous policy space and need not constrain itself for want of revenues. With some dampening of inflationary pressures as well as a receding threat of a current account deficit crisis due to falling international oil prices and high inflows of foreign exchange, the government did have a great opportunity to enhance spending in 2014. At the same time, it is imperative that any increased government expenditure would have had to come with greater attention on governance and raising output and productive capacity of the nation so that the long-term objectives of macroeconomic policy are realized.

The question is why the fiscal deficit target garners so much attention in the media and now even amongst the government itself. It would seem that governments would resist such targets and instead want to increase spending, keeping in mind their own interests. The answer perhaps lies in the hegemonic influence of neoliberal ideology that focuses on private sector led growth as the solution to the problem of growth, employment and poverty. For decades after the Second World War the advanced nations of the world were seen as 'welfare states' that protected and promoted the socio-economic well-being of its citizens through active government interventions in the economy.

Joe Hockey, who went on to become treasurer of Australia under Prime Minister Tony Abbott, remarked that the 'age of entitlement' had come to an end and added that,

> The fiscal impact of popular programmes must be brought to account no matter what the political values of the government are or how popular a spending programme may be.[31]

In the recent past, free market ideals have been propagated worldwide through think tanks like the Cato Institute, the Liberty Institute (now with a chapter in India), the Adam Smith Institute, the Institute of Economic Affairs and the Centre for Policy Studies. The decline of the welfare state and the rise of neoliberalism began in the West in the 1980s—the Reagan-Thatcher era—and have spread across the world. The problem is in fact a larger and a more deep rooted one; capital *vs.* labour. In the West, this trend in rising inequalities of income and wealth is now gaining the attention of several economists including Piketty, Krugman and Stiglitz. In India too, we find a similar situation; the rise in productivity of labour has not been accompanied by a commensurate increase in real wage rates in India (Figure 15.5).

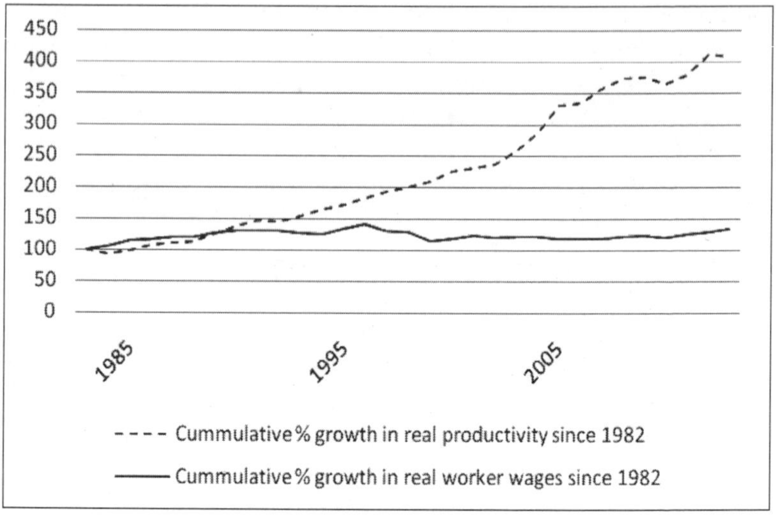

Source: Prabhat Singh, 'Higher Productivity Equals to Higher Wages?: Not for the Indian Industrial Worker', *Livemint*, 22 January 2015, http://www.livemint.com/Opinion/Vxmd5HHO8qeLuqYUiobbpM/Higher-productivity-equals-higher-wages-Not-for-the-Indian.html

Figure 15.5: Divergence in Real Wage and Productivity Growth in India, 1983-2014

Although the government faces increasing pressure on multiple fronts—a slow GDP growth coupled with jobless growth and unemployment, stressed corporate balance sheets and profitability, agrarian distress—it is steadfastly adhering to its fiscal deficit and public debt targets, until now at least. There is still an overwhelming stress in popular macroeconomic discourse on the need for structural/supply-side reforms to bring the private sector out of its present predicament to propel growth. But whether this will provide the necessary impetus to output remains to be seen. Meanwhile, given the signs of deleveraging by the corporate sector, sluggish export growth and stagnant capacity utilization, the dire need for the government to step up spending is palpable. At the same time, the priority accorded to fiscal deficit target numbers is holding back the government from increasing spending. But for how long? Given the present current account deficit, further deleveraging by the domestic private sector warrants fiscal accommodation. If not, the economy will inevitably be drawn into a lower growth trajectory.

While fiscal policy plays an important role, monetary policy in India is also seen as active and significant in managing inflation as well as influencing the real economy. In spite of (repo) rate cuts amounting to 1 per cent since January 2015, the Reserve Bank of India in its bi-monthly review meeting in February 2016 stated that:

> In the first two months of Q3 of 2015-16, industrial activity slowed in relation to the preceding quarter. This mainly reflects weak investment demand with some deceleration of capital goods production. Stalled projects continue to remain high, and there is a decline in new investment intentions, perhaps on the back of low capacity utilisation.[32]

At the same time India constantly faces a threat of food inflation, over the last several years, although it seems to have been tentatively contained at less than 4 per cent. With greater emphasis of the Reserve Bank of India on inflation, rate cuts to boost investment will remain cautious. Moreover, with increasing capital account convertibility of the rupee, the impact of rate cuts on the exchange rate will also be an important factor limiting the Reserve Bank of India.

It is apparent that the primary issue facing India is excessive stress on the primary drivers of growth, in particular exports and private sector investment demand. From leveraging to deleveraging, the cycle is playing out. With limited scope for monetary policy, an accommodative fiscal policy will be the key to ensuring that India does not slip into a 'balance sheet recession'. This runs contrary to recommendations that accord priority to fiscal consolidation and structural reforms.

The SFB analysis clearly delineates the constraints to arbitrary cuts in fiscal deficits without considering the realities of the external sector as well as the leveraging/deleveraging cycle of the domestic private sector.

NOTES

1. The IS-LM model is the mainstay of neo-Keynesianism.
2. Accounting Quest of Steve Keen by JKH, cross posted from Monetary Realism, by Cullen Roche, http://www.pragcap.com/the-accounting-quest-of-steve-keen/
3. R. Wray (2011), 'The Basics of Macro Accounting', *New Economic Perspectives*, http://neweconomicperspectives.org/2011/06/mmp-blog-2-basics-of-macro-accounting.html
4. Recall that the NCM model assumed that the private sector spends all that it earns.
5. $(X-M) > 0$ implies capital outflows from the domestic to foreign economics.
6. If $(X-M)$ is negative to begin with, higher $(X-M)$ could also mean lower $(M-X)$.
7. To reiterate, I falls exogenously while S falls endogenously when Y falls.
8. The increment in savings of households that takes place from an increment in income.
9. Some countries like Norway are able to meet equation (7) with large trade surpluses so that they run budget surpluses along with positive net domestic private sector savings.
10. Richard C. Koo (2015), *The Escape from Balance Sheet Recession and the QE Trap*, Singapore: Wiley, p. 147.
11. https://tradingeconomics.com/india/imports
12. https://tradingeconomics.com/india/current-account-to-gdp
13. Deepak Nayyar, 'Great Fall of India's Exports', *Livemint*, 22 January 2016, http://www.livemint.com/Opinion/RAIxZQM6kafh6a5Hp41wgL/Great-fall-of-Indias-exports.html
14. https://tradingeconomics.com/india/government-budget
15. India's current account deficit increases sharply to 2.4 per cent of GDP in Q1, *Financial Express*, 15 September 2017, http://www.financialexpress.com/economy/indias-current-account-deficit-increases-sharply-to-2-4-of-gdp-in-q1-10-points/856776/
16. V. Anantha Nageswaran, 'An Over-leveraged Sector', *Livemint*, 30 March 2015, http://www.livemint.com/Opinion/3Mps70418gz HeKGJi JUSbM/An-overleveraged-sector.html
17. OECD Economic Surveys Brazil, November 2015, https://www.oecd.org/eco/surveys/Brazil-2015-overview.pdf (p. 23).
18. Sean Brodrick, 'China's Debt Mess . . . Worse than Greece's?', Investment U, 12 August 2015, http://www.investmentu.com/article/detail/47056/china-debt-mess-worse-than-greece#.Vv4hG_l96M8

19. https://tradingeconomics.com/india/gross-fixed-capital-formation-percent-of-gdp-wb-data.html
20. Reserve Bank of India, 2015. 'Private Corporate Investment: Growth in 2014-15 and Prospects for 2015-16', *Monthly Bulletin*, September, p. 61, https://rbidocs.rbi.org.in/rdocs/Bulletin/PDFs/03BB4F1750CFF084696922BE468D0BA81FA.PDF
21. Madhura Karnik, 'Narendra Modi Needs to See These Three Charts—and Turn the Charm on India Inc.', *Quartz India*, 25 February 2015, http://qz.com/349997/narendra-modi-needs-to-see-these-three-charts-and-turn-the-charm-on-india-inc/
22. Mahesh Vyas, 'Economic Outlook', *CMIE*, 12 January 2016, https://www.cmie.com/kommon/bin/sr.php?kall=warticle&dt=2017-01-12%2018:43:14&msec=056
23. Ira Dugal, 'India Inc.'s Credit Quality Woes', *Livemint*, 30 October 2014, http://www.livemint.com/Money/1RKFePHwJ1I5oXKSotkMvK/India-Incs-credit-quality-woes.html
24. Vishwanath Nair and Aparna Iyer, 'Listed Banks' NPAs Surge by Rs. 1 Trillion in December Quarter', *Livemint*, 15 February 2016, http://www.livemint.com/Industry/ZQhav7x8FESxfLT1tHp0aO/Listed-banks-NPAs-surge-by-Rs1-trillion-in-December-quarter.html
25. Ravi Krishnan, 'The Danger in External Debt', *Livemint*, 2 April 2015. http://www.livemint.com/Money/x5lgmLKuf1YYNrovkfURLM/The-danger-in-external-debt.html
26. 'India's Growing Corporate External Borrowing', *Urbanomics*, 11 October 2014, http://gulzar05.blogspot.in/2014_10_01_archive.html
27. Anand Adhikari and Mahesh Nayak, 'Money from Junk', *Business Today*, 2 August 2015, 22 January 2016, http://www.businesstoday.in/magazine/cover-story/distressed-assets-market-in-india-witnessing-unprecedented-boom/story/221604.html
28. *Financial Express*, 27 May 2017, http://www.financialexpress.com/industry/poor-show-by-banks-private-investors-challenge-challenge-for-economy-arun-jaitley/688997/
29. 'India's Savings Rate in Need of a Boost: DBS', *Economic Times*, 2 September 2016, http://economictimes.indiatimes.com/news/economy/finance/indias-savings-rate-in-need-of-a-boost-dbs/articleshow/53978512.cms
30. This could happen in many ways; an increase in *S* and a fall in *I* or even a fall in both but *I* falling more than *S* and so on.
31. Dominic Kelly, 'Free-market Think-tanks Waged War on Entitlement, Conscripted an Australian Joe', *The Conversation*, 30 May 2014, http://theconversation.com/free-market-think-tanks-waged-war- on-entitlement-conscripted-an-australian-joe-27170

32. S.V. Krishnamachari, 'Indian Economy "Lost Momentum" in Third Quarter', says Reserve Bank of India, *International Business Times*, 2 February 2016, http://www.ibtimes.co.in/indian-economy-lost-momentum-third-quarter-says-reserve-bank-india-665375

CHAPTER 16

A Summary of Insights from MMT

In the preceding chapters we have discussed some of the basic tenets of MMT. I will present these as an overview for the reader.

1. Most major economies of the world today are economically sovereign; they issue their own fiat currencies and adhere to a floating exchange rate regime. The European Union is the major exception to this rule.
2. MMT is based on an accurate description of how the modern monetary system works—its institutions and their mandates; it is not a 'theory' based on conjections, postulates or axioms.
3. All money arises from debt, someone's liability.
4. Anybody can create money things, the problem, however, is to get it accepted.
5. Money is everywhere and always hierarchical.
6. The state—the central bank as the mandated institution—is a monopoly issuer of currency.
7. The state uses money to move resources from the private sector to the public sector.
8. Taxes drive money; the state accepts its own liability in settlement of obligations owed to it.
9. In a modern money economy, the state creates money through keystrokes when it spends.
10. The central bank acts as a scorekeeper of debits and credits of the government, the private sector as well as the foreign sector.
11. Spending are credits into the account of the private sector.
12. Taxes are debits from the accounts of the private sector.
13. Fiscal deficits are net credits into the accounts of the private sector.

14. In addition to driving state money, taxes also drain excess credits in the accounts of the private sector, which may lead to increased demand for goods and services and consequently inflation.
15. One reason the government issues bonds to the private sector is to drain excess reserves injected into the system when it spends.
16. The issue of bonds in not a fiscal policy operation to raise funds for government spending; instead, it must follow spending because the government will (like taxes) only accept its own tokens in exchange for bonds.
17. When the government issues bonds, it is a liability of the government but the private sector gets an income-yielding, risk-free financial asset.
18. Fiscal deficits create net financial assets for the private sector.
19. Public or national debt is the liability of the government but assets of the private sector.
20. MMT views the issue of government bonds as a monetary policy operation. When the government spends, reserves are injected into the banking system and the overnight interest rates for reserves in money markets will tend to fall towards zero. To prevent this, the government/central bank sells bonds and maintains its interest rate target (and its inflation target as well).
21. The central bank can set any interest rate it wants to. It does not depend on fiscal deficits or surpluses. For instance, Japan has large fiscal deficits with interest rates close to zero.
22. The crowding out theory is myth.
23. Governments are not financially constrained. All caps on spending are self-imposed; for example FRBM in India.
24. The rule that the government cannot sell bonds directly to the central bank in exchange for currency or reserves to spend is easily circumvented with the system of primary dealers that has been put in place.
25. The size of the fiscal deficit is a political question; how large a public sector does the government desire – how many public schools, how many courts, how many hospitals, how large a

defense force, etc. In other words, the state decides how much resources it wants moved from the private to the public sector.

26. Although there are no financial constraints on the government to spend in its own currency, there can be repercussions on inflation and foreign exchange rates.
27. MMT also accepts endogenous money theory (EMT). Banks create money ex nihilo.
28. Interbank transactions can be settled only with reserve (state) money.
29. Central banks are obliged to provide reserve money against collateral (usually government securities).
30. Central banks do not 'lend' reserves—reserves are not an asset of the central bank.
31. Reserve money is the central bank's IOU and therefore a liability of the central bank.
32. Central banks can, however, set the rate at which they swap reserves against securities; the repo rate. This can thereby influence the demand for credit and expansion of the private sector.
33. The demand for quality credit limits the expansion of commercial bank credit to the private sector.
34. Credit is demand-constrained not supply constrained.
35. Credit is not constrained by savings deposited into the banks as propounded by the loanable funds model.
36. Investment drives income and savings. Savings do not drive investment.
37. Macroeconomic theory must be consistent with double entry book keeping. MMT emphasizes the need for stock-flow consistency.
38. Stock-flow consistency requires the satisfaction of the sectoral financial balances equation;
    $(S - I) = (G - T) + (X - M)$
39. The SFB equation is derived from double entry book keeping and is not based on assumptions.
40. MMT calls for the (re)centering of full employment as the single-most important objective of macroeconomics.

These insights of MMT literally turn mainstream macroeconomics on its head. And all this is derived from a careful examination of actual monetary institutions that exist in a modern money economy. In spite of its relevance, MMT remains unacceptable to the (dubious) mainstream, which continues to wield its twisted grip over macroeconomics and even popular macroeconomic discourse.

PART IV

REFRAMING INDIA'S MACROECONOMIC DISCOURSE

CHAPTER 17

Maximum Government, Maximum Governance

For Keynes unemployment could never be a 'natural' disaster, like an earthquake or a flood. He knew that it is a failure of social and economic organization, a failure by society and social institutions to achieve a desirable goal. Quite simply, when millions of people are out of work, we have failed to organize our society so that full employment is secured. And being a problem of social organization, there must be a solution if only society is willing to take the steps necessary. This doesn't mean that either finding or implementing a solution will be easy. Our society and our economy are complicated institutions, linking a multitude of firms and people at home and abroad, each with their own goals and their ways of doing things. Moreover, achieving full employment may clash with other goals we consider to be important. But it is irrational simply to accept unemployment, as if it were a fact of nature. Unemployment is our failure. At the very least, we must spell out clearly the choices that must be made if we are to attain full employment.

JOHN EATWELL
'Citizen Keynes', *The American Prospect* (1994)

THE CURSE OF UNEMPLOYMENT

I actually found the title of a book co-edited by the founder of neoliberal macroeconomics, Thomas Sargent on the purpose of macroeconomics to be rather fitting; *Macroeconomics at the Service of Public Policy*. The book supposedly 'answers key questions about how the economy functions and how policy should be conducted'.[1] The issue, however, is whether mainstream thinking on these aspects is a true depiction of the institutional reality of a modern money economy. MMTers argue that it is incorrect and there is a need to examine its overriding objective of price stability and repeatedly pointing out that without financial constraints inflicted by mainstream economists, the state could strive to achieve full-employment.

Full employment as the primary objective of macroeconomic policy is justifiable on many counts. First, it enhances productivity; a safety net will mean that people would 'risk' moving from lower to higher productivity jobs. Second, the explicit objective of full employment stabilizes aggregate demand and thereby business confidence—firms can be more confident that sales will not slump on account of people losing jobs. Third, full employment also alleviates, to an extent at least, some of today's most worrying concerns; inequalities and discrimination. This in turn also addresses a key target of macroeconomic policy that is often missed in public debates; social stability. Fourth, when we look at the alternative to full employment—unemployment—there are even stronger reasons for making it the overriding objective of economic policy. The economic cost of unemployment is straightforward—a waste of resources that if employed would not only benefit workers but also businesses to sell more and increase profits. But apart from the economic cost, there are social and moral costs; crime, degrading of the human spirit, dysfunctional families, alcoholism and substance abuse, and so on. In spite of the benefits of full-employment being many and unequivocal, the mainstream macro-economics argument that legitimized unemployment as a buffer stock that ensured price stability has become *commonsensical* in macroeconomics discourse.

From a short-run stabilization point-of-view the MMT argument for full employment rests on solid ground. But this is not a new proposition; it draws heavily upon the lessons of *functional finance* as propounded more than 60 years ago by the Keynesian economist, Abba P. Lerner. When an economy faces unemployment the government must increase its spending to reach full employment. In a modern money economy, there is no financial constraint on the government to spend more; it merely credits its tokens into the system. There is absolutely no sense in trying to achieve a particular fiscal deficit target or even worse, a balanced budget rather than targeting full employment.

Moreover, in an economy which has slipped into recession, the existence of surplus capacity across industries will ensure that government spending and increased aggregate demand does not put pressure on the general price level to rise. Inflation will, therefore, not be a major concern in such situations. This has been exemplified in the aftermath of the 2008 GFC—in spite of large fiscal deficits, Japan, UK and the US struggled to achieve a + 2 per cent inflation target. The question then is why governments in these countries did not undertake more direct measures to employ people and instead chose to spend large sums of money in rescuing banks and financial institutions.

MMT economists have being advocating for the government to institute a job guarantee (JG) programme to create a buffer stock of employed people, rather than a buffer stock of unemployed. Under a JG programme, the government guarantees to employ people gainfully at all times, at a specified wage rate. During a slowdown, as workers are laid-off by the private sector, the JG programme absorbs them and keeps them working in productive jobs at the specified wage. As the slowdown eases and the private sector begins hiring people, the workers would transit back to the private sector. In normal times, the JG programme wage would act as a minimum wage as the private sector would have to offer more than this wage in order to recruit people. Moreover, the JG programme, by keeping people working in jobs, would ensure that they remain employable when a recovery is underway. One of the key issues facing unemployed people in many advanced countries of the world is that the private sector is often not willing to employ people currently 'unemployed' as they lose touch with job discipline and application of skills. MMT argues that the JG programme is a counter-cyclical automatic stabilizer[2] that could replace many other programmes and remains active at all times. In fact, its existence will raise business confidence and perhaps even prevent to some extent, a possible crisis.

India's Mahatma Gandhi National Rural Employment Guarantee Scheme (MGNREGS) has often been considered by MMTers to be public policy action in the right direction. However, as Bill Mitchell points out it is at best a partial JG programme;[3] a fully operational JG would have no conditions attached as in

MGNREGS like the number of days of work (more than 100 days) and/or limitations on the kind of work (unskilled manual labour) or sectoral applicability (agriculture, industry or services). Nonetheless, MMTers have often argued that advanced countries like the US and Australia need to emulate such a scheme or an even broader scale.

An important debate is, however, emerging in the West over the introduction and advantages of Universal Basic Income (UBI)[4] and/or JG programmes. Economies across the world are facing a chronic industrial unemployment problem, especially with an automation revolution underway. Even as productive capacity is expanding exponentially, the prospect of jobless growth and widening inequalities in incomes implies a lack in aggregate demand. Who is going to buy what industries can potentially produce? With this trend manifesting itself at an alarming rate, economists and policy makers are contemplating a UBI programme that will provide individuals some purchasing power to consume what's being produced to prevent recessions. But can a subsidy or distribution of cash be a substitute for a work?

While UBI guarantees every citizen a basic monthly income, a JG programme, as stated above, guarantees every citizen a job at a stipulated wage. It is true that in both cases the person is assured of a basic living standard; however, a job provides many psychological benefits including a sense of personal self-esteem, having purpose in life by contributing to the community and society. A well-run JG programme could engage people in meaningful work that is in many communities underprovided—geriatric care, environment protection, child care, teacher training and small businesses. On the other hand, there are those who are in favour of UBI simply because in reality government job programs become meaningless—like digging holes and filling them. A UBI could instead motivate people to do things they really want to without having to worry about their survival. As one commentator put it; '[A JG program] runs the risk of pushing people into that soul destroying existence that a UBI seeks to liberate us from.'[5]

MMTers, however, argue that in pure economic terms, UBI is not sustainable because if people do not engage themselves in 'productive' activities and raising the potential of an economy, rising inflation rate will be inevitable. In fact, the UBI could actually shrink the active labour force and definitively reduce the potential output of an economy. Over time, more and more people will be claiming larger and larger sums as UBI just to beat inflation and maintain a (basic) standard of living. Without gainful employment, the labour force could lose touch with the culture of 'work' and atrophy into 'useless' citizens.

While the debate is an important one,[6] our purpose here is not to argue on the pros and cons of JG and UBI; instead, what we emphasize here is the *financing* of such programmes. It is important not to fall into the trap that even supporters of such programmes often fall into: 'Australian taxpayers have had to take on a greater burden of debt to support themselves.'[7]

The logic for the introduction of a JG programme or UBI must draw upon MMT's fundamental tenet that a government in a modern money economy faces no financial constraint; there is no 'ideal' target for the fiscal deficit and no burden on taxpayers. This is the essence of MMT and one that any true MMTer must abide, however, extreme is seems at times.

A JG or even an UBI programme when an economy is in recession is difficult to argue against, especially with the existence of excess capacity. In such a situation increases in aggregate demand will not be problematic in terms of inflation until we approach full employment. MMT also effectively dispels mainstream arguments against government intervention including the crowding out effect and concerns over growing fiscal deficits and rising public debt.

But an equally important, if not more important question is what happens as the economy approaches full employment levels? What are the policy implications to be drawn from MMT in such a situation in which governments, especially in developing economies, still need to play a key role in shifting an economy to a higher growth trajectory? Or provide jobs to millions of unemployed and underemployed people (typically in the agricultural sector) even though there are limitations on the availability of productive capacity in various sectors of the economy (typically agriculture and manufacturing sectors). While a JG programme will create demand for goods and services, even MMTers concede that the threat of inflation and depreciating exchange rates do pose a serious challenge. In the case of India, for instance, while full employment is an issue of grave concern, issues like food inflation and fuel prices can be equally destabilizing given their adverse impact on the lives of millions of poor. Politicians too dread inflation; after all 'the Indian political class understands well that nothing is a bigger vote-killer than inflation'.[8]

FRAMING THE MMT NARRATIVE

In many discussions over MMT, people resist the idea that at the macro level, there are no financial constraints for an economically sovereign country—the government can create as much money as it desires and as EMT-MMT establishes, commercial banks too can. In the latter case, aggregate savings do not constrain investment spending; it is the demand for quality loans that constrains bank lending. The reaction to this fundamental idea is always; 'perhaps true, but what about inflation and exchange rates?' As mentioned above, MMTers cannot but help in agreeing to the fact that inflation and exchange rate depreciation are indeed limitations to large fiscal deficits. MMTers are forced into a defensive position even as they may provide a rational explanation of why inflation occurs or why it may not be a threat. The main contention then of skeptics is that while government spending constraints may not exist—technically speaking—the likelihood of inflation and exchange rate instability makes it safer to impose a blanket cap on spending rather than explain to politicians the economic nuances of MMT that could lead to unwanted outcomes. It is safer and less complicated to rely on rules rather than discretion (especially of politicians). The political class may favour this narrative too; they have a widely accepted excuse that their hands are tied by financial constraints— just like a household or a firm—and therefore must not be expected to achieve a target like full employment.

We need to change this narrative. But how? MMTers now acknowledge that this change is the biggest challenge they face today, more than 'proving' or extending modern money theory. In the recent past, there has been a strong emphasis by MMTers on framing and marketing of their ideas. MMT must begin in agreement with the notion that constraints to full employment and high growth do exist. To say that there are no constraints makes it rather unrealistic and puts people off in the first instance itself. It is therefore my contention that MMT must reframe its punch line by pointing out the actual constraints—real resource and governance constrains—in achieving the goals of full employment and high growth while repudiating the financial budget constraint. In other words, if we were to rewrite the macroeconomic problem of the state, it would read as follows: Maximize employment and growth, subject to real resource + governance constraints.

MMT argues for the deletion of the intertemporal budget constraint from the constrained macroeconomic optimization problem. Instead the constraints are—real resources and governance—and without overcoming these, pursuit of macroeconomic objectives would indeed have adverse effects.

With real resource and governance constraints, what results from government spending is therefore greater amount of money in circulation with a corresponding increase in aggregate demand (AD) but inadequate increase in productivity capacity of the economy, resulting in inflation and falling exchange rates. Here then is the problem—and it's not finance—it's the availability of water in dams and canals, soil condition, food grain, technology, pilots, doctors, teachers, and energy. The list of real resource constraints is endless in any economy. It is imperative that the government first assess the economic constraints a country faces with the help of economists, whose role must be redefined to evaluating real or economic constraints faced by the economy, produce a menu of choices in real terms, suggest ways to mitigate resource constraints and communicate these to elected representatives. Economists must not harp on financial constraints. And politicians need to perform in terms of governance to maximize employment in the wake of real resource constraints.

But let us also be clear on the conclusions that we need to draw from MMT; if the government wishes it can literally finance any number of projects in a country—dams, highways, airports, irrigation canals, roads, schools, hospitals—and it can do even more—it can waive all loans be it personal, agricultural or industrial, it can recapitalize the banks, write off the loans of state governments and municipalities, even build any number of statues, it can do whatever it wants in terms of rupees. All this would just put more rupees (either currency and or reserves with banks) in circulation, which are liabilities of the government (the central bank), which may even distort incentives and lead to chaos. But it does not change the fact that the government *can spend* according to its choosing—as it would do in case of war. But obviously the government *must not spend* according to its choosing but on the basis of the constraints it faces; namely real resource and governance constraints, and directed at loosening the real constraints on production and output.

Governance is the most complex but also the most crucial aspect in a country realizing its economic goals. A workable definition of economic governance is provided by the EU Parliament:

> Economic governance refers to the system of institutions and procedures established to achieve Union objectives in the economic field, namely the coordination of economic policies to promote economic and social progress for the EU and its citizens.[9]

Although pertaining to corporate governance, the following definition could also be useful in articulating the importance of economic governance in our context:

> Establishment of policies, and continuous monitoring of their proper implementation, by the members of the governing body of an organization [economy]. It includes the mechanisms required to balance the powers of the members (with the associated accountability), and their primary duty of enhancing the prosperity and viability of the organization [economy].[10]

Politics is the art of governance, running the government, management of the economy at the highest level, balancing interests and ultimately getting things done. Limiting ourselves to the macroeconomics goals of full employment and high growth, politicians must govern effectively and efficiently in managing the use of limited resources.

To illustrate our argument more vividly, I use the aggregate demand-aggregate supply (*AS-AD*) model. The aggregate demand as illustrated in Figure 17.1 is nothing but the aggregate expenditure (the sum of private sector consumption and investment spending, government expenditure as well as net exports) at any given price level.[11] A decrease in the price level all else constant will mean a movement down the *AD* curve so that output increases. Why does this happen? Economists give several reasons; let me elaborate one here. When the domestic price level falls, given exchange rates, domestic exports become more competitive in international markets so that net exports and aggregate expenditure may increase. When, at any given price level, we have an increase in government expenditure (expansionary fiscal policy) or private sector investment spending (say, due to cut in interest rates or monetary policy), the *AD* curve will shift outwards or rightwards.

The aggregate supply curve is shown in Figure 17.2; it is flat for output levels way below full employment but gradually begins to

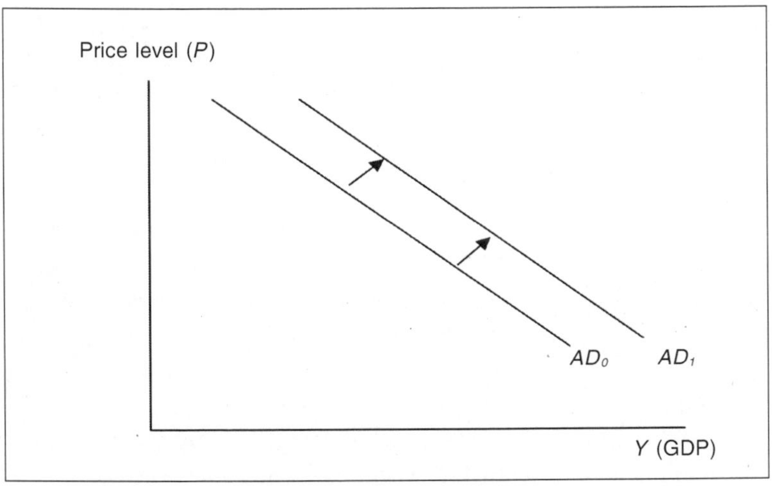

Figure 17.1: The Aggregate Demand Curve (AD) and Shifts in the *AD* Curve

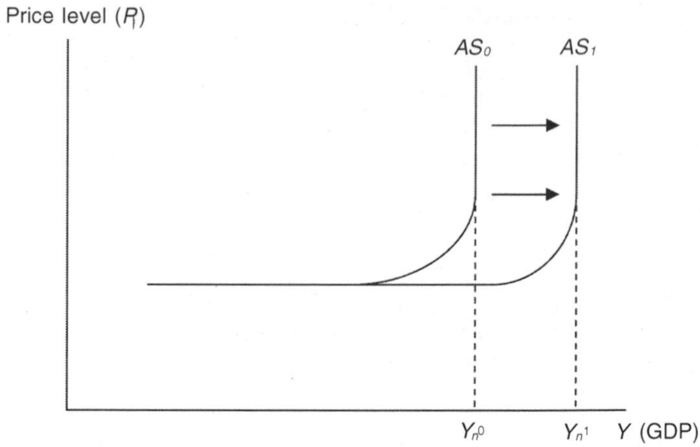

Figure 17.2: The Aggregate Supply (AS) Curve and Shifts in the *AS* Curve

slope upward as the economy approaches full employment. When it reaches full-employment, even with higher price levels, no output will be forthcoming from firms. In other words, beyond the output level Y_n[12] no increase in output is possible; a country has reached its full potential.[13] When a country is, however, operating way below its potential (during a depression) it may be possible to raise output without an increase in price even as *AD* increases. An outward shift in the *AS* curve could be used to represent growth or raising the potential output of a country over time.

From a pure Keynesian perspective, expansionary fiscal and monetary (if the economy is not in the liquidity trap) through shifts in *AD* alone will be sufficient to create jobs without inflation. When the capacity utilization rate (CUR) say below Y_n^0, neoliberal policies through shifts in *AS*, may not be successful in bringing the economy out of recession. This is illustrated in Figure 17.3. However, as the economy approaches full employment output, inflation is inevitable with increases in *AD* unless the *AS* curve shifts outwards too.

It is useful to differentiate the pure Keynesian perspective from the free market neoliberal policy stance; in the latter case, the gov-

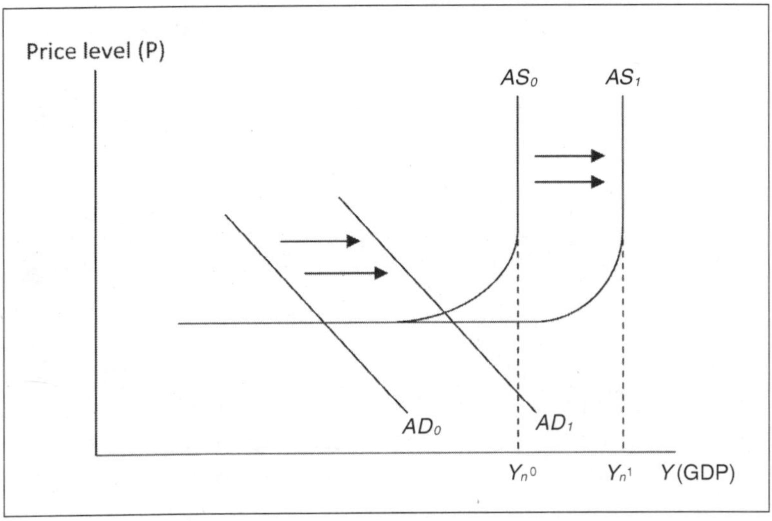

Figure 17.3: The Pure Keynesian Situation

ernment is supposed to play a minimal role in the economic affairs of the country by leaving business to the private sector. Market forces will not only automatically take the economy towards Y_n but also raise the country's potential over time. This is possible with alleviating supply side constraints alone, without the necessity of increased government expenditure. With supply increasing, according to Say's law, so will demand, automatically, since supply creates its own demand. There is healthy growth in the economy with price stability. In other words, to achieve longer-term growth, neoliberal policies call for free market supply-side measures—they focus primarily on changes in legislation that shift the *AS* curve outwards. In terms of Figure 17.5 shifts in *AS* lead to automatic shifts in *AD*, resulting in sustainable growth with low and stable inflation.

Supply side measures in the neoliberal discourse encompasses four main elements: encouragement of savings (the supply of loanable funds) to bring down interest rates, reducing the costs of doing business or raising the ease of doing business (lower costs shift the supply curve outwards as firms are willing to supply the same quantity at a lower price), inducing greater labour market flexibility (to hire and fire) and removing minimum wage legislation or weakening trade unions and finally, shifting the supply curve of labour outwards by lowering the marginal tax rate. An additional word on the last point; as each one of us understands, the marginal tax rate increases with higher incomes or profits, which may impose a penalty or a disincentive to strive for greater surpluses. Lowering marginal tax rates could correct this distortion, raise aggregate supply of labour and induce higher levels of output and employment, while at the same time lower inflation rates. Supply-side measures are a natural policy extension of laissez-faire or 'minimum government'.

The big question, however, is whether free-market supply-side measures would automatically lead to an adequate increase in aggregate demand that can take the economy to full-employment (or at least higher levels of growth). The government's supply-side measures may shift the *AS* from AS_0 to AS_1; however, without adequate shifts in *AD* there will be only small increases in output and income. This is what happens with the failure of Say's Law—when supply does not create its own demand for the reasons Keynes argued. Figure 17.4 illustrates this possible scenario.

One kind of Keynesian policy which seems to satisfy many

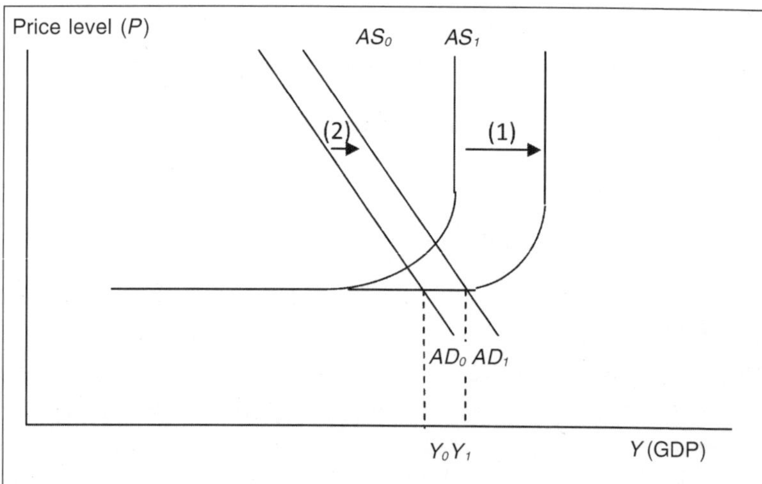

Figure 17.4: Shifts in *AS* without Shift in AD—Inadequacy of Pure Supply-side Measures

neoliberals, especially in countries like India where some state intervention during slowdowns become exigent, is government spending on infrastructure (roads, railways, sea and air ports, dams, etc.). However, such spending comes with a warning; the state has limited financial resources so that any increase in infrastructure spending must be accompanied by revenue expenditure cuts and moreover, if the government were to borrow money in the loanable funds market, it would crowd out private sector investment demand. In a recent article, former Deputy Chairman of India's Planning Commission echoes this view:

> There is talk of expanding public investment to make up the slack. We could certainly do with more public investment in infrastructure, but this will run into fiscal deficit constraints. . . .[14]

This brings us to MMT perspective, which argues that there are no financial limitations on the government to increase *AD* – it can be shifted outwards to whatever extent desired. The problem is with shifting aggregate supply curve, *AS*. Here it is not financial constraints that limit the shift in the *AS* curve but real resource and governance constraints that do so. Shifting the *AS* curve does not imply just building[15] infrastructure, educational institutions, hospitals or whatever but how successfully and how soon these projects actually raise productivity or the country's potential to produce a greater quantum of goods and services across sectors. Shifts in *AD* that bring about adequate shifts in *AS* can deliver growth with price stability as illustrated in Figure 17.5. When governance does not lead to adequate shifts in the *AS* curve, government spending shifts the *AD* without shifts in *AS*, leading to inflation (and a depreciating exchange rate). This is illustrated in Figure 17.6.

The realm of macroeconomic policy therefore lies in effectively shifting the *AS* curve. And most importantly, the state can play an active role in realizing this through spending, which, at the same time, shifts both *AD* and *AS*. It also moves the centre of action to the political arena rather than being with economists who take on the role of raising the alarm bell on fiscal deficits. At the same time, a government's performance must not be judged in terms of

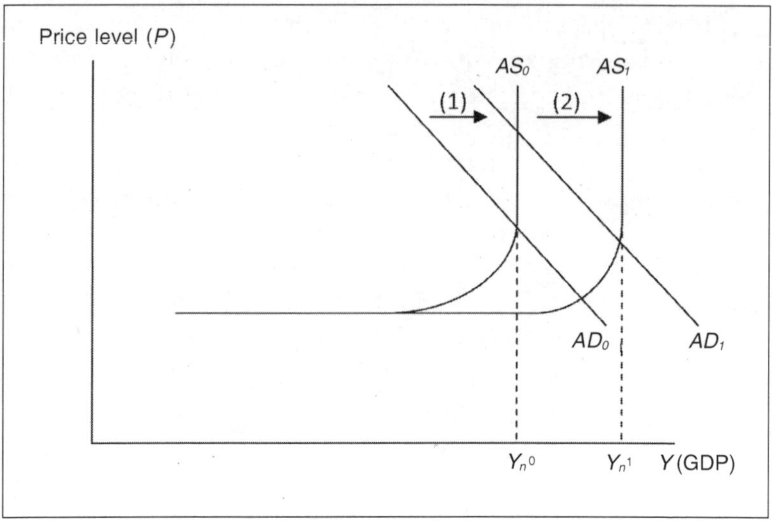

Figure 17.5: The MMT Argument

adherence to fiscal deficit targets but instead by its ability to maximize employment and growth—or shifting the *AS* curve. It is moreover important that governments do not succumb to the threats of rating agencies that pressurize adoption of policies that minimizes government spending. In other words, a government's ability to choose and implement projects that deal with the real resource constraints most effectively—such capacity to deal with real resource constraints could in fact be defined as 'governance'—is what could lead or retard a nation's economic progress.

Poor governance which, for instance, manifests itself in widespread corruption or ineffective and inefficient policies, would mean that an economy is unable to alleviate the resource constraints it faces. As illustrated in Figure 17.6, large shifts in *AD* when not accompanied by sufficient shifts in the *AS*, results in high inflation, low growth and poor employment generation.

It is inevitable that the pursuit of maximizing employment even with effective governance will inevitably lead to some increases in the rate of inflation. This leads us to the obvious question; what is an 'acceptable' rate of inflation? Neoliberalism has always built its edifice of macroeconomic policy on the need for *low and stable*

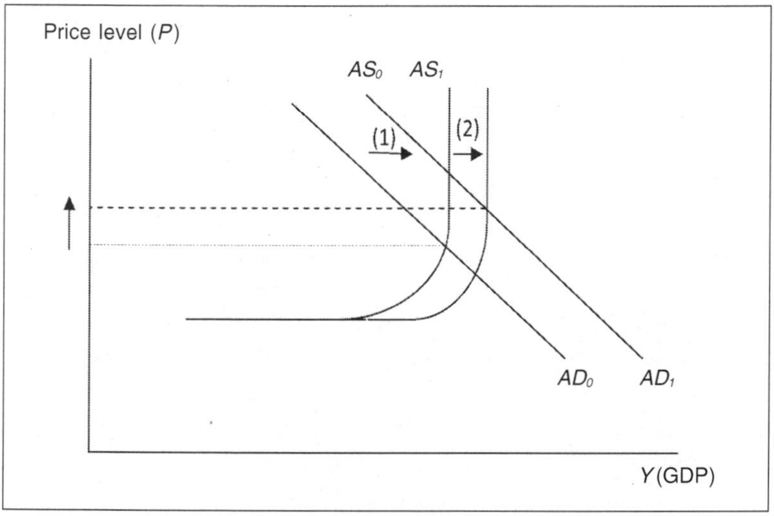

Figure 17.6: Increased Expenditure without Adequate Increases in AS

inflation to ensure 'full employment' and maximum growth through the expansion of the private sector. But is there scope for a more accommodative inflation target; first, with regards to growth and second, on who decides the acceptable inflation target. On the relationship between growth and inflation, the empirical evidence remains tentative. While several studies have shown that inflation targeting does enhance growth, there are others which claim that no such generalized conclusion can be drawn, especially for developing countries. It also wouldn't be out of place to mention, though not as proof, that a study done by the IMF in 2010 found that inflation up to a threshold of 10 per cent brought positive increases in real GDP, although this threshold may be even higher for emerging markets.[16] Another paper published by the International Labor Organisation in 2011 computed that the threshold limit of inflation for positive or zero increments in real GDP growth in developing countries could be as high as 17 per cent.[17]

On the second question—are people willing to settle for higher growth of output and employment opportunities with more flexibility on inflation—it is legitimate to argue that the growth-inflation trade-off is ultimately a challenge that must be confronted by political parties and not 'unaccountable technocrats' (central bankers as referred to by *The Economist*[18]). Moody's Analytics commented on the revised India Finance Code that 'politics would drive decisions',[19] but is this necessarily wrong? The standard argument in favour of central bank autonomy is that governments will be irresponsible in containing expenditure. Once again, is this insinuation always valid, say for instance, in the Indian context? Corruption and inflation are after all two issues which can bring down governments. Political parties may therefore be extremely cautious in taking chances with just a higher inflation rate, let alone an accelerating one. The government is also in a better position than a professional economist to judge the aspirations and perhaps desperation of people at the grassroots for jobs and economic opportunities. Of course, there is a concern that elected representatives may act irresponsibly, taking the country into a scenario of spiraling inflation and instability, is a serious one and cannot be dismissed lightly. But cannot central bankers and mainstream economists in general cause damage too by prodominantly focusing on inflation while taking a rather nonchalant stance on job creation?

If governance is effective, then with relatively positive increases in incomes and safety nets for the poorest of the poor, the population at large may tolerate higher price levels too. This is evident when we take a longer term view; inflation does not really hurt so much because real incomes have grown and standards of living have by-and-large improved. Take, for instance, the headlines: 'What cost Rs 100 in 1947 would cost Rs 5,920.91 now!'[20]

Most people would be oblivious to such a comparison simply because it dosn't matter when people have experienced a higher standard of living. Similarly, inflation may also be bearable even in the shorter-run if people feel a perceptible improvement in opportunities and living standards.

Ultimately the decision on an acceptable inflation target is also an issue of governance; the government will have to convince people that a trade off exists and some hardship may be necessary in the short-run. An important component of governance is exhortation or what Glazer and Rothenberg term as 'persuasion and the art of equilibrium selection'.

> Exhortation makes policies more effective than the policy's mere content may lead one to expect . . . it touches on the vicissitudes of politics rather than on the sterile world of the policy expert. Yet exhortation may affect what the government can accomplish . . . it can improve the inflation/unemployment trade off. . .[21]

A stark example of the power of exhortation was the demonetization decision made by Indian prime minister, Narendra Modi. Although most economists and other experts unilaterally predicted the massive disruption it would cause in the economy[22] (and which it indeed caused), there was widespread support for the move, especially from the very people who had to endure greatest hardship. If the prime minister could have exhorted the masses to accept lower growth (with lesser corruption and black money) post-demonetization, couldn't the political leadership convince people of a high growth-high employment trajectory, perhaps with a dose of higher inflation but with adequate safety nets, especially for the poorest of the poor? However exhortation cannot be an end in itself; ultimately, people must experience that the government is delivering in terms of better job opportunities and higher *real* incomes within a reasonable period of time.

Finally, no developing country can afford to overlook the effects of growth on the external sector; after all MMT only argues that an economically sovereign country does not face a financial constraint in its *own* currency but will in all probability face one in US dollars or other major foreign currencies. Therefore, even policies that succeed in raising real GDP growth along with an acceptable rate of inflation may still lead to a situation of increasing imports, all else constant. This per se may be not be considered a matter of serious concern in a floating exchange rate regime as it would restore a balance in BoP as a depreciating currency would make exports more competitive and dampen imports. However, as the Marshall-Lerner condition reveals, relative inelasticity in the demand for imports and exports could mean a free fall in the price of the domestic currency vis-à-vis foreign currencies.

In such situations, governance once again plays a key role. The neoliberal policies of export led growth and attracting FDI to tackle external deficits through continuous devaluation of domestic currency has only thrown developing countries into a vicious circle of higher import costs, increases in domestic inflation rates and the consequent need for further depreciation of domestic currency. Many developing countries in fact face structural issues that increase their dependence on the external sector; their dependence on oil, food grains and other agricultural products, high value-added manufactured goods and technology. In the case of India, energy imports (including oil and coal) amount for more than 30 per cent although oil price increases can raise this figure to 40 per cent of total imports. Indian agrarian imports of food grains have also seen a phenomenal increase from just Rs. 1.34 billion in 2014-15 to more than Rs. 90 billion in 2016-17.[23] Rather than depend on an export led strategy to correct imbalances in the current account of the BoP, countries need a longer term vision and planning to address these structural issues. For instance, investment in research and development, education and skills training for value added manufacturing, incentives for adoption of renewable energy technologies and adoption of modern farming technologies and techniques can provide solutions to chronic external sector imbalances. Dismissing such initiatives as unviable due to fiscal deficit constraints, countries instead pursue export promotion policies to earn foreign exchange, which are, however, often not in sync with a country's resource endowments. As the MMT economist, Fadhel Kaboub points out Tunisia a drought prone region, encourages strawberry exports (which demands huge amounts of water and fertile land to grow) rather than investing in growing food grains for domestic consumption.[24] India's concerted effort at agricultural self-sufficiency in the 1960s through the Green Revolution is an example of how the government was able to reduce food grain imports and in fact achieve an exportable surplus in the matter of a few decades. Although these policies did have unintended ecological consequences, the advancement of agriculture technology provides scope for a more sustainable revolution; drip irrigation methods, acquaponics and vertical agriculture could become financially viable on a large scale with adequate state support in research and development as well asadequate incentives. Similarly, advancements in renewable energy sources, green building technologies and public transportation must reduce a country's dependence on fossil fuel imports.

In spite of policies to overcome structural imbalances in the BoP, developing countries are still prone to shocks in their external sector that are beyond their control; for instance, an increase in interest rates by the US Federal Reserve or an increase in international oil prices. We can therefore assert that the ability to shift the *AS* curve is essentially a governance issue, which requires us to reframe the objective of macroeconomic policy as: Maximize employment + growth through maximum government spending and maximum governance subject to real resource constraints, an acceptable rate of inflation and management of structural imbalances in the BoP.

Whatever may be the political position on the acceptable rate of inflation and foreign exchange rate, it does not take away from the essence of MMT, which shifts the narrative of growth from *economies to politics*, from financial to real resource constraints and from reigning in the *fiscal deficit to governance.* And this is the essence of Keynes as Steindl put across so succinctly. But are economists ready to hand over the controls to the politician? And are politicians ready to take full responsibility for their actions? And most importantly, how do we communicate to the common person on the street the true constraints and trade offs to economic development? More than ever, the need for macroeconomic literacy from an MMT perspective is imperative if modern money economies—India included—are to realize their full potential.

NOTES

1. https://global.oup.com/academic/product/macroeconomics-at-the-service-of-public-policy-9780199666126?cc=us&lang=en&
2. Spending on the JG programme increases during a recession and reduces during an upswing in private sector economic activity.
3. Bill Mitchell, 'Large-scale Employment Guarantee Scheme in India Improving

Over Time', 1 September 2014, http://bilbo.economicoutlook.net/blog/?p=28845

4. The topicality of UBI is also on account of the global phenomenon of jobless growth that is un-constraining production while demand is unable to keep up on account of joblessness and widening inequalities.
5. John Maycock, 'Downward Envy: A Job Guarantee versus Universal Basic Income', Independent Australia, 25 May 2017, https://independentaustralia.net/politics/politics-display/downward-envy-a-job-guarantee-versus-universal-basic-income,10334
6. Readers can watch some debates on this issue on YouTube channel by Real Progressives; for instance interviews with Steven Hail (https://www.youtube.com/watch?v=i9Q-0nNYp54) and discussion with Pavlina Tcherneva (https://www.youtube.com/watch?v=iPx7pIdYwxM).
7. Claire Connelly, 'Why a Universal Basic Income is a Poor Substitute for a Guaranteed Job', ABC News, 19 January 2017, http://www.abc.net.au/news/2017-01-19/universal-basic-income-vs-job-guarantee/8187688
8. Janmejaya Sinha, 'All the Bank's Men', *Indian Express*, 2 May 2016, http://indianexpress.com/article/opinion/columns/all-the-banks-men/
9. European Parliament at your service, http://www.europarl.europa.eu/atyourservice/en/displayFtu.html?ftuId=FTU_4.1.4.html
10. http://www.businessdictionary.com/definition/governance.html
11. Aggregate expenditure = $AE = CI + G + (X - M)$
12. Corresponding to this full employment output is a 'natural rate of unemployment'. Here, even as the labour market is in full employment equilibrium or all those willing to work at the going wage rate, find work there are people in the labour force who, although they are willing to work at the equilibrium wage rate cannot find work because of frictional (moving from one job to another) or structural (people do not have the right skills) reasons.
13. It is useful to abstract a little here. Every country has a potential to produce a certain level of output given their resources, people's skills, health, education, and so on. It's difficult to sustain an increase in output beyond this potential level. However, over time with improvements in health, education, infrastructure, etc., this potential level of output would increase.
14. Montek Singh Ahluwalia, 'The Slow Growth in the First Quarter is a Warning Signal', *Livemint*, 7 September 2017, http://www.livemint.com/Opinion/qCpQ6RNfRGD6NdKD6YIddL/The-slow-GDP-growth-in-the-first-quarter-is-a-warning-signal.html
15. The process of *building* infrastructure, etc., actually induces outward shifts in the *AD* curve as the government spends money into the economy.

16. Raphael Espinoza, Hyginus Leon and Ananthakrishnan Prasad, 'Estimating The Inflation–Growth Nexus: A Smooth Transition Model', IMF Working Paper WP/10/76, 2010, https://www.imf.org/external/pubs/ft/wp/2010/wp1076.pdf
17. Sarah Anwar and Iyanatul Islam, 'Should Developing Countries Target Low, Single Digit Inflation to Promote Growth and Employment?', Employment Sector Employment Working Paper No. 87, International Labour Organization, Geneva, 2011, http://www.ilo.org/wcmsp5/groups/public/@ed_emp/@emp_policy/documents/publication/wcms_160448.pdf
18. Buttonwood, 'Rethinking Central Bank Independence', *The Economist*, 17 November 2016, http://www.economist.com/blogs/buttonwood/2016/11/unaccountable-technocrats-or-convenient-scapegoats
19. 'Government must Deliver on Promises to Drive Higher Growth: Moody's', *Business Today*, 30 July 2015, http://www.businesstoday.in/current/economy-politics/moodys-on-narendra-modi-govt-higher-growth-promises/story/222267.html
20. Rediff.com, 23 September 2011, http://www.rediff.com/business/slide-show/slide-show-1-how-inflation-has-changed-in-india/20110923.htm
21. Amihai Glazer and Lawrence S. Rothenberg, *Why Government Succeeds and Why It Fails*, Harvard University Press, Cambridge, 2001.
22. Advait Rao Palepu, 'Not a Single Macro Economist Thinks Note Ban was a Good Idea: Gita Gopinath', *Business Standard*, 22 December 2017, http://www.business-standard.com/article/economy-policy/not-a-single-macro-economist-thinks-note-ban-was-a-good-idea-gita-gopinath-117122101525_1.html
23. Ajit Singh, Jitendra, 'Rs 1,402,680,000,000: India's agrarian import bill for 2015-16', *Down to Earth*, 25 May 2018, https://www. downtoearth.org.in/news/rs-1-402-680-000-000-58217.
24. Hopping Mad with Will McLeod and Arliss Bunny, Fadhel Kaboub of the Binzagr Institute,Podcast, https://www.buzzsprout.com/50892/659073-fadhel-kaboub-of-the-binzagr-institute-must-listen?client_source=twitter_card&player_type=full_screen

Bibliography

Bell, S. (2000), 'Do taxes and bonds finance government spending?', *Journal of Economic Issues*, 34: 603-20.

Bell, S.A. and L.R. Wray, (2002), 'Fiscal Effects on Reserves and the Independence of the Fed', *Journal of Post Keynesian Economics*, 25 (2): 263-71.

Fullwiler, S.T. (2006), 'Setting Interest Rates in the Modern Money Era', *Journal of Post Keynesian Economics*, 28 (3): 495-525.

Innes, A.M. (1913), 'What is money?', *Banking Law Journal*, May: 377-408. Republished as 'What is Money?' in L. Randall Wray, ed. (2004), *Credit and State Theories of Money*, Cheltenham: Edward Elgar.

—— (1914), 'The Credit Theory of Money', *Banking Law Journal*, January: 151-68. Republished as 'The credit theory of money', in L. Randall Wray, ed. (2004), *Credit and State Theories of Money*, Cheltenham: Edward Elgar.

Kaboub, Fadhel (2013), 'The Fiscal Cliff Mythology and the Full Employment Alternative: An Affordable and Productive Plan', *Review of Radical Political Economics*, 45.

Knapp, G.F. (1924) (1973), *The State Theory of Money*, Clifton, NY: Augustus M. Kelley.

Lavoie, Marc (2014), *Post-Keynesian Economics: New Foundations*, Cheltenham, Edward Elgar.

Lerner, Abba P. (1943), 'Functional Finance and the Federal Debt', *Social Research*, 10: 38-51.

Minsky, Hyman P. (1977), 'The financial instability hypothesis: An Interpretation of Keynes and an Alternative to "standard" theory', *Challenge*, 20(1): 26.

Mitchell, W.F. and W. Mosler, (2002), 'Public Debt Management and Australia's Macroeconomic Priorities', Working Paper No. 2-13, Center for Full Employment and Equity.

Mosler, W. (1995), *Soft Currency Economics*, 3rd edn., West Palm Beach, FL (self published), http:\\www.warrenmosler.com

—— (2010), *The 7 Deadly Innocent Frauds of Economic Policy*, Valance Co Inc.

Murray, Michael J. and Mathew Forstater (2013), *Employment Guarantee Schemes: Job Creation and Policy in Developing Countries and Emerging Markets*, New York: Palgrave Macmillan.

Sivramkrishna, Sashi (2015), 'Decentring Fiscal Deficit Target Numbers in the Macroeconomic Policy Debate', *Economic & Political Weekly*, L(19): 15-18.

—— (2015), *In Search of Stability: Economics of Money, History of the Rupee*, New Delhi: Manohar and London/New York: Routledge.

—— (2016), 'China's Macroeconomics Policy Options: A Sectoral Financial Balances Perspective', *Studies in Business & Economics*, 11(1): 152-63.

—— (2016), 'Cracks in BRICs: A Sectoral Financial Balances Analysis and Implications for Macroeconomic Policy', *Theoretical & Applied Economics*, XXIII (3-608): 53-78.

—— (2016), 'Can a Country Really Go Broke? Deconstructing Saudi Arabia's Macroeconomic Crisis', *Real World Economics Review*, 76: 75-94.

—— (2016), 'The Ornithology of Macroeconomic Policy: India's New Monetary Policy Framework', *NMIMS Journal of Economics and Public Policy*, 1(1): 45-55.

Steindl, Josef, 'J.M. Keynes: Society and the Economist', in *Economic Papers 1941-88*, Palgrave Macmillan, New York, 1990, pp. 277-8.

Tcherneva, Pavlina R. (2012), 'Permanent on-the-spot job creation—the missing Keynes Plan for full employment and economic transformation', *Review of Social Economy*, 70(1): 57-80.

Tymoigne, Éric (2014), 'Modern Money Theory and Interrelations between the Treasury and the Central Bank: The Case of the United States', Working Paper No. 788, Levy Economics Institute of Bard College.

Wray, L.R. (1990), *Money and Credit in Capitalist Economies: The Endogenous Money Approach*, Aldershot, UK and Brookfield, US: Edward Elgar.

——, (1992), 'Commercial Banks, the Central Bank, and Endogenous Money', *Journal of Post Keynesian Economics*, 14(3): 297-310.

——, (1998), *Understanding Modern Money: The Key to Full employment and Price Stability*, Cheltenham, Edward Elgar.

——, (2012), *Modern Money Theory: A Primer on Macroeconomics for Sovereign Monetary Systems*, London: Palgrave Macmillan.

Index

Austerity 65, 71, 74, 112, 117, 189

Bretton Woods 12, 128, 136

call money market 175-7, 180-1
Cash Reserve Requirement (CRR) 177
crowding out 52-4, 78, 208, 225
current account deficit 100, 187, 190-1, 195, 198, 202

Dynamic Stochastic General Equilibrium (DSGE) 63-7, 100, 102, 108, 134, 149, 168

embedded liberalism 51, 56, 83, 89
Endogenous Money Theory-Modern Money Theory (EMT-MMT) 162, 164, 167, 170-2, 209, 218

fiat currency 128, 135-6, 152-3, 156
fiscal deficit 18, 21-2, 47, 62, 81-2, 102-11, 113, 116-17, 139, 141, 143-4, 184, 193, 195, 198-9, 201-2, 207, 214, 225-6, 231
fiscal discipline 95-6, 103
fiscal policy 21, 51-2, 54, 57-60, 62-3, 65, 68, 70, 78, 95, 143, 193, 203, 208
fiscal Responsibility and Budget Management (FRBM) 107-8, 113, 182, 208
fiscal surplus 68, 141, 189, 193, 208
Friedman, Milton 11, 57-9, 62, 168
full employment 49, 51-2, 57, 69, 71, 82, 174, 209, 213-14, 217-18, 222, 224

Gandhi, Indira 87
global financial crisis (GFC) 17, 23, 65, 71, 74, 84, 88, 100, 112, 149, 193, 215, 223
Golden Age of Capitalism 51, 54, 73
governance 19, 24, 219-20, 225, 226, 228, 230-1
Great Depression 35-6, 39, 44, 49, 64
Great Moderation 65, 73

hierarchy of money 46, 149-52, 155-6, 165-6, 207

independent central bank 62, 82-3, 95, 112-13, 228
Indian Financial Code (IFC) 113-14, 228
inequality 13, 19, 83-4, 88-9, 116
inflation 18, 45, 47, 52, 56-60, 62, 70, 73, 79, 81-2, 88, 95, 111-18, 132-4, 139-40, 143-4, 168, 172, 174-7, 181, 199, 203, 217-18, 222, 227, 228

Job Guarantee (JG) 215

Keynes 11, 35, 38-40, 42-9, 53, 62, 67, 74, 136, 171, 213, 224
Keynesian 11, 35-6, 39, 40, 42, 45, 48-9, 51, 53-4, 62, 64, 69, 71, 84, 89, 95, 99, 171, 174, 193, 222, 224

legal tender 128-9, 132
Liquidity Adjustment Facility (LAF) 176-8, 180

liquidity preference 46, 171
liquidity trap 44-5, 51
loanable funds 42-3, 46-8, 53, 65, 82, 97-100, 159
Lucas critique 63

Marginal Standing Facility (MSF) 177-8, 180-1
Modern Money Theory (MMT) 12-3, 21-5, 118, 133-4, 141, 143-6, 160, 178-9, 182, 185, 187, 207-10, 213-20, 225, 229-31
Modi, Narendra 18, 88, 105, 229
monetarism 11, 56-7, 60, 69, 168
monetary policy 21, 52, 54, 57-60, 63, 67, 73, 83, 92, 95, 106, 113-14, 174, 177-8, 180, 203
Monetary Policy Committee (MPC) 114-16
money multiplier 53, 158-60, 168

NAIRU 58
Neo Keynesian 36, 51-4, 56-60, 63, 65, 69, 73, 75, 87, 111, 168, 180
Neoclassical Synthesis 64
neoliberalism 17, 20, 24, 57, 76, 82-4, 87, 95, 115, 226
net financial asset accumulation 68, 145, 185-95, 198, 207
neutrality of money 22, 65
New Classical Macroeconomics (NCM) 62-7, 69, 100, 102, 145
New Keynesian 36, 40, 64-6
Phillips Curve 52, 59
Post-Keynesian 20, 36, 185

Quantity theory of money 170

rational expectations 62
Real Business Cycle (RBC) 63-4
repo rate 174-5, 178, 209
reverse repo rate 175, 177
Ricardian Equivalence 109

Say's Law 37-9, 41-2, 46-8, 65, 224; public debt 21-2, 65, 108, 144-6, 181, 184, 195, 208
Sectoral Financial Balances (SFB) 184, 187-8, 190-6, 209
Stagflation 56, 60, 83
Statutory Liquidity Requirements (SLR) 177
sticky price 39
structural reforms 70, 77, 91, 96, 110-11, 202-3
supply side 63-5, 77, 81, 90-1, 113, 202, 223-4

unemployment 13, 19, 38-40, 46, 49, 52-4, 56-60, 64-5, 70, 78, 83-4, 53, 88-9, 92, 95, 116, 132, 200, 202, 214
Universal Basic Income 216, 218

Washington Consensus 78